# FLYING FORWARDS
# FACING BACKWARDS

# FLYING FORWARDS FACING BACKWARDS

Captivating Tales from a Vulcan and
Nimrod Air Electronics Officer

## JIM WALLS

GRUB STREET | LONDON

Published by
Grub Street
4 Rainham Close
London SW11 6SS

A CIP record for this title is available from the British library

ISBN-13: 978-1-911667-32-2

Design by Myriam Bell Design, UK

Printed and bound by Finidr, Czech Republic

DEDICATION

This book is dedicated to all of those who strive to preserve freedom and
democracy. It is also dedicated to those members of the Royal Air Force
Benevolent Fund and the Royal Air Force Association who offer care and
support to our aviators and their dependents when tragedy strikes.

# CONTENTS

# PREFACE
# A WORD FROM THE AUTHOR

This book does not pretend to be an authoritative source of technical and historical information. It is simply a distillation of personal memories, observations and opinions garnered over 40 years of serving as both ground crew and aircrew in the Royal Air Force.

The book selectively describes my pre-service days, my years serving as an air radar mechanic and technician and later, as aircrew, on both the Nimrod MR1 and R1. But most of all, it describes events that took place during the period of 1977–1981 when I served as an air electronics officer on the Vulcan B2s of No. 617 Squadron.

In writing this book I have made no effort to refer to formal documents other than my flying logbooks, but I have used online media and other open-source literature to jog my memory regarding dates and events of historical interest. I have avoided naming some of those that I served with as I am unable to reach them to obtain their permission for inclusion in this book. Similarly, I am unable to contact most of those that feature in the photographs. I trust they will not be offended.

It would be remiss of me not to take this opportunity to acknowledge the assistance provided by those who have helped me to gather and describe some of the information contained in the chapters that follow – they are too many to name, but they know who they are. I must also thank my dear wife, Jessie, who suffered in silence throughout the countless months that it took for me to recall, and put in writing, many of the experiences gained during my air force days. Her patience and help have not gone un-noticed. Finally, I would like to thank the small, but heroic team at Grub Street Publishing who took a big gamble in publishing this book. I will forever be indebted to them for their unflinching support, professional guidance and their belief in me and the story I had to tell.

In spite of my best efforts to ensure the general accuracy of the book's content, there will undoubtedly be parts that some readers will see as being incorrect, controversial and perhaps even provocative. This is only to be expected. Despite the caveats, I hope you will enjoy reading my personal recollections of flying forwards, facing backwards.

# PROLOGUE
## "SH*T HAPPENS"

During the late morning of 25 April 1979, V Bomber crews at Royal Air Force (RAF) Scampton and Waddington were making final preparations to fly Exercise Cloudy Chorus, a hi-lo-hi nuclear strike exercise over Western Europe. I was an air electronics officer (AEO) serving on 617 Squadron at Scampton and my crew had been allocated Vulcan B2, XL317 for the exercise. As we carried out our final preparations prior to take-off, we knew that North Atlantic Treaty Organisation (NATO) fighter and land-based air-defence (AD) elements based in Western Europe were gearing up to act as the defending forces. During pre-flight briefing, the Scampton meteorological officer advised us that the cold air mass settled over Europe should provide sunny weather with good visibility throughout the day. Contrary to what you might think, this was bad news for us as the combination of sun and cold air would give rise to a fair amount of overland convection, thus guaranteeing us a rather bumpy ride during our low-level penetration to the target. The excellent visibility and lack of cloud would also simplify the air defenders' task.

We got airborne just before noon and set course on an easterly heading across the North Sea whilst climbing to our cruising altitude of 43,000 feet. During the climb I closed down the auxiliary airborne power plant (AAPP) and connected the No. 4 alternator to the synchronising busbar as per standard operating procedure (SOP). When we reached our cruising altitude, the captain eased back the throttles of our four Olympus 201 engines to their cruise power setting. This provided the Vulcan with sufficient power to maintain a cruising speed of around Mach 0.84 – 84 per cent of the speed of sound. Upon reaching the Dutch coast we turned onto a southerly heading taking us across Belgium and northern France, a leg of the sortie clearly designed by the 'masochistic exercise planners' to serve us up as lambs to be slaughtered by NATO fighters waiting on quick reaction alert (QRA) at their bases in Europe or already orbiting impatiently on their combat air patrols (CAP). It wasn't long before my radar warning receiver (RWR) display flashed a warning strobe indicating that we were being illuminated by a sector scanning, I-Band radar from somewhere in our seven o'clock position. I transmitted a few sweeps on my Red Steer rearward-looking radar and noticed a contact slightly below us at a range of about five miles, and closing. My RWR indicated that the contact was gradually moving around towards our six o'clock position and that the pilot had changed the operating mode of his radar from its sector-scanning search mode to the high-threat locked-on mode. Taking a quick look through my rearwards-looking periscope I saw that it was a F-15 Eagle, almost certainly from the United States Air Force Europe (USAFE) base at Bitburg in Germany. As the F-15 closed in on our tail, I knew that the American pilot would be manoeuvring his fighter to align our Vulcan with the weapon-aiming symbol on his head-up display (HUD) then, upon hearing the 'locked-on' tone from his Sidewinder missile, would press the button that, for real, would have launched a missile to bring about an explosive end to our flight. Thankfully, being an exercise, there was no missile launch and no sudden end to our flight and we continued on our planned route unharmed. The F-15 pilot, having completed his simulated attack, banked sharply and dived away to the east. A short while later we were attacked again, this time by a French air force Mirage F1. Like the pilot in the F-15, the Mirage pilot closed to about 1,000 yards in our six o'clock position and executed what I guess was a simulated missile launch. He then edged in closer to within a hundred yards or less for what, I assumed, was a practice gun shot. Whilst keeping the captain and crew informed of our 'double execution' there was little I could do to defend our aircraft as any serious attempt at evasive manoeuvring would have caused us to deviate significantly from our authorised course, heading and altitude. Besides, manoeuvre on its own was unlikely to prevent us from being shot down by the fighters. Energetic manoeuvring combined with the use of chaff, infrared (IR) countermeasures (flares) and radar jamming, on the other hand, would certainly have given us a fighting chance or, at least, it would have seriously complicated things for the fighter pilot. Unfortunately, the use of chaff and IR countermeasures was strictly forbidden over mainland Europe. Also, as Scampton-based Vulcans were not equipped with I-Band jamming equipment, there was nothing I could do in terms of active electronic countermeasures (ECM) to disrupt the operation of the fighter's radar. So, all I could do was log the time of the intercepts for debriefing back at base. Very frustrating!

We soon arrived over our southerly turning point in France and changed course onto an easterly heading which, if maintained for more than 20 minutes or so, would have taken us across the Inner German Border (IGB) – the dividing line between West Germany and the communist-ruled German Democratic Republic (GDR). To avoid infringing GDR airspace and setting off a diplomatic/military commotion, we started our descent early and, a short while later, turned onto a northerly heading. This placed us on a track that ran parallel to, but at a safe distance to the west of, the IGB. During the descent, I removed No. 4 alternator from the synchronising busbar and replaced it with No. 3 alternator as per Vulcan SOPs. Later, as we descended through 3,000 feet, our co-pilot closed down communications with the area air traffic control centre (ATCC) and the crew set about configuring their systems for flight at low level. As was normal for the Vulcan, we chose to fly at a height of around 500 feet above the undulating ground while maintaining an air speed of around 240–300 knots, both parameters largely determined by peacetime exercise rules and a modicum of consideration for the Vulcan's age. Having established ourselves at low level, we turned onto a westerly heading taking us towards our planned 'target for the day' which was a point or structure located some distance to the south of the four 'RAF Clutch Bases' at Wildenrath, Geilenkirchen, Laarbruch and Brüggen. As we made our way along the planned route, I carefully monitored the RWR, checking for radar activity from NATO fighters and ground-based air-defence systems, such as US Army HAWK surface-to-air missile (SAM) and German Gepard anti-aircraft artillery (AAA) units. I also maintained an intermittent search of the airspace above and behind us with the Red Steer to watch for fighters that might 'eye ball' us from their CAP and close in for a rear hemisphere visual attack. Meanwhile, the moderate to severe convection forecast by the Scampton met office proved to be accurate and our Vulcan was already lurching up and down, sometimes quite violently, as we flew through the columns of rising and falling air. It reminded me of a comment made by another AEO who opined that "working as an AEO in the back of the Vulcan at low level was like sitting in the small dark cupboard beneath the stairs of your house trying to read the gas and electricity meters while the whole house was being severely shaken by an earthquake!"

"Quite a few birds about," said the captain in a matter-of-fact tone. For some reason I flicked my gaze across to the electrics panel situated to the right of my seat. Everything was as it should be with each of the aircraft's four engine-driven, 40kVA alternators dutifully providing electrical power to the Vulcan's systems and, vitally, to its ten powered flying control units (PFCUs). The PFCUs moved the Vulcan's elevons and rudder flying control surfaces in response to inputs from the pilot's control column and rudder pedals. "Captain from nav, come right five degrees onto a heading of 265 degrees." "Roger, 265 degrees," replied the captain. Our nav plotter was monitoring his navigation equipment and checking the progress of our flight on his chart. Meanwhile the nav radar was concentrating on his H2S radar display, checking that what he saw agreed with the picture he expected to see from his pre-flight planning. Up in the cockpit our young co-pilot was peering through the Vulcan's small and less-than-ideal cockpit windows, attempting as best he could to maintain a methodical visual search ahead of the aircraft. We were not under any form of air traffic control, so it was vital that the pilots did their best to see and avoid other aircraft, balloons, gliders, birds, and anything else that could pose a risk of collision. Suddenly a strong, pulsing tone erupted in my earphones and a solid flashing strobe appeared at the six o'clock position on my RWR display. We were being illuminated by an I-Band radar from somewhere behind us. Within seconds the tone became steady and threatening as the radar was switched to its lock-on mode. I quickly flicked my intercom switch. "Captain from AEO, high threat six o'clock, possible AAA." "Roger AEO." We must have flown over a NATO air-defence unit. The operator, having possibly acquired us visually, had locked his tracking radar on to our aircraft and would now be simulating opening fire with his radar-controlled cannon.

In a real war situation, the captain would have immediately reduced height, accelerated and made use of any topographical cover available. Our Vulcan, being void of I-Band jamming equipment, meant that I only had chaff to break the AAA radar's lock, but once again, being peacetime – and for very good environmental reasons – we were not allowed to fly below our authorised minimum height, or dispense chaff over the European mainland. Such limitations were frustrating, but they were a natural consequence of practising our wartime role over the populated areas of Western Europe. We soon flew out of the range of the AAA system and I logged the time and its estimated position for the debriefing back at base. We continued on our planned track across Germany when the captain suddenly burst in loudly on intercom, "Crew from captain, bird strike, bird strike, climbing out!"

There was a sudden surge of acceleration and an onset of G forces as the captain simultaneously pushed forward on the Vulcan's throttle levers while easing back on the control column causing our Vulcan to rotate into a steep climb. This left the three of us in the back of the aircraft dangling from the safety straps that held us into our rearwards-facing seats. I immediately started the AAPP, checked its electrical output was within limits and made the required switch selections to connect it to the aircraft's synchronising busbar, replacing number three alternator. The AAPP would provide a standby source of electrical power to the aircraft's systems in the event that the bird strike caused us to lose one or more of our engines and alternators. The nav plotter quickly reached into his aircrew bag and fished out the charts and other documentation he would need to navigate our aircraft towards our declared emergency diversion airfield at Ramstein, a USAFE airbase in Germany. The co-pilot, being impressively fast off the mark, was already transmitting a PAN call to inform air traffic control (ATC) of our situation. I was about to raise the periscope from inside my desk to check the outside of the aircraft for damage, when we must have entered cloud because the inside of the cabin suddenly went from being its usual gloomy darkness to being very dark indeed. This was followed almost immediately by an almighty BANG. "My God! What the hell was that?"

My first instinct was that birds had gone down our engine intakes and caused one or more of our engines to explode. But a quick check of my electrics panel showed that all four engine-driven alternators were still working normally and feeding electrical power to their individual busbars. I raised the periscope from under my desk and had a quick look outside, checking the top and bottom surfaces of the wings and fuselage for fire, airframe damage and/or loss of fluids. Everything seemed to be okay. I re-checked my electrics panel; everything was as it should be. During this period, I noticed that the intercom had suddenly fallen silent. Not a word had been heard from the pilots on intercom since the captain had made his bird strike call. I attempted to call the captain, but there was no reply. The three of us in the back looked at each other in anticipation – the silence was eerie. The nav radar, perhaps being uncertain about what was going on, decided to take up his abandon-aircraft position by the crew escape hatch. He placed his hand firmly on the opening handle. If things turned bad, he would be the first of the rear crew to exit the aircraft. Further seconds passed with nothing being heard from the pilots. The three of us in the rear cabin were definitely becoming concerned – what was happening up on the flight deck? I swivelled my seat around and looked up into the cockpit. The co-pilot seemed to be busy flying the aircraft as well as communicating on the radio. I can only guess that the captain must have been busy checking his engines and other systems. I called the captain once more, but got no reply. The nav plotter, clearly as concerned as I was, looked at me quite intently and moved his hand towards the switch that would electrically open the escape hatch – a back-up procedure for the nav radar who would be expected to open it with the manual handle. His steady stare told me that, given the order to abandon aircraft, or if the pilots ejected, he was ready to follow me out of the aircraft. "Come on captain, say something!" I thought to myself. "What the hell was going on?" The silence seemed to last for minutes. Suddenly, at last, the captain broke in on intercom, "Crew, can you hear me?" "Captain from AEO you are loud and clear" I replied with some relief. "Okay, crew check in." We all checked in on intercom, then the captain called me directly. "AEO, I have lost some of my flying controls, my main rudder and numbers 4 and 5 elevons! "WHAT?!" I looked again at my electrical panel and confirmed that the AAPP was still connected to the synchronising busbar and that the No. 3 alternator that fed power to the PFCUs in question was still connected to the No. 3 busbar with its output stable and within normal operating limits. In fact, everything was the same as it was about 20 seconds earlier, except now I noticed that the meter showing the electrical load on the No. 3 busbar was lower than normal. "What on earth was going on?" After a few more checks of the electrical system I called on the intercom, "Captain from AEO, all is okay with the electrics, you are clear to restart your rudder." "Roger AEO, starting the rudder." There was a short pause then, "Rudder back online." "Roger captain, re-start your elevons." Another short pause, then. "Okay AEO, all the PFCUs are now up and running. Crew carry out a systems status check and report. AEO have a look outside and check for any damage then we will run through the Flight Reference Card (FRC) check list." "I have already checked outside captain, no sign of fire, airframe damage or fluid leaks." "Roger AEO." At that point the co-pilot interrupted, "Captain from co-pilot, ATC has rejected our planned diversion to Ramstein due to a thunderstorm over the airfield and they recommend that we divert to the USAFE base at Zweibrücken instead." "Roger Co," said the captain. "Nav, can you dig out the information that we will need for Zweibrücken?" "Will do captain."

After carrying out the essential FRC checks and with our captain following instructions from the ATCC, things started to settled down. We all agreed that in addition to having a possible bird strike, we had probably suffered a fairly major lightning strike. As we transited towards Zweibrücken I noticed that my Red Steer tail warning radar was no longer working so I turned it off. At the same time the ATCC instructed us to change frequency to Zweibrücken approach. Listening to the Zweibrücken approach controller during our descent towards the airfield I noticed that there was a certain strain in his voice and that his instructions seemed to be somewhat less than reassuring. A short while later, the approach controller passed us over to the Zweibrücken local controller who, for some reason, was also showing signs of stress. Things became even more bizarre when we landed. Our Vulcan was immediately surrounded by a swarm of vehicles carrying armed personnel in full combat gear. "Looks like we have upset the locals," suggested the captain. Taking advice offered over the radio, the captain taxied our aircraft to a position close to where the ATC controller wanted us to park. However, this left the base defence troops rather uncertain as to what they should do next. The captain, becoming a bit impatient, piped up on the intercom. "Nav radar from captain, will you go outside and ask them what they want us to do, but stay on intercom using the long lead." "Roger captain, will do." The nav radar opened the wooden locker-cum-passenger seat located behind and below his seat and fished out the long intercom lead. Then, having connected it to the aircraft's intercom system, he opened the crew entry/exit door and slid down to the ground. He was immediately forced to adopt the spread-eagle position on the ground and was thoroughly searched and checked over by the armed troops. After being allowed to stand up, the nav radar initiated some form of dialogue with the armed party. This, apparently, involved much arm waving and pointing but, eventually, he got the message through to the troops that we needed to park the aircraft somewhere that would provide us with plenty of clear space when the time came for us to taxi for departure. At last, and with some belated help from a senior USAFE officer who had just arrived on scene, we were marshalled to a spot where it was safe for us to shut down. When we got out of the aircraft our crew was met by the USAFE officer who immediately appraised us of the situation. Apparently, we had landed in the middle of a Tactical Evaluation Exercise (TACEVAL) and our unplanned arrival was being used by the exercise directing staff to assess the performance of base personnel when confronted with the arrival of a defecting Russian bomber!

As we waited for the captain to finish making necessary arrangements with the American officer, I strolled around the aircraft looking for any obvious signs of damage and was amazed by what I saw. The radome covering the Red Steer radar at the rear of the Vulcan had been totally blown away by the lightning and the radar dish was hanging loose, pointing down rather forlornly towards the ground. This explained why the Red Steer had stopped working. It also told me where the lightning's exit point was. I continued my walk around the aircraft checking for further damage when a young American airman shuffled up towards me. Having cast a serious eye over what remained of our Red Steer radome, he said, "Sir, I work in the base fabrication shop and if you like I could either construct a cover for your radome that will get you home, or if you have the time I could build you a new radome." At first I looked at him in disbelief, then I realised that he was deadly serious. I was absolutely flabbergasted by this young man's offer of help. I explained to him that arrangements would be made for a replacement radome to be flown out from the United Kingdom, and I thanked him for his kind offer. I was far from certain that the airman really did have the skill and materials to perform the promised task, but it was his belief that he could do so, coupled with his sincerity and willingness to help, that I found quite uplifting.

I can't remember much of what happened after we got to the local hotel where we would spend the night. All I can recall is the five of us sitting at a table in the bar-cum-restaurant looking rather tired and dishevelled and still wearing our flying suits, because that was all the clothing that we had with us. In fact, my last memory of that evening was trying to explain to the young German waitress that we needed five large beers – fast! The following morning, after a quick breakfast, we boarded the transport that took us back to Zweibrücken and to our aircraft. During a thorough check of the external airframe, and the inside of the engine intakes for indications of bird strike and other damage, we came across the lightning's point of entry to the aircraft. It was a small hole, about the size of a penny, located on top of the fuselage just ahead of the cockpit; such a small hole for such a loud bang. We continued to look for any other signs of damage, but nothing further was found. After fitting the replacement Red Steer radome that had been flown out from the UK that morning, we all climbed on board the Vulcan. With engines started I took the opportunity to carry out a thorough check of the aircraft's electrical system. Everything seemed to be working as it should and without further ado, we took off and flew back to Scampton.

A day or two later I was called to an impromptu meeting in the 617 Squadron operations office. My captain, accompanied by the senior AEO instructor from the

Vulcan Operational Conversion Unit (OCU) and another AEO instructor were in attendance. We talked through the sequence of events leading up to the loss of the aircraft's PFCUs over Germany. All the possible causes were covered, but we could not arrive at a logical reason that would explain why the PFCUs should have rundown. I sensed that patience was in short supply and tempers were becoming frayed. Also, the meeting was gradually morphing from being a gathering of informed individuals, to becoming an interrogation of one individual – me. This, to be fair, was quite understandable, as loss of power to the PFCUs could definitely be caused by the AEO mishandling the controls and switches on the aircraft's electrical panel, although to be honest, I am not sure what, precisely, that mishandling would have entailed on this occasion. I was certain that I had carried out the proper switch sequence on the aircraft's electrical panel after the captain had made his bird strike call. I didn't do anything differently to what I had done very many times before, both on the OCU electrical training rig and in the aircraft. The reliability of the Vulcan's electrical system was such that I had only ever experienced one failure during my four years flying on the aircraft (one alternator had dropped offline while taxiing for take-off on my very first OCU sortie). Nevertheless, the questioning continued.

"No sir, as confirmed by the captain, we inspected the airframe and the engine air intakes and found no indications that we had actually suffered a bird strike." "No sir, to my knowledge we did not suffer any kind of temporary spool down or failure of number three engine," I said looking at the captain for his agreement. "No sir, number three alternator did not fail at any time during the sortie." "Yes sir, when the captain made his bird strike call I started AAPP and connected it to the synchronising busbar in accordance with Vulcan SOPs. No sir, I cannot for the life of me explain what had caused the PFCUs to fail while all the other services supplied from that busbar remained working." "No sir, short of the captain accidentally or deliberately switching off the said PFCUs (possible but unlikely) or some transient current associated with the lightning strike causing them to 'switch off' (possible but also unlikely), or me messing up the switch sequence on the aircraft's electrical panel in some obscure way (definitely possible, but equally unlikely as far as I was concerned), I couldn't really say what caused the three PFCUs to run down." Obviously, my interrogators didn't have much of a clue either because they looked at each other, shrugged their shoulders, and called a halt to the meeting. That was the last I heard from them and the subject was never raised again.

In summary, as for Exercise Cloudy Chorus, we had been 'shot down' by two fighters and one AAA system. We had abandoned the sortie due to a potential bird strike. During the climb out we suffered a major lightning strike resulting in some damage to the airframe and the Red Steer radar. The captain, for some obscure reason, had lost intercom with the crew. We lost three of our ten PFCUs (subsequently re-started). Our planned diversion to Ramstein had been disallowed by ATC causing us to be re-routed to Zweibrücken. We had landed at Zweibrücken in the middle of a full-scale TACEVAL where we were 'used' to simulate a defecting Russian bomber. I had been subjected to a rather pointed interrogation by senior staff from the OCU who, naturally, wanted to find a cause for the loss of electrical power to the PFCUs. Oh, and of course, we had failed to bomb our target. I couldn't help but wonder what curse had caused this string of events to visit themselves on my crew. Then I recalled the words of an ancient Roman philosopher – or was it a Vulcan crew chief – who once said, "Sh*t happens!"

# CHAPTER ONE
# EARLY DAYS

## Pre-Royal Air Force Days

In 1948, when I was five years old, our family moved from a tenement flat in central Edinburgh to a brand-new council house located on the outskirts of the city. The house also happened to be located below the approach path to runway 31 at RAF Turnhouse – now Edinburgh Airport. By the time I was 12 in 1955, I had become fascinated by the range of aircraft that swooped low over my house on their way to and from the airfield, and I took great interest in learning everything I could about them. Vampire FB.5s of No. 603 City of Edinburgh Royal Auxiliary Air Force Squadron and Meteor F8 and T7s from RAF Leuchars were regularly seen as was British European Airways DC-3s and visiting Percival Pembrokes, Avro Ansons and de Havilland Tiger Moths. Lincoln and Washington bombers and Neptune maritime patrol aircraft (MPA) were occasional visitors too. When the Royal Navy (RN) aircraft carrier, HMS *Ocean*, was in its home port at the nearby Rosyth naval base, it was quite common to see RN Fleet Air Arm aircraft such as Hawker Sea Furies and Sea Hawks, Fairy Gannets and Fireflies, Avengers and the occasional Sycamore and Whirlwind helicopter.

One balmy evening in September 1956 I was watching a Meteor F8 performing aerobatics over Turnhouse from the kitchen window of my house. I was unable to follow the Meteor's manoeuvres all the way down to low level due to my view being obstructed by nearby houses, but I was able to observe

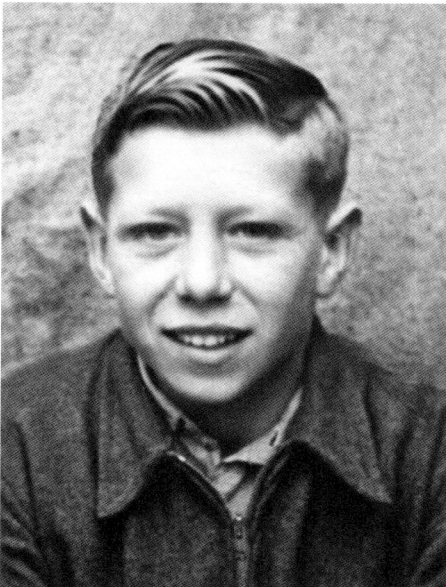

Author aged 12 in 1955.

most of the pilot's aerobatic sequence. My assumption was that he was practising his display routine for the Battle of Britain Air Show that was due to take place on the coming Saturday. I watched as the Meteor climbed and dived performing loops and other aerobatic manoeuvres. Then, to my surprise, upon completing a loop, it dived down behind the houses and didn't re-appear. I waited for it to zoom skywards again but it wasn't to be. Instead, all I saw was a large pall of smoke rising from where it had disappeared. It didn't take long for the gut-wrenching truth to dawn on me that the pilot must have left it a bit too late when pulling out from the dive and crashed into the ground. Although I was just a distant onlooker, the crash had quite a profound and emotional impact on me and it left me feeling confused and sad for many days. It was the first time I had witnessed what proved to be a fatal accident, albeit from a distance. A year or so later, perhaps around 1957, I became intrigued by the regular appearance of an all-black-painted Canberra that was fitted with a small, sharp-pointed nose radome. I later found out that the Canberra was being used by the Edinburgh-based, Ferranti Electronics Company to test the airborne interception radar and pilot's attack sight system (AIRPASS) that would eventually become the target acquisition and fire control radar for the RAF's next generation fighter; the English Electric Lightning F1.

Over the months that followed, I became an ardent aeroplane 'anorak'. I spent most of my free time at Turnhouse armed with my *The Observer's Book of Aircraft*, watching and identifying aircraft as they arrived at the airfield. Civilian aircraft would have their registration letters jotted down and marked as 'seen' in my Ian Allan book of civil aircraft registrations. Evenings and wintery days would be filled reading old *Flight* magazines 'borrowed' from the local barber shop or, with pencil and paper, trying to sketch aircraft that I had seen that day. Another favourite pass time was helping my older brother to build and fly his Keil Kraft, balsa-wood model aeroplanes.

The skeleton, or frame, of a Keil Kraft model was assembled using partly stamped-out balsa-wood bulkheads, spars and stringers supplied with the kit. These were glued together with balsa cement in accordance with the provided plan. When complete, the skeleton was covered with lightweight tissue paper that formed the skin. The paper was then doped, causing it to shrink tight against the balsa-wood frame, thus providing additional strength to the model. During the war, my dad was employed in a factory in Glasgow that built wings for Lancaster bombers and he informed me that the process used to build the model closely resembled the way that real aircraft were built. Constructing the models was quite an intricate undertaking requiring a great deal of care and patience. However, even the most carefully built model rarely led to a successful first flight. In fact, flying the models proved to be the most disappointing part of the whole process. They definitely looked better than they flew, and sometimes they didn't get a chance to fly at all. It soon became clear to my brother and I that our string of first-flight failures was down to my dad's 'helping hand'. Despite his experience building wings for Lancasters, he clearly didn't have much of a clue when it came to flying model aeroplanes. My brother had just about finished building a model Fairy Gannet, when my dad advised him to double the number of rubber bands used to operate the propeller as "this was sure to provide more power and make it fly better". Come the first test flight, and determined to give the model full power, my dad overwound the propeller's elastic bands causing the aircraft to collapse, concertina fashion, down to something approaching half its original length. We didn't have better luck with the F-86 Sabre. Whilst trying to hold the model steady during the lighting of the little Jetex 50 rocket motor, my dad set fire to the cuff of his shirt and, in the panic that followed, managed to drop the Sabre and stand on it. I didn't know whether to laugh or cry, but my brother was visibly furious – another four shillings and hours of diligent model-making wasted. Later, and in an effort to improve the first flight success rate, my brother and I avoided telling my dad when a model was ready to be flown. Instead, we sneaked out of the house and quietly made our way to the open field nearby. Although we managed to avoid any of

the previous first-flight disasters, mounting successful flights still proved to be elusive and somewhat frustrating. They certainly failed to satisfy my mind's image of carefree, soaring flight. No doubt one of the many pitfalls of being a dreamer.

Getting back to real aeroplanes, I vividly remember seeing a flight of six brand-new Hawker Hunter jet fighters overflying Edinburgh on their way to take up residence with 43 Squadron at Leuchars. I also remember my intense excitement when a squadron of Gloster Javelins arrived at Turnhouse on temporary detachment from somewhere in England. Another highlight was when, on my way home from school, I spotted a Supermarine Swift arriving at Turnhouse. I raced home, dropped my school satchel, picked up my bike and raced off to Turnhouse, heart pounding. When I arrived at my secret viewing point, I saw the all-silver Swift parked on the far side of the airfield near the Ferranti Company's hangar. There was lots of activity around the aircraft and my heart was thumping when I saw it start up and taxi for take-off. It quickly lined up on runway 31 then, after a short pause, the pilot opened the throttle and the Swift roared off, getting airborne just before the end of the runway. It remained low down and on a steady heading until it must have been over the Firth of Forth at which point it suddenly pitched up into a rocket-like vertical climb, silver wings glinting in the evening sun. It then banked into a wingover and dived back down towards the airfield, rapidly gaining speed. When it looked as it would surely hit the ground, it pulled out of its dive and thundered back down the runway, very low and incredibly fast, passing several hundred yards from where I was standing. I watched in awe as it climbed away to the south soon to disappear from view. A few days later an airman who worked at Turnhouse, but lived nearby, told me that the pilot was none other than the famous Supermarine test pilot, Mike Lithgow.

Canberra B(I)8 used to conduct flight trials for the Ferranti AIRPASS radar for the Lightning and, later, the Blue Parrot radar for the Buccaneer.

Building wings for Lancasters. My father is in the front row, far left.

Levitation and flying aeroplanes were a constant subject of my dreams. So you can perhaps imagine my excitement when I used ten shillings of the cash I earned delivering milk before school every morning for a 15-minute trip over Edinburgh in a Dragon Rapide bi-plane. It was an absolutely glorious experience. To this day I can still remember the unique smell of the inside of the aircraft, the soft bouncing motion as we accelerated across the grass during take-off, and the thrilling sensation when we lifted off the ground and soared skywards. I remember being able to identify parts of Edinburgh from the air; Princes Street, Edinburgh Castle, the old volcanic shape of Arthur's Seat, the silvery Firth of Forth with the Fife coast in the background; they were all so easy to see. I can also remember Corstorphine Hill and Edinburgh Zoo coming into view as we started our descent back to the airfield. When I climbed out of the aircraft after landing, I felt somewhat giddy and I simply could not stop smiling. It was without doubt the best ten bob I had ever spent.

When I was 14, I attended the annual Battle of Britain Air Display at RAF Turnhouse and was astonished to catch my first glimpse of three of the RAF's brand-new V Bombers; the Vulcan, Victor and Valiant. Unbeknown to me, on the day before the display, the trio of V Bombers had arrived at Turnhouse to take part in the static display. The aircraft were parked well away from the crowd, but even at a distance they looked magnificent with their futuristic shapes and their brilliant white anti-flash paint. Little did I realise that 20 years later I would fly as an AEO in Vulcan B2s of 617 Squadron.

# Boy Entrant Training

In the spring of 1958, just before I was due to finish my time at Carrickvale Secondary Modern School, I mentioned to my form tutor that I was hoping to join the RAF Technical Apprenticeship Training Scheme. Being a kindly gentleman, he took the time to research my application and, later, tactfully suggested that my English Language skills were not up to the mark (no surprise to me!) and that it would be better if I applied to join the RAF Boy Entrant Training Scheme for which the educational requirements were somewhat lower. This I did, and after attending an initial assessment board at the RAF Careers Office in Hanover Street in Edinburgh, I was selected to travel to RAF Cosford, near Wolverhampton, for further assessment. My mother insisted that I take a flask of tea and a sandwich for the journey and she gave me a wave from our living room window as I walked up the street to catch the bus to the Caledonian Railway Station at the western end of Princes Street in Edinburgh. The journey to RAF Cosford required two train changes and it took the best part of a day. I suspect that not many mums would allow their 14-year-old sons or daughters to make such a solo journey today. Nevertheless, I arrived at Cosford safe and sound and the following day I was guided through the assessment phase by some very helpful and friendly sergeants and corporals; a duo of ranks that would prove to be significantly less helpful and definitely less friendly after I started my training.

After some written tests and a number of interviews, a young flying officer called me forward to his desk. Studying what looked to me like a cribbage board with lots of coloured pins in the holes, he advised me that the RAF could accept me for training as a photographer, a radar mechanic or a cook. Now, I don't know very much about career profiling, but to this day, I still wonder what magical algorithm was used to derive such a diverse selection of trades from my test results. Upon returning home to Edinburgh, I asked my dad what he thought I should do. "Go for training as a cook," he said, "people will always have to eat and you will have no trouble getting a job when you leave the RAF." I understood his logic, but it wasn't really what I wanted to hear. My mother must have noticed my disappointment and she quickly added her tuppence worth to the discussion. She suggested that, having read about how radar had helped our country win the Battle of Britain during World War II, I should look to the future and apply for training as a radar mechanic. This I did I and I can honestly say that I have never had reason to regret her advice as it set me off on a career in the

RAF that lasted 40 years. I suppose the moral of this paragraph is: listen carefully to what your dad says, then do what your mother tells you.

It must have been sometime in June or July 1958 that I wrote to inform the officer responsible for allocating training positions at RAF Cosford that I wished to take up the offer of training as an air radar mechanic. Within a month or so I was informed that I would be joining No. 35 Entry Air Radar Mechanic Course in October of the same year. So, at the tender age of 15 years and two months, I left home to join the RAF. As I walked up the street to catch the bus to the railway station I looked back over my shoulder and saw my mother, once again, waving me farewell from our living room window. Only this time I could see that she was crying. I was about to turn back to reassure her that everything would be okay, but I decided not to do so. Instead, and despite welling up a bit myself, I waved back to her in a jaunty and confident fashion and quickened my pace until I was out of sight.

After what seemed to be a never-ending rail journey, I arrived at Albrighton railway station on 13 October 1958 along with lots of other young lads that had made their way from all over the UK. Military police and disciplinary non-commissioned officers (NCO) were awaiting our arrival and they soon divided us up into our respective trade groups. These groups were then further divided into sub-groups, each of which was assigned to take up residence in a long wooden hut or billet that would become our accommodation for the whole of the initial training period. I think there were about 16 Boy Entrants per hut, and each hut was supervised by a disciplinary corporal whose room was positioned close to the entrance door. After a meal and a sleepless night, our group was escorted to breakfast and then, later, to a hall where I was formally inducted into the RAF and gifted with the Queen's Shilling. This short but formal ceremony represented a very important and life-changing moment for me. It also seemed to have a life-changing impact on the behaviour of our escorting disciplinary NCOs who, up until that moment had been paragons of friendship, helpfulness and bonhomie. They suddenly became significantly less helpful and friendly and adopted a rather threatening persona. They wasted no time in telling us that, as newly inducted Boy Entrants, we were the absolute lowest rank in the RAF, and that if any trouble landed on their heads due to transgressions made by any one of us, it would very quickly find its way back to the transgressors in significantly enhanced form. They then corralled us into some semblance of a group and marched us off to clothing stores where we were issued with two pairs of grey overalls, underwear, socks, boots, a pair of pyjamas, a towel and a beret with a RAF brass badge. Back in the billet, we were told to change out of our civilian clothes and don our newly issued temporary 'uniform'. We were then ordered to gather up all of our civilian clothes and carry them to a large hall where a stern and somewhat ancient flight sergeant issued us with two large sheets of brown paper and some string. "I want you to parcel up your civilian clothes for sending back to your homes," he said. "You will not be needing them anytime soon." Interestingly, some of the young lads didn't know their home address; they knew where they lived, but they couldn't describe it in address form. Luckily, the flight sergeant had a list of all our addresses in anticipation that this would happen. When I handed over my parcel I remember thinking, "that's it – definitely no turning back now!"

RAF Cosford was well-equipped and organised to indoctrinate young lads into the ways of service life and to provide them with the level of technical knowledge they would need to allow them to take up employment in their chosen trade group. Looking back, I can now appreciate what an excellent training regime it was. The course lasted 18 months and was roughly divided into three major parts or phases. The first initial training phase was what one would describe as an introduction to military service. It included daily drill on Cosford's large parade ground, physical fitness training, briefings on RAF history and military discipline, lectures on the Queen's Regulations and lots of other subjects that would become important in the days ahead. A good number of training periods were also set aside for educational revision focusing on mathematics, physics and general science. This, we were told, would prove to be very important once we started the trade training phase. As you would expect, this early part of the course weeded out those that were clearly unsuited to life in the RAF. But even those that 'survived' lived in fear of making a mistake. My first big error was when I lost the rather flimsy piece of paper that was issued to me just after taking the Queen's Shilling. The piece of paper was called a 'Temporary RAF Form 1250'. I hadn't a clue what that meant and, not understanding its importance, I probably left it in the pocket of my jacket which, by that time, was on its way back to my home in Edinburgh. When our group was

Boy Entrant Jim Walls in 1959.

being issued with webbing belts and side packs, the issuing corporal looked at me and asked to see my RAF Form 1250. Not understanding what he meant, I simply said "Pardon?" "PARDON? PARDON? WHAT DO YOU BLOODY MEAN, PARDON? IT'S PARDON, CORPORAL, TO YOU SONNY!" I was stunned. "Sorry, I don't know what it is you are asking for corporal," I said meekly. "WHAT? YOU HAVE BEEN IN HER MAJESTY'S ROYAL AIR FORCE FOR SEVERAL DAYS AND YOU STILL DON'T KNOW WHAT A BLOODY RAF FORM 1250 IS?" Not knowing what to do, I stood rigidly to attention, stared straight ahead and took my first official bollocking as best I could. He ranted on for a few more seconds before calming down a notch. "Look here lad," he said, "I am asking you to identify yourself so that I can enter your details on the equipment issue register and then issue you with your personal webbing. That piece of paper that you lost was your temporary identity card. It included the relevant details needed to prove your existence. It was your means of proving that you were a Boy Entrant member of the RAF. Do you understand me?" "Yes corporal." "Right, at tea break you will report to the squadron office and tell the flight sergeant that Corporal XYZ has sent you to be issued with a replacement temporary Form 1250, understood?" "Yes corporal." Come tea break, I quickly made my way to the squadron office and reported my transgression to the flight sergeant, upon which I was subjected to another terrifyingly loud dressing-down. This verbal onslaught was made all the more unbearable by being carried out in full view of a very attractive female secretary who was busy typing out my new temporary Form 1250, whilst, at the same time, trying not to laugh at my misfortune. I vowed that from that day onwards I would guard my RAF Form 1250 with my life.

Those of us that survived the first few months were slowly becoming model trainees. Our movement as a flight no longer resembled a herd of startled sheep. Instead, our drill movements became very polished indeed. So much so, that when we marched around the parade ground and along the camp roads, it was as if we were stuck together in the correct formation with some form of invisible glue. My confidence grew daily and I was even beginning to enjoy my time at Cosford. However, there was one thing that was really starting to niggle me. It concerned the weekly pay parade. Boy Entrants were paid around 30 shillings a week, a portion of which I had arranged to send home to my mum to help support the family. Ten shillings of what was left was paid to each Boy Entrant at the weekly pay parade, and what little there was leftover was held back and issued to the boys when they were sent home on leave. The weekly pay parade was held in one of the station hangars, and just before teatime on every Thursday hundreds of Boy Entrants would turn up and arrange themselves in loose alphabetical order, with those whose surname began with the letter A making their way to the front. Having a surname that began with W meant that I was always at the back of the crowd and was always paid last.

It also meant that I always missed the Thursday evening meal. You can imagine my delight, therefore, when on one memorable pay day the issuing officer announced that, for a change, pay would be issued in reverse alphabetical order. I excitedly made my way to the front of the mass of Boy Entrants. There would only be one or two Boy Entrants with surnames beginning with "X, Y or Z" ahead of me. The routine was that when the senior NCO (SNCO) shouted out your name, you would come smartly to attention and shout back "Sir" followed by the last three digits of your service number, as written on your F1250. Upon hearing the SNCO shouting out my name I came smartly to attention, but instead of shouting back "Sir, 955," I shouted "Sir, ten shillings." The hangar fell silent and the face of the SNCO standing beside the paying officers turned deep crimson as he glared at me in disbelief. He then called me forward and bellowed in my ear, "It is the paying officer who will decide how much a Boy Entrant gets paid, not you. Do you understand that, Boy Entrant Walls?" "Yes, flight sergeant." "Right, get yourself to the back of the queue and take it as a lesson." I could hardly believe my bad luck. It was just an accidental slip of the tongue, but it resulted in me missing yet another Thursday evening meal.

Just before the end of the initial training phase, our flight was taken to the camp rifle range to observe a firepower demonstration by a RAF Regiment NCO. He showed us the workings of the 7.62 self-loading rifle and demonstrated its firepower by gradually breaking down a small brick wall with repetitive rounds of fire – very impressive! But even more impressive was when we were all allowed to fire the Lee Enfield .303 rifle for the first time. Until then, Boy Entrants were only allowed to fire the much smaller .22 training rifles. My little Irish friend, John T, who was knee high to a grasshopper, could only, with extreme effort carry his .303 Lee Enfield rifle let alone use it for target practice. The regiment corporal ordered John to lie down and take aim at the target in front. I could see the barrel of John's rife waving all over the place. Upon being given the order to fire John pulled the trigger and fired his first round. I swear to God that John flew backwards as fast as the bullet flew forward. The kick from the rifle was much greater than anything he had expected, a situation no doubt compounded by his very small stature and light weight. Bruised, but not beaten, John remembered from that day forth to hold the rifle very firmly against the shoulder and lean into the direction of fire before pulling the trigger. In truth, there were quite a few bruised shoulders at the end of that day. The repetitive nature of the training continued unabated until one day we were ordered to move out of our wooden-hutted billets to take up residence in a billet located in the Fulton Block; a grand brick building that could house hundreds of Boy Entrants. This move marked the end of the initial training phase and the focus of learning shifted from drill, physical education, maths and science, towards electronic circuit theory and practical electronics work.

Electronic systems in the late 1950s relied almost exclusively on thermionic valve technology and I soon learned an awful lot about diodes, triodes, pentodes, beam-tetrodes and other valve types. There was a mass of other electronic components with strange names that would soon become part of my daily lexicon. Things like magnetrons, klystrons, carcinotrons, resistors, capacitors, series and parallel-tuned circuits, waveguides, dipoles, reflectors, directors and scanners, to name but a few. The list was endless, but I lapped it all up. Mind you, handling some of the electronic components was not without risk. There were a number of wags in our class who would charge up some fairly large capacitors and leave them lying around so that anyone who innocently picked them up and touched their terminals received quite a nasty shock. Looking on the bright side, the experience did help to instil in all of us a modicum of caution when handling and working on anything to do with electronics. Moving on, I decided fairly soon after arriving at Cosford that I wanted to work on fighters and I grafted hard and lobbied my instructors to achieve that aim. Electronic circuitry was taught to my class by a very nice civilian gentleman called Mr Fell. He was the epitome of kindness and understanding. He and his wife would invite small groups of us to his house in Albrighton for tea on a Saturday evening where we would watch 'Boy Meets Girl' (or was it 'Six-Five Special') on his little monochrome television whilst we would simultaneously dig into Mrs Fell's delicious cakes and biscuits. Afterwards Mr Fell would run us back to the camp in his car. During class work he really inspired us to work hard by getting us to compete for the best weekly test results against other classes following the same curriculum. I loved it and I am sure you can imagine my relief when, at the end of phase two training, I was told that I would be going on to study three fighter-associated radar systems during the final training phase. One of the radars was an airborne interception (AI) radar built in Britain by – I believe – the EKCO Electronics Company. It was called AI Mk. 17 and it was fitted to most of the odd-numbered marks of Gloster Javelin fighters, such as Javelin Mks. 5, 7 and 9.

In addition to learning the complex workings of AI-17, I was taught all I needed to know about the Cossor identification friend or foe (IFF) Mk.10 transponder and another small transponder called fighter identification system (FIS). The purpose of AI-17 and IFF was generally self-explanatory, but FIS was, I believe, unique to the Javelin. Its purpose was to identify Javelins as being friendly, whenever they were illuminated by the AI radar from another Javelin. Essentially, FIS was there to prevent one Javelin from shooting down another Javelin. If a transmission from AI-17 (or from the AI-22 radar that was fitted to most even marks of Javelin) was detected by the FIS receiver, the system would broadcast a response on a different frequency that would be picked up by another part of the FIS system on the Javelin conducting the search. This would result in a 'blip' being displayed next to the primary radar return

Author working on an AI-17 scanner.

on the navigator's radar display, thus identifying the target as friendly. The good news about the FIS system – at least from the maintenance perspective – was that it was very reliable and the crystals in the little centimetric-band FIS receiver only needed to be checked periodically to ensure the system was working at optimum performance. The bad news was that this receiver was mounted in the most inaccessible position on top of the Javelin's tailplane. This meant that the unlucky tradesman ordered to test the crystals would have to manoeuvre a tall 'cherry picker' ladder system up behind the Javelin, climb up its wobbly steps and reach out across the tailplane to carry out the fiddly and finger-numbing task of checking the crystals – an extremely dodgy process when carried out on the squadron flight line, especially during cold, wet and windy nights.

The maintenance philosophy adopted by the RAF at that time was based around three levels of repair; first line, second line and third line. First-line repairs were carried out at flight-line level and mainly involved isolating a reported fault to an individual line replacement unit (LRU), or 'black box' as they were often referred to at that time. A black box suspected of being faulty would be returned for second-line servicing at the Radio Servicing Flight (RSF). Once at RSF, the faulty unit would be installed on a bench-testing rig where the nature of the fault could be investigated in some depth and rectification carried out to render the unit serviceable again. This normally involved changing sub-units, thermionic valves and, in some cases, individual resistor, capacitor and other small electronic components. Black boxes deemed to be beyond repair at RSF were sent to the appropriate maintenance unit (MU) where third-line repair work and/or refurbishment could be carried out. Boy Entrant training at Cosford was mainly designed to prepare students for first and second-line work.

First-line training for Boy Entrants destined to work on fighters was carried out in one of the large hangars that overlooked the station parade ground. It contained a selection of aircraft types that were currently in service with the RAF at that time, including a Gloster Javelin and several Hunters and Meteors. There was also a Mosquito and a Venom night fighter for the lads to clamour over. During a typical training session, one of the instructors would deliberately install a faulty LRU on one of the aircraft. The trainee would then be ordered to apply electrical power to the aircraft, carry out a system test, and then attempt to find and isolate the fault to a specific LRU/black box. Once the faulty unit was identified, the student would be expected to replace it with a serviceable item. He would then have to re-test the system in accordance with the proscribed test schedule to ensure that the replacement unit was working properly and that the aircraft was ready for operational use. Details of all rectification carried out would then be entered in the aircraft's dedicated RAF Form 700, a document that contained a record of all work carried out on the aircraft. It also held details of the aircraft's history including its total number of flying hours, replenishment records, details of modification work that had been carried out, plus other bits of information too numerous to mention here. I found first-line maintenance training extremely interesting. But what I secretly loved most of all was the chance to sit alone in the cockpit of the various aircraft types pretending that I was the pilot or navigator. Training for second-line maintenance was carried out in purpose-built laboratory facilities located inside another of Cosford's many hangars. There, students were trained to conduct in-depth fault finding and repair procedures down to sub-unit and component level. This required a deeper level of system knowledge and I found it to be particularly satisfying when I could find the obscure faults introduced inside the black boxes by the instructors.

One of the big disappointments during my 18 months at Cosford was when I was told that I would not be allowed to partake in the gliding activities that took place on the airfield at weekends. Gliding, I was told, was reserved for air training cadet (ATC) members only. So all I could do was gaze forlornly out of the window of my billet and watch the gliders being winch-launched then slowly circling about before descending back to the launch site. There was some consolation when, on one fine Saturday morning, the members of our flight were taken for an air experience flight around the local area in an Avro Anson – a WWII, twin-engine, light transport aircraft. This was only my second flight in an aeroplane and I loved it. My third flight took place

Avro Anson. (Aviation Photo Company)

towards the latter part of my time at Cosford when the members of my course were individually taken up in a de Havilland Chipmunk two-seat light-training aircraft for a flight around the Wrekin Hill in Shropshire. During my flight the pilot allowed me to take control of the aircraft, but being scared that I might do something wrong and endanger the aircraft, and also probably being a bit under-confident, I soon asked the pilot to take back control.

At the culmination of 18 months of intense training, and after successfully passing the final theory and practical examinations, the 35th Entry of Boy Entrants was given a formal farewell from Cosford at a graduation parade held in their honour. Our squadron, supported by the junior squadrons, marched onto the parade ground with boots shining, uniforms pressed and Lee Enfield rifles at the slope. A senior air officer from Bomber Command was our reviewing officer and he gave us a rousing speech to see us on our way. He also arranged for one of his Victor B1 bombers to overfly the parade ground during the presentation of arms – all very exciting. The parade went very well but, unfortunately, the Victor crew failed to find the parade ground. Instead they carried out their fly-past over some remote rural area in Staffordshire, an event that must have surprised all of the village-dwellers and farmers. Whilst news about one of the RAF's brand-new Victor bombers getting lost over the UK would certainly raise a laugh in the Kremlin, I don't think it went down particularly well at HQ Bomber Command. Our reviewing air officer was definitely not impressed.

# The Real Air Force

In the spring of 1960, and at the 'grown-up' age of 16, I left Cosford to enjoy two weeks' leave at home in Edinburgh before taking up my first 'proper job' in the RSF at RAF Leeming in Yorkshire. I was still officially a Boy Entrant and would remain so until I reached the official adult service age of 17 and a half. Until then, I was required to continue wearing the four-propeller, brass badge on my uniform. It was all a bit embarrassing and was a source of much ribbing from the older airmen, NCOs and National Servicemen. However, I tried not to let it get to me and after reaching the magic age that signified adult service, I quickly replaced my Boy Entrant badge with the cloth, twin-bladed propeller badge signifying that I was now a leading aircraftman in the real Royal Air Force.

Leeming in 1960 was home to No. 228 OCU, where pilots, navigators and radar observers were trained to fly and operate the Gloster Javelin night fighter. My time in RSF required me to carry out maintenance work on the Cossor-built IFF Mk.10 equipment, and carry out routine maintenance on the AI-17 antenna/scanner unit. As previously mentioned, AI-17 was fitted on Javelin Fighter All Weather (FAW) 5, 7 and 9. Even-numbered marks of Javelin including the FAW 6 and 8, were, in the main, fitted with the American-built AI-22 radar. AI-22 was effectively a dual radar system, one part of which was used to search ahead of the Javelin for targets, and the other part was used to lock on and track a target that had been acquired. Thus AI-22 offered Javelin crews a track while scan (TWS) capability. That is to say the equipment could lock on and track an enemy aircraft while simultaneously maintaining a search of the airspace out in front. Unfortunately, AI-22 proved to be rather unreliable in RAF service and it was also difficult to maintain. AI-17, on the other hand, was a simpler system offering reasonable reliability, but it did not have a TWS capability. Instead, the Javelin navigator or observer had to select either the search or the track function, a limitation that, I was told, could prove disadvantageous during certain air-to-air war-fighting scenarios. Later, when talking with one of the navigator instructors, he told me that the maximum range offered by the AI-17 against the tail-on aspect of a medium bomber was somewhat less than the 40 nm advertised for the system. However, he said that the system was definitely better than the radar he had previously operated when flying in Meteor NF11 night fighters.

Pilots destined to fly the Javelin received familiarisation training in a ground-procedure trainer located in the OCU building before progressing to the flying training phase on the Javelin T3. The T3 was a pilot training version of the Javelin. Instead of having AI-17 installed in the nose, it was fitted with the small radar-ranging radar that fed target-range information to the aircraft's gyro gunsight. This was the same type of radar that was fitted in the nose of the Hawker Hunter day fighter. The Javelin

T3 also had dual flying controls to allow both the instructor and the trainee pilots to fly the aircraft. Navigators and radar observers received lead-in instruction on Varsity aircraft followed by specialist air-intercept training in Canberra aircraft that had been modified to carry AI-17. Old Meteor NF11 aircraft were flown by the OCU staff to act as training targets. Finally, when deemed ready, pilots and navigators were crewed up together and completed their conversion training flying the Javelin FAW 5.

I enjoyed my time at Leeming. My boss, Warrant Officer (WO) Ormerod, was an observer/air gunner who, much earlier in his career, had flown in Westland Wapiti bi-planes in India and around the North West Frontier. He was an amazing gentleman whose kind and humorous leadership remains firmly ensconced in my memory. Another highlight of my time at Leeming was learning to fly gliders at the Leeming-based Cleveland Gliding Club. I lived and breathed everything to do with gliding and my friend, Bob McLuckie, and I would regularly find ourselves at the sharp end of our sergeant's tongue for gazing out of the RSF window and observing the different cloud types forming over the Yorkshire Dales instead of getting on with our work. Bob would later be commissioned as a pilot and fly Vulcans on 617 Squadron.

Possibly as a sop to RAF physical fitness requirements and to get us out of RSF and into the fresh air, about 12 of us, including our SNCOs and WOs would play volleyball on the grass area in front of the RSF building during tea breaks and at lunchtime. This most enjoyable pastime was brought to an abrupt halt when a group of officers and SNCOs from what I think was the inspectorate of radio installations and services (IRIS) realised that our game of volleyball was taking place directly in front of the radar benches, thus exposing us to microwave transmissions from AI-17 and radar-ranging transmitters. Our volleyball pitch was very quickly fenced off and 'Radiation Hazard' signs liberally set up around its perimeter. When word got around that those of us that worked in RSF had, unwittingly, been irradiated with microwaves for many weeks and months, airmen from other sections on the camp laughed and suggested that we would probably start glowing in the dark. They were also very keen to suggest that our future ability to father children would almost certainly be compromised. I am pleased to report that since that time, I have successfully fathered two healthy children and, to date, I have shown no signs of glowing in the dark.

When 228 OCU closed down in 1961–62, I was posted to RAF Waterbeach where I worked in RSF on the IFF Mk. 10 and an associated unit called selective identification feature (SIF). This unit served as a coding unit for IFF Mk. 10. It allowed an aircraft to respond to interrogation from ground-radar sites with an aircraft-specific identification code thus allowing the ground operators to identify specific aircraft rather than just whether they were friend or foe. Later, I was posted to RAF Leuchars where I worked on GEE III, a miniaturised and updated version of the GEE hyperbolic navigation system used in Lancaster and Halifax bombers during the latter years of WWII. In early 1963, and at the age of 19, I was called forward to attend a radar fitters course at RAF Yatesbury in Wiltshire after which I was awarded the rank of junior technician and given what at the time was deemed to be a significant pay rise. A short while later, I was posted to RAF Wyton where I worked on radar and special receiver and analysis equipment installed in Comet R2 and Canberra aircraft belonging to No. 51 Electronic Reconnaissance Squadron. My time on 51 Squadron was short-lived and I was soon posted back to RAF Leeming which, by then, had been re-rolled as a flying training station equipped with Jet Provosts. It was during this time that I met Jessie, my future wife-to-be. It was also during this time that I was treated to a night-time flight in a Jet Provost. It was a 'cowboy' flight tasked with 'rounding up' students that got lost on their night navigation exercises. Thankfully, being a clear night, no one got lost and my pilot treated me to some night-time aerobatics in the open airspace just south of Darlington. Very exciting! However, my time at Leeming was marred when I was involved in a gliding accident.

I had re-joined the Cleveland Gliding Club and, as an introduction back to gliding, my instructor, an ex-Javelin pilot, was asked by the club's chief flying instructor to take me for a familiarisation trip in the DFS Kranich. This was a rather old-fashioned, gull-winged, dual-controlled German-built glider of wood and fabric construction. It was a very heavy machine which made it hard to manually move about on the ground, but once airborne, it flew beautifully. It also had a cockpit canopy that would not have been out of place on a Messerschmitt 110. At the pre-flight briefing, my instructor told me that I was to sit in the front seat of the glider and he would sit in the rear. He also told me that he would do the take-off and landing and that I could fly the bit in between.

The winch launch was uneventful and after the instructor released the cable at around 1,000 feet, I was allowed to take control of the glider. I flew straight and level for a short while then did a couple of gentle turns before heading off on the downwind leg. I must have misjudged my positioning in the circuit as it soon became clear that we would arrive at base leg somewhat higher than I judged to be ideal. Still in control of the glider, I cracked open the airbrakes to help lose some height. Upon turning onto base leg my instructor advised me that he was taking back control of the aircraft. I said, "you have control," let go of the controls and put both my hands on either side of the canopy where he could see them. As we continued on base leg, I noticed that the instructor had further extended the airbrakes. We were now down to a height that I deemed ideal for landing, however, my instructor seemed determined to lose even more height and as we turned onto finals, I was aware that the airbrakes were now fully out and our airspeed was bleeding away. The next thing I remember is when the Kranich shuddered, executed a swift roll to the right and entered a steep dive towards the ground. I don't remember the impact. Then I saw that club members were running towards me while I remained strapped in the cockpit of the glider. I turned to ask the instructor if he was all right and was amazed to find that there was nothing whatsoever behind me. The nose of the glider with me inside had broken off, bounced into the air, and landed many yards away from the rest of the aircraft. Amazingly, apart from a few scratches and bruises, I was completely unhurt. Unfortunately, my instructor, who had clearly taken the brunt of the crash, was severely injured.

It was later decided that with the airbrakes extended the glider had lost flying speed during the turn on to final approach, stalled, entered a spin, and crashed about 300 yards short of the touchdown point. Later, after a formal investigation had been carried out, I was told that the crash was caused by the instructor failing to take proper control of the aircraft during the base leg and allowing the glider's airspeed to fall below that required for safe flight. Despite being told that no blame would be attached to me, I nevertheless sensed, correctly or incorrectly, that my presence at the club was no longer welcome. The instructor was a well-liked individual and I was a 'new boy'. Furthermore, the club had just lost an old, but valuable glider. Although the accident happened many years ago, I still think about the tragic injuries sustained by the instructor and wonder if I could have done something, anything, to prevent the crash.

In early 1965, I was told that I was to report to RAF Yatesbury for a three-month course on air navigation radar systems. On completion of the course, I was posted to No. 210 Shackleton Squadron at RAF Kinloss. This was an interesting time for me. Working on the Shackleton Mk. III and flying off on detachments to Bodø and Ørland in Norway and Ballykelly in Northern Ireland was much more interesting than working on Jet Provosts and going nowhere. In November 1965 and at the ripe old age of 22, I tied the knot with my fiancée, Jessie – aged 19 – at All Saints Parish Church in Northallerton, North Yorkshire. After our weekend honeymoon at Berwick-on-Tweed (yes, I know, but money was scarce in those days) Jess and I set up home in a cottage in the village of Findhorn, not far from Kinloss airfield. Life was wonderful there and we were very happy indeed, but things got even better when, in the autumn of 1966, I was told that I was being posted to No. 390 MU at RAF Seletar in Singapore. Better still, Jessie would be going with me.

My work at 390 MU involved doing overhaul and repair work on Rebecca Mk. 4 and Mk. 8 equipment. Both were distance-measuring equipment (DME) navigation systems, the Mk. 4 system being fitted in the Blackburn Beverley transport aircraft that flew from RAF Seletar located at the north of Singapore Island, and the Mk. 8 being fitted to Hunter fighters that flew from RAF Tengah on the western side of the island. The work was easy, and I was never required to do night shifts. This proved to be a distinct advantage as my wife was soon to give birth to our daughter, Juliet, at the

No. 390 Maintenance Unit at RAF Seletar.

British Military Hospital at Alexandra Road, a few miles west of Singapore city. One of the big advantages of living with my wife in Singapore was that in addition to my normal pay, I was also entitled to receive the rather generous local overseas allowances (LOA). This not only meant that Jessie and I could enjoy a comfortable lifestyle in our hired bungalow at 51 Jalan Chengam in Sembawang Hills Estate, it also allowed me to join the Singapore Flying Club at Paya Lebar Airport where I gained my Private Pilot Licence. This was an exciting period of my life and I enjoyed flying my wife and friends in Piper Cherokee and Cessna 172 aircraft on sightseeing trips over Singapore city, and doing circuits and bumps at Paya Lebar between arriving and departing jet airliners.

The Flying Club would occasionally organise 'barbeque fly-outs'. One such fly-out took us to Rompin, a small airfield that belonged to a tin mining company located on the east coast of Malaya. Once there, we held spot-landing and flour-bombing competitions followed by all of us enjoying a group swim in the East China Sea. Later, we feasted on barbequed food before packing things up and flying back to Singapore. Being able to fly Cessna 172 and Piper Cherokee aircraft around Singapore and Malaya definitely gave me the urge to apply for aircrew. However, I still enjoyed working with radar and other electronic equipment. So, in order to have the best of both worlds, I applied for SNCO aircrew training as an air electronics operator (AEOp). I was ordered to attend an initial aircrew selection board at RAF Changi, which I must have

Above: With my daughter, Juliet, at the Singapore Flying Club.
Below: Singapore Flying Club fly-out to Rompin in Malaya.

passed, because upon returning to the UK in 1968, I was told to report at the Officer and NCO Aircrew Selection Centre at RAF Biggin Hill for final assessment. I must have done reasonably well there too, because not long afterwards I was ordered to attend No. 21 AEOp and Flight Engineers Course at RAF Topcliffe in Yorkshire.

# CHAPTER TWO
# AIRCREW TRAINING

When I arrived at RAF Topcliffe in the summer of 1969 it was with a feeling of great excitement, but also some trepidation. I wasn't sure what to expect and, naturally, I was wondering how well I would blend in with, and be judged against, other members of the AEOp course. I had arranged for my wife and daughter to move down from Kinloss and live at Jessie's parent's house near Richmond in Yorkshire where they would stay until I could move them into a RAF married quarter (MQ). But before I could be allocated a MQ, I would have to successfully complete the aircrew initial training course (ITC). This required all cadets to stay on base at RAF Topcliffe for a number of weeks. The ITC involved lots of room inspections, drill, some outward-bound challenges, survival skills and, of course, lots of physical training. I found this part of the course not too challenging, and I was glad when it was over as I was impatient to start work on the infinitely more interesting, technically oriented, part of the training syllabus. Having completed the ITC, I was able to apply for a MQ and, as luck would have it, I was soon allocated a small, but comfortable, semi-detached house at nearby RAF Dishforth. My wife and daughter moved in a few weeks later.

The ground study part of the course was fairly wide ranging and included both voice and Morse radio communication procedures, radio and radar theory, aviation medicine, meteorology, survival training and, of course, more physical training. As the course progressed, I was introduced to the magic of Q and Z codes, three-lettered code groups that acted as a form of shorthand for aircrew. Each three-lettered group has a specific meaning, and collectively, they cover a vast range of aircraft-related subjects such as flight operations, weather and communications etc. Although Z codes have pretty much fallen into disuse, a small number of important Q codes are still used regularly throughout aviation today. However, in earlier times, the full ledger of Q and Z codes resided firmly within the wireless operator's domain and they formed a vital part of his communications tool kit, particularly when using Morse code. The high-frequency (HF) communications equipment used in RAF aircraft at that time was called STR-18. It was a crystal-controlled radio comprising a number of black boxes and a control unit. It was a rather complicated and awkward piece of equipment to set up and tune and I was pleased to learn that the RAF had started the process of re-equipping some of its front-line aircraft with modern, and much easier to use,

Collins 618T and Marconi AD-470 HF radios. However, at Topcliffe, I was stuck with the STR-18, the workings of which I would have to learn, and the use of which I would have to master. A common fear amongst students was being handed a box of crystals by their instructor and being told to re-tune the STR-18 whilst in flight – a nightmare scenario. Lucky for me I was only ever asked to tune one transmit and receive channel during a ground-training session, and no one was more surprised than me when it worked.

Despite there being a fairly large amount of technical subject matter to grasp, there was little or no doubt that the main focus of the course was on mastering the art of communicating using Morse code, a means of communication which, at that time, was the radio operator's bread and butter. I soon became fairly proficient on the Morse key and had no trouble sending messages, but receiving plain text (normal sentences) Morse messages proved to be a problem for me. I knew that I would have to master the skill before I could progress on to the flying phase of the course and this kept me motivated. Without realising it I had fallen into what – I would discover later – was the well-known trap of trying to guess what the message was about after writing down the first few lines of text instead of transcribing the whole message first before trying to read it. It was only after weeks of Morse training that the penny dropped and I realised that the secret to accurately receiving plain text Morse code was to simply ignore the meaning of what you were writing down and simply concentrate on receiving and translating the message onto paper.

Receiving military-encoded messages made up from four-letter code groups did not pose a problem, because reading them directly off the page made no sense whatsoever, so it never occurred to me to try. However, at the time, so difficult did it seem for me, and some others, to get to grips with correctly translating plain text messages, that we began to question whether we would ever be able to master the art. A good friend of mine, Tony Rollo, who was also suffering the same problem, decided that "being a person with higher-than-average intelligence and capable of sophisticated, logic-based analytical thinking, he was probably too advanced in human terms to revert back to the skills of yesteryear and communicate using dots and dashes!" This caused much laughter amongst the other class members who were coping well with their Morse lessons. But it didn't go down at all well with our civilian instructor who seemed to take it as a personal insult. Needless to say, with perseverance and an abundance of periods allocated for Morse training, we all gradually got the hang of it and before long we could reliably send and receive code groups and plain text messages at more than 16 words per minute.

Although the course curriculum was quite broad, it only delved into subjects to a depth that was deemed necessary to prepare us for future training at one of the front-line OCUs. Our course was very lucky to have Flt Lt Peter Fownes as our instructor.

His lessons were always well prepared and his logical, step-by-step, method of instruction made learning very easy indeed. This was helped along by his propensity to deliver regular and humorous anecdotes about life on the front line. Overall, I had no difficulties mastering the academic part of the course, helped perhaps by my previous training as a radar technician. That said, there were other technically trained individuals on the course and the race to come top in progress tests soon engendered a competitive spirit within the class. Somehow, when all the exam results had been added up, I emerged as the overall winner and for that I was awarded the Ground Studies Award at graduation. It was around this time that my wife gave birth to our son, James, in Ripon Hospital.

With the technical study phase of the course finished, it was time to move on to the flying phase. I could hardly wait! You can perhaps imagine the excitement I felt when I was told to report to clothing stores at Topcliffe to pick up my aircrew boots and socks, flying suits, gloves and all the other paraphernalia that goes with being aircrew. Along with other course members, I had to make my way down to the RAF Aeromedicine Training Centre (AMTC) at RAF Lindholme to be fitted with an oxygen mask, inner helmet and bone dome. This, at last, was the real thing. The feeling of excitement and anticipation was overwhelming. But before our instructors allowed us to get anywhere near an aeroplane we were subjected to many hours of tuition on pre-flight planning. This included preparing communications plans, drawing routes on maps, recognising the different types of airspace and the rules pertaining to each of them, analysing meteorology forecasts, and studying the daily Notices to Airmen (NOTAM). NOTAMs provided up-to-date information on airfields, navigation beacons, airspace restrictions and a plethora of other things needed to ensure that flights could be planned and conducted in a safe and efficient manner. We were also issued with all the essential charts and documents needed for pre-flight planning and for reference during flight. By the time I had collected all the required documents and charts my newly issued flight bag was bulging at the seams. After several weeks, it was time to undertake my first instructional flight and I could feel the butterflies fluttering around inside me. What would the air instructor ask me to do? Would I be able to remain calm and work in a methodical manner or would I become a jabbering wreck and end up making a complete mess of things?

The aircraft used for training AEOps was the Vickers Varsity, a twin-piston-engine aircraft that entered service in 1951. Although it was rather old, slow and noisy, it was an ideal platform for students to gain real-life very high frequency (VHF), ultra-high frequency (UHF) and HF air-related communications experience. Each training flight carried two trainee AEOps, one sitting in what would normally be the co-pilot's seat and the other sitting at a rearwards-facing desk further back in the aircraft – my first experience of flying forward while facing backwards. The trainee in the co-pilot's seat

Vickers Varsity. This was one of the Varsity aircraft that I flew in during aircrew training at RAF Topcliffe. (Aviation Photo Company)

was expected to conduct all of the V/UHF voice communications associated with the flight and assist the pilot with minor tasks associated with flying the aircraft. All of this helped to engender good crew cooperation and airmanship.

The trainee in the back of the aircraft was expected to use the STR-18 HF equipment to conduct two-way HF communications with the training cell at RAF Topcliffe – call sign PR7W. In addition, he was expected to carry out flight safety tasks mandated by the captain and the on-board AEO instructor. Trainees would swap positions from flight to flight such that both students covered the full air-training syllabus. In total, the flying phase comprised around 20 sorties, most of which were out-and-return flights from Topcliffe each lasting around four hours. Routeing at that time took us from Topcliffe back to Topcliffe via Whitby, Aberdeen, Bonar Bridge in the north of Scotland, and RAF Leuchars. Other flights involved patrolling over the North Sea and reporting back to Topcliffe via HF, shipping contacts observed (or made up) by the captain. Trainees were also expected to obtain regular weather updates and perform other tasks whilst always being prepared to don parachutes and/or man fire extinguishers if a practice emergency was called by the captain.

Although I had eventually mastered the art of sending and receiving Morse messages in the classroom, I found it rather more awkward doing so while being bounced around in the back of a Varsity. But, like others on the course, I gradually got the hang of it and my confidence soared. To introduce some variety into the training, one of the training flights involved landing at another RAF airfield in the UK which, in my case, was RAF St Mawgan. Later on, we did an overseas flight to RAF Wildenrath in Germany which offered us some experience in conducting voice communications with foreign ATC agencies. As you may already know, English is the mandated language for voice communications with ATC agencies throughout the world. However, it is not unknown for foreign aircrews to occasionally revert to their own language when communicating with their own ATC authorities. I am told that on one occasion, a Topcliffe student tried to impress his instructor by opening communications with the French ATC authorities using his state-school version of the French language. This resulted in the French ATC controller replying in rapid and heavily accented French. This left the poor student dumbstruck, and with the sad realisation that his Grade C, O Level in French was never going to cut the mustard when it came to communicating with French ATC agencies. Worse still, the poor devil was left with the humiliating task of trying to recover the situation in grovelling English.

HF Morse communications could have their humorous moments too. One of the elderly Morse instructors manning the HF ground station at Topcliffe must have suffered from some form of arthritis in his hand as his Morse would include unnatural pauses which would render parts of his messages unreadable, or at least, odd. Asking for a repeat usually resulted in another totally different and equally incoherent version of the same message. Gradually, students got to understand his multiple variations of the Morse code, but it did prove challenging at times.

The penultimate training flight was a long-range sortie to Malta with a refuelling stop at Istres in the South of France. This provided students with ample opportunity to communicate with foreign ATC and other civilian and military agencies. It also allowed students manning the HF positions to conduct realistic two-way HF communications with the Maritime Headquarters (MHQ) at Malta. Elated at having successfully completed this outbound training flight, some of the students, myself included, decided to let off steam by visiting some of the 'interesting' bars lining the back streets of Valletta. Having grown accustomed to good Yorkshire brown beer, the Maltese beer proved to be something of a disappointment, being described by one person in our group as being rather like the output from the urinary tract of a very small insect. That said, it must have had some delayed potency as, come the morning, some of the students had trouble getting out of their beds and were wishing that they had stayed on base the night before. I think it would be fair to say that the average performance of the students on the flight home was somewhat less gilded that that on the outbound flight. The final training flight from Topcliffe was an 'anything goes' sortie with a few practice emergencies thrown in. I thoroughly enjoyed the flying phase of training, but I was also happy and relieved when it was over and I was told that I had passed the course. I graduated as a sergeant AEOp in September 1970.

# CHAPTER THREE
# PRE-VULCAN DAYS

After completing AEOp training at Topcliffe and despite being told that I would be joining 120 Squadron at RAF Kinloss, I was somewhat confusingly posted to 42 Shackleton Squadron at RAF St Mawgan. At the same time, a fellow course member whose surname also began with 'W', found himself being posted to 120 Squadron at Kinloss despite being told he would be going to 42 Squadron. Clearly, an admin error had occurred. So, upon arriving at St Mawgan I discussed the problem with the personnel services staff in Admin Wing HQ. They quickly established that a mistake had, indeed, been made. However, instead of ordering me to proceed to Kinloss, I was told to stay at St Mawgan and remain on 42 Squadron for a few weeks after which I would join Crew 7 from 120 Squadron when it arrived from Kinloss to begin conversion onto the Nimrod MR1. This was a fine solution, and I quickly made plans to ensconce my family in a MQ at nearby RAF St Eval. Having very little to do other than make tea and wander around the 42 Squadron crew room, I asked if I could tag along as supernumerary aircrew on a Shackleton sortie scheduled for the following day.

Having never done any training as aircrew on the Shackleton and knowing less than nothing about maritime operations, I failed to understand most of what was said at the crew briefing. However, I did gather that we were going to take part in a combined anti-submarine exercise (CASEX) in the English Channel, and this would require our Shackleton crew to work with the crew of an RN helicopter to jointly detect and prosecute a cooperating RN submarine. At the briefing the captain informed us that we would be practising vectored-attack (VECTAC) procedures, where the helicopter, having acquired and located the submarine with its dipping sonar system, would call in the Shackleton to drop a simulated torpedo on the target. The Shackleton captain would do this by flying his aircraft from a position directly above the helicopter out on a heading and to a distance dictated by the helicopter crew that would position the Shackleton directly above the required weapon release point. It all sounded very interesting and when the briefing was finished the crew, with me tagging along behind, left the briefing room and boarded the Shackleton. Once in the aircraft, I was instructed to sit in the starboard beam seat near the rear door of the aircraft. There was lots of chat on the aircraft's intercom, most of which went over my head, but soon, with the pre-start checks complete, the engines were started and we taxied to the holding point near the entrance to the runway. After carrying out magneto checks on all four Rolls-Royce Griffon engines and carrying out the pre-take-off checks, the captain taxied the Shackleton, brakes squeaking and engines grumbling at low RPM, onto the runway for take-off.

As the throttles were eased forward the growl from the Shackleton's four engines changed to a frantic and deafening roar added to by the scream of the Shackleton's two Viper jet engines as they, too, reached their take-off power setting. I couldn't help thinking that the deafening crescendo of engine noises plus the vibrations that rattled and buzzed throughout the aircraft would surely play havoc with the on-board electronic systems which, in that era, relied almost exclusively on thermionic valve technology. Power checked and set and with the brakes released our Shackleton started its surging acceleration down the St Mawgan runway. As the speed built up the captain initially used the nose-wheel steering and later the rudder to keep the aircraft running straight. At 'V-Rotate', the calculated take-off airspeed, the captain eased the Shackleton into the air and commenced a gentle climb. "Undercarriage up please co-pilot." "Roger captain," replied the co-pilot. A few seconds later the captain ordered the flaps to be raised and, after another short pause he instructed the radio operator to read out the after-take-off checks. When the checks were complete the navigator piped up on the intercom, "Captain from nav, when you are ready, please turn on to heading XXX." "Roger nav heading XXX, turning on." The Shackleton's starboard wing dipped below the horizon as the captain commenced a gentle turn on to the new heading. I think it was around this point that he ordered the flight engineer to shut down the two Viper jet engines and we settled into the climb using 'piston power' only. We were on our way.

Upon reaching the designated altitude for transit to the exercise area, the pilots reduced power and the four Griffon engines settled down to a steady, and less frantic, drone. I listened to the intercom and tried to make sense of what was going on, but it was all a bit difficult to follow. Looking out of the beam window, I could see the towns and roads of Cornwall pass slowly behind us as we crossed the south coast and headed towards the restricted airspace above the English Channel. Upon arriving in the exercise area there was a 15-minute lull in the proceedings during which a member of the crew rustled up a most welcome round of coffee and tea. The beam seats in the Shackleton were well known for their comfort, and with warm air making its way down to the back of the aircraft and the intercom chat falling off, I started to feel quite drowsy. The master AEOp (MAEOp) sitting on the beam seat on the other side of the aircraft seemed to be having difficulty keeping his eyes open too. It was a short, but most welcome, lull in the proceedings.

"We have good radio contact with the chopper, captain," someone said as we continued to orbit in the exercise area. The crew waited in anticipation for attack details to be passed to us by the helicopter crew. I had just finished drinking my second cup of coffee when one of the navigators, who must have nipped down to the back of the aircraft to visit the Elsan toilet, suggested that I might like to get involved by dropping a smoke marker through the nearby chute in the Shackleton floor when he gave the command. He said that when we reached a point on top of the submarine, I would hear him say "Now, Now, NOW," and I should drop the marker on the third now. It seemed simple enough.

As our Shackleton continued to drone around in circles the co-pilot announced that he had visual contact with the helicopter. A short while later the level of intercom chat started to increase and someone announced that the helicopter, using its dipping sonar, had acquired the submarine and that we should standby to execute a VECTAC procedure. With a smoke marker in my hand, I made myself ready at the launch chute. I heard someone saying, "Okay captain, take up a heading of XYZ degrees from on top of the helicopter." "Roger turning on," said the captain. There was a bit more chat, then I heard someone saying, "keep turning, keep turning, steady, steady on top Now, Now, NOW!" I launched the smoke marker, but before it had covered the short distance from my hand to the chute the MAEOp who was crouched beside me snatched it with his fingertips, looked at me and, with a wide grin, informed me that we were on top of the helicopter, not the submarine. He handed the canister back to me and told me to stand by. The navigator culminated his range countdown to the simulated weapon-release point with a second "Now, Now, NOW!" I let go of the canister. This time it made into the chute, out of the bottom of the Shackleton and hopefully, down to a point in the sea, beneath which the submarine was lurking. As the captain turned the Shackleton on a new heading and ordered the bomb doors to be closed, I thanked the MAEOp for his unbelievable quick reactions and apologised for my stupidity. He calmly replied in soft West Country accent, "It's all right my lad, not your fault, bloody navigator shouldn't have asked you to do something you hadn't been properly briefed to do." I tried to hide my embarrassment, but I realised that I should have declined the navigator's suggestion that I drop the smoke marker. I had tried to appear confident, but instead ended up looking foolish. It was a good lesson well learned, and I sincerely hoped that I wouldn't have to learn any more lessons that way. A few weeks later and not long after I had stopped blushing at the thought of nearly downing a RN helicopter with a smoke marker, I met up with my new crew from Kinloss and, together, we started the Nimrod MR1 conversion course at No. 236 OCU.

# The Nimrod MR1

The 236 OCU Nimrod course was very well organised. The purpose of the course was to arm the crews with the information, procedures and skills needed to safely and efficiently operate the Nimrod MR1 MPA. Those that had already served on

Shackletons were already aware of the 'lingo' associated with maritime operations and they probably found most of the course work a simple walk down memory lane. But for me it was all brand new. As the course progressed, I started to appreciate the 'cat and mouse' challenges involved in trying to detect, localise, track and attack submarines. Destined to be a 'dry' operator, I received fairly detailed briefings on the Nimrod's air-to-surface vessel Mk. 21 (ASV-21) radar, the magnetic anomaly detection (MAD) equipment and the French-made ARAR/ARAX electronic support measures (ESM) sensor. I was also introduced to the AD-470 HF radio, which proved to be a vast improvement over the STR-18 radio used in the Varsity. There were multiple briefings on communication procedures associated with the many types of operation that the Nimrod would be tasked to perform. These included CASEX sorties, close and distant support to surface task forces, and procedures to be followed during search and rescue (SAR) operations, to name but a few.

To provide a rounded understanding of Nimrod MR1 operations, dry operators were provided with familiarisation briefings on the roles and responsibilities of the 'wet' team. We were told how they would detect and locate submarines using the Nimrod's Jezebel underwater detection system. They would do this by analysing the underwater acoustic information transmitted up to the aircraft from sonobuoys dropped from the Nimrod into the sea earlier in the sortie. Both wet and dry teams also received some minimalist instruction on how to take photographs out of the Nimrod's beam window using the aircraft's handheld camera. It was drummed into us the importance of holding on tightly to the light meter when taking light value readings through the open beam window prior to a photographic run. Even a small light meter was sure to cause extensive damage to one of the Nimrod's Rolls-Royce Spey engines if it was snatched from the operator's hand by the slipstream and ingested down the engine air intake. I was reliably informed that a number of light meters had indeed been lost out of the Nimrod's beam window, albeit none had so far found their way into an engine. While the OCU staff were most proficient at teaching the basic concepts of operating the Nimrod MR1 and its systems, it would be later, when flying real operational sorties in the Nimrod, that vital experience would be gained and operating techniques refined.

# Maritime Operations

Having completed the Nimrod OCU, Crew 7 of 120 Squadron, with me in tow, moved back to Kinloss. The first thing I did upon arrival was get my wife and two children safely settled in our allocated MQ at 34 Portal Road. This was a fortunate location as the house was situated less than 100 yards from the 120 Squadron building and proved to be very convenient for walking to work in the morning and for trotting home after happy hour on Friday nights. Life on 120 Squadron was wonderful. We had brand-new aircraft to fly, everyone on the crew seemed to get along well, and morale, in all its forms, was high. Although I was just beginning my first operational tour, most of the other aircrew were experienced maritime operators that had previously served on Shackletons and, in a few cases, Lockheed P-2 Neptune MPAs. Crews were constituted, that is to say that each crew, once assembled, tended to stay together for a long time. This provided ample opportunity for crew bonding and for them and their wives to get to know each other socially. It also offered other benefits in terms of crew cooperation and getting to know each other's foibles. However, this tight-knit crew arrangement had some very strange and unintended consequences.

The job of the 120 Squadron planning team was to ensure that crews were kept busy on a range of different daily, weekly and monthly tasks. These included flying on operational or training sorties, undergoing simulator training, deploying on overseas detachments, carrying out SAR standby duty, partaking in ground training, completing essential crew admin and, of course, going on leave. This meant that each crew rarely had time to meet up with and get to know the other crews on the squadron. Indeed, on the fairly rare occasion when there was a whole squadron gathering, it could sometimes feel like a gathering of stand-offish, distrusting and long-separated families. As an extreme example of this phenomenon, in 1975 when I moved from Kinloss to start the Special Operators Course on 51 Squadron at Wyton, there was another operator from 120 Squadron – Flt Sgt George Lash – who was also on the course. His time on 120 Squadron had overlapped mine by no less than three years, yet I didn't know him, and he didn't know me. To this day both George and I still find it astonishing that such a thing could occur. This crewing arrangement was seen as being analogous to that of a Mafia family as portrayed in films and on television. The commanding officer (CO), acting as the 'Don', was responsible for organising, commanding and sometimes pacifying his seven or so suspicious, distrusting and somewhat distant crews. At the bottom of the food chain, individual crew members would try to encourage their skipper to approach the CO for special favours such being sent on interesting overseas detachments, or having their summer leave coincide with school holidays etc. Being endlessly lobbied and harassed by their crews, skippers would succumb to the pressure and tenuously approach the Don in low-bowing and hand-wringing fashion to make their requests for preferential treatment known. Despite this rather dystopian analogy, squadron COs always did their best to ensure that flying, detachments and leave etc. were spread evenly and fairly amongst his crews. I went on to spend four glorious years flying on 120 Squadron, first on Crew 7 which, without doubt, was the very best crew on 120 Squadron. Until, that is, the CO carried out a reshuffle of his crews that resulted in me being transferred to another crew. At that moment, my

Nimrod MR1 over the Moray Firth.

allegiance changed and my new crew became the very best crew on 120 Squadron.

Looking back, my first impressions of the Nimrod MR1 was one of mixed surprises. The interior of the aircraft was painted in refreshingly light colours, mainly light blues, greys and creams. The aircraft also had an airline-style toilet and a fairly good galley and dining area. There were several rows of comfortable passenger seats in the rear of the cabin for ground crew personnel earmarked to fly on detachment with the Nimrod. Some thought had clearly been given to the layout of the crew positions, but perhaps not quite enough. For reasons best known by the aircraft's interior designers, it was decided that at least one crew member's seat should be made to face backwards and that it should be the radio operator's position – one of the seats I would have to occupy on a regular basis. The seating arrangement for the two navigators was rather odd too, because instead of facing forward, backwards or even sideways, their joint workstation was offset some 45 degrees to the right of the direction of flight. This somewhat bizarre seating arrangement didn't really bother me – because I didn't sit there – but some of the navigators genuinely felt that it accelerated the onset of nausea when the aircraft was being manoeuvred aggressively at low level.

One disappointment regarding the Nimrod MR1 was the decision to retain use of the rather ancient ASV-21 radar that had been fitted in the Shackleton. I honestly hoped that the aircraft would be fitted with a new, state-of-the-art, radar system. That said, and despite its reliance on thermionic valve technology, ASV-21 proved to be a reasonably reliable sensor that offered a fairly good performance. It could display coastlines out to and beyond 100 miles, destroyer-sized shipping out to about 80 miles and a periscope out to about ten miles, all depending, of course, upon the aircraft's altitude, the viewing aspect to the target and the sea state. One drawback of the Nimrod's ASV-21 installation voiced by some of the more experienced crew members was that unlike in the Shackleton, where the radar scanner could be lowered below the fuselage to give the radar a 360-degree unobstructed 'view' around the aircraft, the Nimrod's fixed-scanner installation in the nose resulted in the radar having a blind arc to the rear of the aircraft. Some ex-Shackleton operators felt that this was a significant disadvantage during the submarine attack phase, but having never operated the radar on the Shackleton, I just took this limitation as fait accompli and I didn't let it bother me. On the other hand, the ASV-21 and Nimrod combination had a number of important advantages over the Shackleton's installation: it allowed radar operators to semi-automatically transfer radar contacts from their radar display through to the large computer-driven tactical display mounted at the tactical navigator's (tac nav) position. Also, because the Nimrod's was able to operate at high altitude, surface targets could be acquired on the radar at a greater range than that offered by the Shackleton. Later, an IFF interrogator was installed at the radar operator's position to allow friendly naval contacts of be positively identified.

The ARAR/ARAX ESM installed on the Nimrod MR1 proved to be a massive improvement over the obsolete and frequency-band-limited Orange Harvest system fitted in the Shackleton. It allowed operators to perform basic analysis on intercepted radar transmissions operating in the S, C and X frequency bands (broadly equal to the E-Band through to I-Band frequencies – see Appendix). The system provided operators with a reasonably accurate indication of a radar signal's radio frequency, pulse repetition frequency, pulse width, and scan period, thus supplying the basic parameters needed for operators to classify the radar type and on certain occasions, the radar's host platform. It also allowed an instantaneous, albeit approximate, line of bearing to be established towards a target radar and for the derived bearing to be automatically transferred through to the aircraft's tactical display. If the radar remained active, this bearing could be significantly refined with a little bit of manipulation of the system's DF bearing controls. Having analysed the intercepted data, the ESM operator would advise the captain, tac nav and AEO of the radar's type, its likely platform and the threat or intelligence it represented. This, when merged with radar contacts passed by the radar operator, and, on certain occasions, information derived from the wet team's Jezebel system, allowed the tac nav and AEO to derive an excellent understanding of the evolving tactical picture.

The Nimrod's MAD equipment system was a welcome addition to the Nimrod's sensor suite. It was operated by the ESM operator and it came into its own during the attack phase against a submarine. As its name suggests, it detected anomalies in the earth's magnetic field, such as those caused by the presence of nearby ferrous objects. In the Nimrod's case, the system would provide an indication to the operator when the aircraft flew over or close to ships, and submarines whether they were surfaced or submerged. Its effective range was around 2,000 to 3,000 feet. The ESM operator was provided with a display not unlike a miniature version of the lie detectors used by criminal investigators. It included a roll of paper that was passed slowly under a pen. When a magnetic anomaly was detected by the MAD equipment, the pen would scribe high-amplitude deflections from its central norm. Seeing this, the operator would instantly press a button which would cause a 'MAD mark symbol' to appear on the tac nav's tactical display showing the exact position where the MAD detection occurred. It also caused a smoke marker to be launched from the aircraft's retro launcher, thus providing a visual marker on the surface of the sea. The MAD system was sufficiently accurate for the captain to authorise the release of weapons such as active or passive homing torpedoes and nuclear depth bombs. Although its rather short detection range meant that the system would only rarely be used as a primary search sensor, it did offer a means of pinpointing the location of submerged submarines once their general position had been established by other sensors. I used MAD very successfully on a number of occasions during my time flying on the Nimrod MR1.

The Nimrod's long-range communication capability was provided by an AD-470 HF transceiver. During my early days on the Nimrod MR1, HF communications were conducted using Morse code, but later in 1972–73 the use of single sideband (SSB) voice was authorised and could be used as an alternative means of communicating with MHQ. Despite the provision of SSB voice facilities, when HF propagation conditions were poor, it was definitely easier to get a message through to MHQ using Morse code. In fact, despite the increasing use of SSB voice on the MHQ HF network, many of the older operators continued, indeed preferred, to keep on using Morse code. Sometime after I had left the MPA force, the use of encrypted radio tele-typewriters (RATT) for HF communications became the norm and the use of Morse was eventually phased out.

The main long-range sensor used to detect and track submarines was Jezebel. This system allowed the wet team to analyse acoustic information received from an array of sonobuoys dropped from the Nimrod earlier in the sortie. A typical sonobuoys array/pattern of, for example, 12 sonobuoys could detect and transmit to the Nimrod, underwater acoustic information from within an area of ocean measured in thousands of square miles. The acoustic information simultaneously transmitted to the Nimrod from each of the sonobuoys was displayed on a number of paper-based, waterfall-type displays. Paper slowly moving from front to rear across a wide metallic plate represented the time domain or Y axis of the display while frequency spectrum data received from a number of buoys would be drawn on the paper's X axis. The frequency lines drawn on the paper as it moved across the plates allowed operators to determine information such as a target's engine type, the number of propeller shafts, shaft rotation rate, the number of blades on each shaft, and much more. Analysis of this information also allowed operators to determine the ship or submarine type and, occasionally, its unique identity. By observing the position of the 'in contact' buoys on the tactical display, noting their relative signal strengths and observing individual changes in audio frequency from each buoy due to Doppler effect as the target passed through the pattern, the tactical team could determine the target's approximate position and its mean line of advance. Detection on only one or two buoys would normally result in more buoys being dropped close by to help refine the position and track of the target.

In addition to Jezebel, the Nimrod MR1 also retained the Shackleton's 1C Sonics system which was used for short-range underwater detection and tracking. This was quite an old system that, when it worked, was very good. However, during my time on the Nimrod MR1, the reliability of the 1C sonobuoys was poor and I cannot honestly remember my crew regularly achieving many attack solutions via its use. Buoys regularly failed to work, which allowed the submarine time to escape before a replacement 1C buoy could be dropped. Furthermore, the sonobuoys used by this system were very expensive. Each one was known to cost about the same as a Morris 1100 car, a small family saloon that cost around £1,500 at that time. This high cost was exacerbated by the fact that it was normal to drop a pattern of three of these buoys in order to obtain an attack solution. For comparison, a single Jezebel buoy at that time cost in the order of £60.

The types of operations flown by the Nimrod MR1 fleet were many and varied and I certainly can't remember them all. However, they mainly fell into two groups. One involved the Nimrod acting on its own, and the second involved sorties where the Nimrod cooperated with other air, surface, and sub-surface forces. A typical example of the first group would include the long-range operational flying exercise (LROFE) where the Nimrod would be tasked to fly to an area of the sea or ocean and conduct some form of surface and/or sub-surface search, report its findings, then return back to base. Examples of cooperative exercises included working closely with friendly submarines, providing close or distant support to surface task forces, and carrying out SAR operations in coordination with other air and surface rescue assets. Working with a task force was a very complex affair that required a great deal of pre-flight preparation and compliance with comprehensive communication plans. However, these sorties were also the most interesting due to the multi-faceted and simultaneous variety of events taking place involving other MPA aircraft, multiple surface and sub-surface units and their indigenous fixed-wing and rotary airborne units.

# Some Nimrod-Related Stories

On one memorable LROFE from RAF Akrotiri in Cyprus, our crew was tasked to conduct a radar and acoustic search of an area within the Ionian Sea to the east of Sicily. I was manning the ESM system as we transited west at around 25,000 feet. About 30 minutes or so after take-off, I picked up an S-band radar emission on the ARAR/ARAX ESM system that had all the hallmarks of a Soviet 'Head Net' shipborne search radar. I reported the contact and passed a bearing through to the tac nav. Subsequent ESM bearing showed that the radar was located somewhere within a fairly large group of small Greek islands. This cast some doubt as to whether I had identified the radar type correctly. However, having taken off a bit earlier than scheduled, the skipper decided we should go and have a look. As we gradually descended and flew north, the ESM contact grew stronger and, after a short while, I started to pick up a number of Soviet I-Band shipborne navigation radars, on approximately the same bearing as the Head Net. The radar operator, who was concentrating his search in the direction of the ESM bearings, could not determine the exact location of the targets due to the plethora of small islands and other contacts close to the ESM fix.

Suddenly, the co-pilot announced that he was visual with a number of large surface vessels ahead of us and that they were positioned between a group of small islands. When we flew closer the excitement mounted as we realised that we had found a large Russian fleet at anchor. I can't remember the actual make-up of the fleet, but it included cruisers, destroyers, several submarines, some oilers and other smaller vessels. Our crew had a great time manoeuvring in and around the ships taking photographs and noting things of intelligence value. However, we still had the briefed task in the Ionian Sea to carry out and it wasn't long before the skipper announced that it was time to leave. It was also time for the ESM and radar operator to carry out their hourly swap of positions. It was deemed bad practice to allow an operator to spend too much on radar as it could result in severe eye strain. So, as we climbed away, I left the ESM position and took up my seat at the ASV-21 radar position.

During our high-level transit to the tasked area I continually adjusted the tilt of the ASV-21 scanner to alternate between searching for surface contacts and nearby airborne contacts. During a stint on surface search, I picked up two good radar contacts, very close to each other, about ten miles ahead and to the south of our track. I passed the contacts through to the tac nav, but the skipper decided that we didn't have time to go south and identify them, so we continued on our way to the briefed area. We soon arrived at our tasked area and having done a radar sweep and investigated a number of radar contacts that turned out to be fishing boats, cruise liners, cargo ships, and ferries etc., it was time for the wet team to do their acoustic search using Jezebel. A pattern of sonobuoys was dropped and we settled down at medium level to let the wet team do their thing. Due to the shallowness of the sea, water temperature gradients and the different layers of water salinity commonly found in the Mediterranean, the paths of underwater sound waves do not always propagate in a straight line. This sound wave-bending phenomenon could, on some occasions, obscure submarine targets. For these reasons, the Mediterranean was considered by some to be less than ideal for conducting Jezebel operations. So it came as no surprise when we ended the on-task period without gaining any interesting Jezebel contacts. With the search task complete, we climbed back up to cruise altitude and started to make our way back to Akrotiri.

During the transit back I picked up two radar contacts to the south of our track that I assumed to be the same ones that I had detected on the outbound leg. I was pretty certain that they were not small fishing boats as the radar returns were persistent despite the moderate sea state. Also, they were sailing extremely close together and in the same direction, something that in my very limited experience most large commercial ships tended not to do when sailing in open waters. I hesitantly suggested to the skipper that it might be worth having a look, but he was reluctant to descend again. At that juncture the AEO piped up and suggested that it was worth investigating as, to use his words, "we didn't have much to lose except several thousand pounds of aviation fuel and the crew missing the 'Early Throats' beer call in the mess bars at Akrotiri." That raised a laugh, but it also did the trick and down we went, descending through what was turning out to be rather murky weather.

The skipper was flying the aircraft while the co-pilot was carrying out a visual search ahead. Two miles from the contacts the co-pilot announced that he had visual contact with the ships and they were not commercial. It turned out that both contacts were Soviet; a Tapir-class landing ship (code-named by NATO as Alligator) escorted by a Kotlin-class destroyer. During the photographic runs we could see that the Alligator was loaded with military vehicles, and the ship's track suggested that they were heading for North Africa, possibly Egypt. With the photographic runs complete, it was time to start our climb back to altitude. It was also time for another radar/ESM changeover. When I opened the curtain to leave the radar position, the wet team had formed a line with their backs to the Jezebel print-outs to prevent me from seeing them "just in case the jammy sod finds a submarine". It was all in jest, of course. Jezebel print-outs were a complete mystery to me. But I have to admit that on that particular sortie, I was a bit jammy. It felt good though!

My four years on the Nimrod MR1 also had some moments of terror. I remember one rather exciting/terrifying post-exercise departure from an airfield in Canada. The Nimrod was fairly heavily laden with fuel for the transit back to Kinloss. Also, we were carrying the usual load of SAR survival gear in the bomb bay and our ground crew and all their tools and personal luggage were loaded in the rear cabin area. We also had on board an extremely large and heavy Nimrod towing arm. As an added bonus, the air and ground crews had liberally loaded the Nimrod with bags of fresh Canadian apples for consumption by their families back at Kinloss. The weather for our departure was poor with some cold drizzle, low stratus cloud and mist hanging over the airfield. So I was glad when our air and ground crews said farewell to their Canadian hosts and we all boarded the Nimrod.

Without further ado, the pilots started the engines and we taxied to the runway for take-off. I was sitting at the radar position and had the window blind up for our departure. With the pre-take-off checks complete, the captain advanced the throttles causing our four Rolls-Royce Spey engines to spool up to the required take-off power setting. Brakes released, we started our acceleration down the runway. Rain was streaked down the outside of my window as our speed increased and, a few seconds after getting airborne, we entered the stratus cloud. With undercarriage and flaps retracted, the radio operator and co-pilot began to action the after-take-off checks. While peering out of the window, my eyes were drawn to some black objects flashing past under the port wing. I couldn't quite make out what they were, but they were becoming more numerous. I suddenly realised that they were the tops of fir trees. My heart froze. I was convinced that we were about to fly into the rising ground ahead of us.

Before I could yell a warning on intercom the co-pilot must have realised what was happening and wrenched back on the control column, rotating the Nimrod into what felt like a very steep climb. The instantaneous G caused me to bang my head on the ASV-21 display and there was, shall we say, some commotion within the crew cabin. A few seconds later the Nimrod popped out of the top of the stratus like a Polaris missile out of the ocean. Our angle of climb was quite steep and our airspeed couldn't have been all that high and I was definitely not looking forward to the bunt manoeuvre that would be required to get the nose of the aircraft down to the horizon. However, our co-pilot deftly turned our steep climb into a wingover by easing forward on the control yoke and applying a fair amount of bank. This combination of actions induced a modicum of zero G within the cabin that caused plastic cups, apples and other odds and sods to 'lift off' and scatter around the cabin. There were shouts of consternation, but not a word was heard from the flight deck on intercom. The co-pilot, having superbly completed his unplanned but beautifully executed wingover manoeuvre, re-established the required heading, re-initiated the climb, and completed the after-take-off checks.

A deafening silence fell throughout the aircraft as crew and passengers realised that something had gone badly wrong on the flight deck, but no one said a word. A short while later, there was a gradual increase in off-intercom whispering as the rear crew began to question each other about what had happened, but the intercom remained eerily quiet for quite a while until one of the crew piped up on intercom with a refreshingly loud "err excuse me, anyone for a cup of tea?" Looking back, it is clear to me that there must have been a momentary lapse in concentration at the pointy end of the Nimrod and had it not been for the fast reactions of the co-pilot and his expert handling of the aircraft, I do believe that I would not be here to tell the tale.

One feature of the Nimrod that I did find somewhat irritating was the tendency for doors and hatches to swing open during landing and when manoeuvring at low altitude after descending from flight at medium to high level. I am not exactly sure why this sort of thing happened. My guess at the time was that when the aircraft was at altitude, the pressure inside the cabin forced the doors and hatches up tight against the framework thus relieving pressure on the lever system that was holding them closed. This, perhaps assisted by vibrations throughout the airframe, allowed the levers to move to the 'open' position on their own volition. Thus, when the internal-to-external difference in air pressure was relieved during landing, or perhaps after descending from medium or high altitude in order to prosecute a target, it was not uncommon for a door to swing open or an overwing escape hatch to drop inwards.

It was particularly common at the ESM position when, at touchdown, the hatch would fall inwards onto the operator. This was made worse by the blast of hot air from the engine's reverse thrust system entering the cabin via the open hatch. If it happened to be raining or snowing at the time, some of that would enter the aircraft too. But perhaps the scariest time of all was when our crew was prosecuting a submarine at very low level using MAD on a bumpy and blustery day not far to the west of the Shetland Islands.

I was standing in the extreme rear of the Nimrod's cabin, close to the starboard/rear entrance door, loading smoke markers into the aircraft's retro launcher. This was a device that fired smoke markers backwards at the same speed as the aircraft was flying forward thus causing the marker to drop vertically into the sea establishing an accurate visual marker on the surface of the water. We were carrying out a MAD trapping procedure around a submarine. This involved the pilots flying the Nimrod in tight – G inducing – circles at very low level around the assumed location submarine in order to 'trap' it using the MAD equipment. Meanwhile, I was trying to load the retro launcher which was difficult enough when flying MAD trapping procedures, but trying to do so during extremely turbulent weather made it even more challenging. With two smoke markers in my hands and doing my best to stand upright, the rear door, which was no more than a few feet from where I was standing, suddenly swung open revealing the open sea whipping past just a few hundred feet below.

The noise from the slipstream accompanied by the blast from the two Spey engine exhausts that were located just forwards of the door was shattering, and the buffeting, turbulent air entering the cabin and swirling around me made me freeze in terror. For a few seconds I was riveted to the spot, scared to move in case I lost balance and fell towards the gap where the door should have been. A few seconds, that seemed like hours, passed before I got moving, put down the smoke markers, dropped down to my hands and knees and then, with some difficulty, carefully moved the door back to the closed position. Breathing a sigh of relief, I couldn't help but wonder how long it would have taken the crew to notice I was missing if I had I fallen out of the door.

Maritime operations in the seas and oceans in different parts of the world present different challenges. As previously mentioned, the Mediterranean was not considered to be ideal for doing acoustic searches using systems like Jezebel, however, when the water was calm, as it regularly was in the Med, it could be fairly easy to pick up a submarine's snorkel and/or periscope on radar. Furthermore, if Lady Luck really was on your side, the clear water of the Mediterranean could sometimes lead to visual sighting of submerged submarines, particularly in the shallower regions of the sea.

On the other hand, conducting an ASV-21 radar search for submarine snorkels/periscopes in the deep waters of the Atlantic Ocean could prove to be a very difficult undertaking given the preponderance of high swell and choppy sea states. But in these situations, acoustic search using Jezebel could regularly prove to be very successful. However, on some occasions the sea state, weather and even Mother Nature's creatures would conspire to cock things up totally.

On one sortie flying from the Canadian Forces Base (CFB) at Greenwood Nova Scotia, we were tasked to search for a Canadian, diesel/electric-powered submarine that was patrolling off the coast of Nova Scotia in the Grand Banks area of the Atlantic Ocean. We were tasked to conduct a radar search of the area to establish a plot of surface vessels while simultaneously laying sonobuoys to prepare for Jezebel operations. What a fiasco! It must have been whale migration season and the radar reflections from hundreds of broaching whales resulted in my radar display looking as if it had caught a severe dose of the measles. It was literally covered with radar contacts appearing and disappearing at such a rate that I hardly knew where to start.

Trying to establish a fix on any given contact was like playing 'Whack-a-Mole'. As soon as I had selected one, it would disappear and be replaced with two or more contacts close by. The acoustic team was having a similarly interesting experience. The underwater noises being transmitted from the sonobuoys to the aircraft sounded like the sea creatures were having a rave accompanied by an aquatic band, high on hallucinating drugs. The rustling, snapping and scraping of millions of shrimps, lobsters and other crustaceans accompanied by the loud whistling and moaning of the migrating whales had to be heard to be believed – what a racket – and no, we did not find the submarine.

In the early days of the Nimrod MR1, the aircraft's armament for anti-surface warfare included two AS.12 wire-guided missiles – one carried under each wing. The AS.12 was a French missile designed and built by Nord Aviation and developed from the SS.11 and SS.12 anti-tank missile systems. In the Nimrod's case, the weapon was intended for use against surfaced submarines, lightly armed surface vessels and Soviet trawlers that had been modified to conduct auxiliary gathering of intelligence (AGI) operations.

However, most crews were very dubious about the utility of the missile. The reason being that the missile was visually guided and could only be used during daytime and during periods of fairly good visibility. Also, it required the first pilot to maintain the Nimrod on a steady descending approach towards the target to allow the co-pilot time to acquire the target, fire the missile and guide it all the way down to the impact point. This, of course, rendered the Nimrod extremely vulnerable to return missile and gun fire from the vessel being attacked.

Despite this, on 7 May 1973 my crew was tasked to fly to the Aberporth Sea Range, off the coast of Wales, to fire two inert AS.12 missiles at a floating target. This task was so out of the ordinary that it generated a great deal of excitement throughout the crew. On the day in question, we got airborne from Kinloss with a AS.12 missile tucked under each wing and flew south to Aberporth. When within range of Aberporth, we established two-way communications with the range controller and readied ourselves for the first launch.

I would guess that almost half of the rear crew were crammed into the flight deck behind the pilots to observe the missile-firing event. Having acquired the target and been cleared 'hot', the captain set the Nimrod on the required flight path to allow the co-pilot to launch the missile and guide it towards the target. The first missile left the port wing with a loud Swoosh and started its jerky flight path down towards the floating target. Meanwhile those observing from behind the pilots started to offer a steady stream of non-expert, but progressively louder, advice to the co-pilot, such as "up a bit…left a bit…you're too high…you're going to miss…get a grip co!" The co-pilot was obviously feeling the strain as he tried to gain control of the missile and steady its flight towards the required impact point. Unsurprisingly, the missile missed the target by a fairly wide margin.

In frustration, the captain ordered the onlookers back to their proper crew positions and then orbited back for another go with missile number two. There was another Swoosh as the missile left its starboard wing pylon and started its zigzagging flight towards the target. We could hear the co-pilot cursing under his breath on intercom as he tried his best to get control of the missile which, a few seconds later, splashed into the water near to, but not on, the target. "Bollocks to this," said the captain as he pushed forward on the throttles and eased back on the yoke. The Nimrod obediently climbed away while the co-pilot sat quietly blushing and muttering to himself in the right-hand seat. A round of tea was made while the self-appointed 'experts' in the back of the aircraft discussed how failure had been grabbed from the hand of victory by the co-pilot's failing to take heed of the simultaneous and increasingly loud 'non-expert' advice offered by the 'back-enders'.

We must have been halfway back to Kinloss when one of our new AEOps piped up on intercom, "Captain from port beam." "Go ahead beam." "There is a bunch of missile control wire wrapped around the port wing…" "WHAT?!" "I said there is a bunch of missile control wire wrapped around the port wing just inboard of the aileron." "For Christ's sake what next?" said the captain. "I don't know," said the young AEOp in the port beam. "It wasn't a bloody question, beam." "Sorry captain." Clearly, the skipper was suffering from sense of humour failure. Meanwhile, the co-pilot was still nursing his embarrassment while the 'experts' in the back had decided that, having seen the missile in action, its use probably posed a bigger risk to the Nimrod than it did to the Russians. We landed safely at Kinloss and the wire around the wing had either fallen off during the descent to the airfield or it was removed by the ground crew – I cannot remember which. However, I do believe that sometime later the AS.12 was quietly dropped from the Nimrod's weapons repertoire.

Another anti-surface weapon intended for use on the Nimrod was the Martel TV/ anti-radar missile (ARM). There was even a position in the Nimrod that was intended to be used by the Martel operator, but I don't remember one ever being fired from a squadron aircraft. In fact, I believe that plans to use the Martel were also quietly dropped, and if my memory serves me correctly, it never found mention in any of the Nimrod tactics manuals.

Having got over some minor teething issues and entry-into-service niggles, the Nimrod MR1 proved to be an extremely successful MPA that provided the UK with an outstanding anti-submarine warfare (ASW) capability over a period of many years. Being a crew member on the Nimrod at that time was surely one of the most interesting and satisfying jobs for AEOps. My only regret is that I didn't get the chance to serve on the Nimrod MR2 with its advanced Searchwater radar, Yellow Gate ESM and improved MAD system. I was also somewhat surprised, and a bit sad, when the MR4 version was cancelled. Perhaps if someone had called a halt to the never-ending requests for additional capabilities and refinements during its development, the MR4 might have had a chance to enter service. Alas, it was not to be.

# A Brief Time on 51 Squadron

In April 1975 I was posted to RAF Wyton to be trained as a special operator (spec op) on 51 Squadron. The squadron's role was to conduct electronic reconnaissance operations against countries that were deemed to pose a threat, or to be of special interest, to the UK. The squadron had recently dispensed with its Canberra and

Comet aircraft and was now – or would soon be – operating three Nimrod R1 aircraft configured to undertake signals intelligence (SIGINT) collection duties. Nimrod R1 missions flown from RAF Wyton were mainly focused on collecting SIGINT from Russia and other Warsaw Pact (WP) countries along the Eastern Baltic, across Eastern Europe, and parts of northern Russia bordering Norway. Less frequent missions were flown around the southern and eastern littoral of the Mediterranean Sea, and very occasionally, a few missions would be mounted to observe signals activity around the southern periphery of Russia close to the Caspian Sea. Most of these less-frequent sorties were flown from countries outside the UK, including Gibraltar, Malta, Cyprus and Iran, which made a pleasant break from the routine sorties flown from Wyton.

The crew on the Nimrod R1 in 1975–76 comprised between 25 and 30 individuals including five flight deck crew – two pilots (one being the captain), two navigators and the flight engineer – and 20-plus mission crew members comprising a number of mission supervisors, about eight electronic intelligence (ELINT) operators and ten or more communication intelligence (COMINT) operators. The number of operators could change from flight to flight depending upon the area under reconnaissance and the nature of the sortie. Despite this rather large crew, the provision of galley equipment for meal preparation was the same as that in the Nimrod MR1. Making tea and coffee to suit each crew member's individual taste whilst simultaneously heating up 25 Cornish pasties in the Nimrod's tiny oven was an art form mastered only by the most experienced crew members.

Nimrod R1 XW665 at RAF Wyton.

My job as a newly trained special operator was to intercept, analyse, identify, record and plot radar and other emissions operating in the A, B and C frequency bands. Radars that operate at these frequencies tend to be adopted by air defence centres to provide early warning and fighter control services. They are also used by civilian ATCC for surveillance and control of commercial and military aircraft operating within large volumes of airspace. The long-range capability of these radars meant that only a few of them were required to satisfy the needs of any given geographical region. Also, being rather large devices, they tended to operate from fixed sites.

As a result, the almost daily sorties into the Baltic rarely offered anything new for me to get my teeth into, and after about a year I was beginning to tire of the repetitive nature of the work. I tried to arrange a swap with operators working other positions on the aircraft but, probably for the very same reasons as those mentioned above, none of them wanted to change positions. With the lack of variety sapping my interest and with the realisation that I could end up doing the same thing for a very long time I decided that I needed to find a new challenge. Don't misunderstand me, the stability offered by 51 Squadron perfectly suited those that had children going through a critical stage of their education. It was also perfect for those that wished to side-step the normal nomadic nature of service life in order to purchase a house and settle down to a more stable family routine. Such thoughts didn't appeal to me at that time and in a bid to seek out pastures new, I decided to apply for a commission.

# Officer Cadet Training Unit

As luck would have it, I passed the commissioning selection process and was ordered to attend the Officer Cadet Training Unit (OCTU) at RAF Henlow in Bedfordshire. The course was interesting but not overly challenging. In fact, it seemed to include many of the same leadership and training tasks that I had covered during my aircrew training at Topcliffe. That said, many of the young direct entry cadets, and even some of those that came from university air squadrons, found the grind of being subjected to moderately rigorous RAF discipline and the stress associated with having to perform leadership tasks, rather daunting. I suppose those of us that had come from a SNCO background had a slightly more mature attitude towards the training, or perhaps we felt that we had rather less to lose if things didn't work out as planned. Whatever, we were not pre-occupied with the same fear of failure that seemed to fill the minds of most of the younger cadets.

One useful part of the training at Henlow was its focus on public speaking. We would be sent off to prepare a two-minute briefing on a subject of our choice. When the time came for the cadets to stand in front of the class and deliver their briefings, some cadets would dry up after 30 seconds while others would still be talking after five minutes had passed. It took some practice to get to grips with what one could achieve in set-time briefings, but most students eventually mastered the art.

Put it down to bad luck, but a day or so before our course was due to graduate, the young cadet chosen to be our flight commander for the graduation parade fell ill and, having insufficient time to train up another 'young blade', I was 'volunteered' by my flight commander to take his place. Gone was my opportunity to relax and enjoy a period of daydreaming in the ranks while others were barking orders and swinging swords around. On the evening before the parade, the disciplinary sergeant arrived at my room to give me a quick, one-on-one, crash course on sword drill and the verbal commands that I would have to deliver during the parade. I did my best to take it all in, and after a final run-through of the parade's order of events, the sergeant deemed my training to be complete, wished me luck, and left.

Some short time later, having done my evening domestic tasks, I wandered down to the mess bar with one of the other cadets. As we walked past the billiard room I overheard a male, coaxing voice. "Open your legs as far as you can, that's it, that's it." My colleague and I exchanged wide-eyed glances, and concerned that

Author marching his flight past the reviewing officer at RAF Henlow during his graduation parade.

something untoward was taking place, I decided to crack open the door of the billiard room and look inside. I was somewhat relieved to see one of our rather short female Woman Royal Air Force (WRAF) cadets marching across the carpet alongside one of our disciplinary NCOs who was measuring the length of her step using his pace stick in a twirling motion. At that point he must have sensed my presence because he spun round and said, "Ah, Cadet Walls, just the man. Come here, I've got something to show you." Blushing at being caught snooping I stepped forward towards him. "Look," he said, walking his pace stick across the floor in a twirling motion. "This is the maximum pace length that the WRAF cadets marching behind you on the parade will be able to manage. You must take care not to lengthen your pace beyond this distance or you will leave the WRAF contingent behind. Got it?" "Yes, sergeant." "Look, have a go," he said. I marched across the carpet while the sergeant marched beside me step by step on the floor. "Keep it short, keep it short," he said. "That's it, make sure none of your steps are any longer than this, okay?" "Yes sergeant, I understand." "Excellent," he said as he walked towards the door. Then with a sly smile on his face he turned and said, "we don't

George and Tony (standing) at my graduation parade.

want to see any spit skirts or split anything else on our parade tomorrow, isn't that so, Cadet Walls?" "Yes sergeant, definitely," I said, at which point he marched out of the billiard room.

The following morning, as we prepared to march on to the parade ground, I tried to concentrate on the verbal commands that I would be expected to deliver at a volume sufficient for all to hear, whilst also trying to avoid skewering other cadets with my sword. I am pleased to say that everything went to plan during the parade with no erroneous verbal commands or sword-swinging cock-ups being made by me. In fact, the biggest distraction during the parade was when I was marching my flight past the saluting base and, to my surprise, I spotted two of my good friends from 51 Squadron – George Lash and Tony Rollo – standing behind the seated dignitaries. They were clearly relishing my discomfort as they were grinning from ear-to-ear.

When the parade was over, the cadets, guests and VIPs were invited to retire to the officer cadets' mess for refreshments. Imagine my surprise when I realised that George and Tony had invited themselves too and accompanied my wife and my parents into the mess where they helped themselves to some light refreshments. It was all strictly against the rules and I had visions of my commission lasting no more than 30 minutes. So I was somewhat relieved when, upon seeing the reviewing officer circulating towards our group, George and Tony decided to make a stealthy departure from the mess. Their audacity still makes me burst out laughing to this day. Newly commissioned as a flying officer, I was impatient to make my way to RAF Scampton where I would join No. 197 Vulcan Course at No. 230 OCU and later, having completed the course, fly as an AEO on 617 Squadron – The Dam Busters!

# CHAPTER FOUR
# NO. 617 SQUADRON AND THE VULCAN B2

## A Bit of Squadron History

No. 617 Squadron is well known for its role in Operation Chastise, the attack led by Wg Cdr Guy Gibson on the German Möhne, Sorpe and Eder dams in May 1943. It was, without doubt, an audacious and courageous raid that reflected the determination of Bomber Command to take the war to the enemy. The weapon used on the raid was a 7,500-lb cylindrical mine designed by Barnes Wallis. For the mine to work effectively, it had to be dropped into the water behind the dam at a precise distance from, and on a heading that was pointing directly at, the centre of the dam wall. Furthermore, at the time of dropping the mine, the Lancaster had to be flying straight and level at 240 mph while only 60 feet above the water.

To enable the crew to determine their exact height above the water, a set of downward-facing lights were fitted to the Lancasters and arranged such that their beams would merge to a spot only when the aircraft was flying at the required 60 feet. To save precious weight, gun turrets and certain other pieces of equipment were removed from the aircraft. The Lancasters also had their bomb doors removed to make way for the cradle arrangement that was needed to hold the mine, semi-recessed, inside the aircraft's bomb bay. Electrical turning gear was fitted to spin the mine at 500 rpm in a rotational direction that was opposite to the direction of travel of the mine when it made contact with the water. This opposing spin caused the mine to skip across the water and, upon hitting the dam, sink beneath the water while maintaining close contact with the dam wall. The hydrostatic fuse in each mine was set to trigger at a depth of around 30 feet. By detonating the mine underwater in this fashion, it was able to impart much more destructive power to the structure of the dam than anything that could have been achieved using conventional bombs.

Although a large number of aircraft and crews were lost on the raid, their sacrifice was not in vain. The Sorpe dam was damaged and both the Möhne and Eder dams were breached causing extensive flooding and a vast amount of damage to the roads, farm land, accommodation and materials needed to sustain life in that part of Germany. It also led to the temporary loss of water supply and hydro-electric power urgently needed for German industrial production. As a secondary effect, the attack compelled the enemy to increase the amount of AAA defences located around its dams thus diverting them away from other important target areas such as industrial complexes around the Ruhr Valley. While the raid led to a significant loss of lives amongst the German military and civilian population, it also, unfortunately, took the lives of many Russian prisoners and people of other nationalities who, at the time of the attack, were being forced to work as slave labourers in the local area.

Another outstanding and famous wartime 617 Squadron commander was Wg Cdr Leonard Cheshire. He was invited to take charge of the squadron at a time when it was experiencing some operational bad luck and a rather high attrition rate amongst its crews. Cheshire immediately agreed to take command of the squadron, despite having to relinquish his rank of group captain and revert to being a wing commander. He was a very experienced bomber pilot, but most of his previous night-time operational flying had been carried out at high altitude. By joining 617 Squadron, he would be expected to fly his Lancaster and lead his other squadron aircraft on raids, not only at high altitude, but also at night and at extremely low level – a 617 Squadron speciality.

At around this time there was an urgent need to destroy or disable a number of well-protected targets in France and Germany, including submarine and E-boat pens, V1 and V2 launch points, and, closer to home, a number of long-range V3 guns that were being installed near Calais. These guns, if allowed to enter service, would have been able to deliver thousands of 500-lb high-explosive shells onto targets located in the south-east of England, including London. However, they were protected by concrete bunkers that rendered them invulnerable to the standard high-explosive bombs used by the RAF at that time. In an effort to overcome this problem, Barnes Wallis was asked to develop a special bomb capable of destroying such targets.

The bomb Wallis designed was called the Tallboy and it weighed 12,000 lbs. But to have the desired destructive effect, it had to be dropped directly on to the target, or very close to it. It also had to be let go from medium or high altitude to allow the bomb time to accelerate to near supersonic speed and thus impart maximum damage onto the target. At that time, even the very best efforts of the RAF Pathfinder Force could not mark targets anywhere near to the 'bullseye' accuracy required for Tallboy operations. It became obvious to Cheshire and his highly experienced and capable Australian subordinate, Flt Lt Mick Martin, that to provide the accuracy required, a new method of target marking would have to be devised. They later agreed that a single, bright, target-marker flare dropped directly on to the target from around 200 feet – a height that was well below the minimum height of 5,000 feet that was currently allowed by higher authority – would satisfy the requirement. Deciding to ignore the official altitude limitation, Cheshire and Martin developed their new low-level method for marking targets. It involved, in the first instance, an aircraft dropping illuminating parachute flares over the target area from around 14,000 feet. With the target now clearly visible, the target-marking aircraft would approach at speed and drop a single bright target-marker flare accurately onto the target from a very low height – typically below 200 feet.

Due to its large size, limited manoeuvrability and rather moderate maximum speed, it was decided not to use the Lancaster for the target-marking task. Instead, Mosquitos and a single Mustang provided on loan from the United States Army Air Force were used instead. With the target clearly marked, the main force of Lancasters was able to overfly the target and deliver their Tallboys from medium level. This procedure proved to be extremely successful and a large number of important targets in Germany and other parts of Europe were destroyed or damaged. After the war, Cheshire, who had been awarded the VC in recognition of his courage and determination, dedicated his life to philanthropy and was responsible for setting up a number of charitable organisations aimed at providing relief to war veterans and their families.

Wg Cdr Willie Tait was officer commanding (OC) of 617 Squadron during September 1944 when Lancaster bombers from both 617 and 9 Squadrons, flying from an airfield near Archangel in Russia, launched an attack using Tallboy bombs against the German battleship *Tirpitz* that was sheltering in Kåfjord in northern Norway. One bomb, believed to be from Tait's aircraft, scored a direct hit on the ship inflicting serious damage, while several of the bombs dropped from other aircraft landed sufficiently close to the vessel to cause some buckling of the hull plates. The damage inflicted by the raid was sufficient to prevent the ship from being used for ocean-going operations and the ship's captain was ordered to sail his vessel south to a fjord near Tromsø for repairs. This move placed his battleship within striking range of Lancaster bombers flying from Scotland.

On 29 October 1944, both 617 and 9 Squadrons flying from RAF stations Kinloss, Lossiemouth and Milltown, carried out a second Tallboy attack on the *Tirpitz*, but only minor damage was inflicted on the ship for the loss of one Lancaster. Determined to succeed, the two squadrons mounted another attack on 12 November. This time the mission was successful and the *Tirpitz* was struck by two or more Tallboy bombs causing it to capsize and sink in the shallow waters where it was moored. One 9 Squadron Lancaster, having been damaged by German AAA, diverted to Sweden where it crash-landed. The remaining Lancasters managed to return to Scotland. Wg Cdr Tait was the mission leader on all three attacks. No. 617 Squadron took part in many other important raids during the war, but there was great relief when, finally, the war ended and air and ground crews were stood down to return to civilian life or to take up new career opportunities within the RAF.

Soon after the war had ended, 617 Squadron was re-equipped with Avro Lincoln bombers and later, in 1952, it entered the jet age with the English Electric Canberra.

After operating the Canberra for just over three years, the squadron was once again disbanded only to be reformed at RAF Scampton in 1958 with the Vulcan B1, and some years later, with the Vulcan B2. No. 617 Squadron was the first Vulcan squadron to be equipped with the Blue Steel thermonuclear stand-off missile and, alongside two other Blue Steel-equipped Vulcan squadrons and two Blue Steel-equipped Victor squadrons, it served for eight years as the spearhead of Britain's nuclear deterrent. In 1969, when the RN took over the nuclear deterrent role, 617 Squadron relinquished its Blue Steel capability and was re-armed with the WE.177B nuclear bomb configured for laydown delivery. It was also re-assigned to serve under the Supreme Allied Commander Europe (SACUER) in the low-level sub-strategic/tactical strike role. The squadron eventually ceased Vulcan operations in December 1981. To understand why the Vulcan was designed, built and brought into RAF service, we have to look back to WWII when, during the ongoing cauldron of war, a number of vitally important and highly classified political and scientific events were taking place.

## The Birth of the Vulcan

During the war, Germany was conducting research aimed at developing an atomic bomb. Britain, too, was undergoing atomic weapon research under a top-secret programme called Tube Alloys. However, due to the huge costs involved and other

Vulcan with Blue Steel missile. (Aviation Photo Company)

demands being placed upon the country by the ongoing war with Germany, the UK did not have the wherewithal to carry forward its research from the scientific arena to the weapon-development phase. At around the same time America, too, was conducting secret atomic research under a programme called Project Manhattan. However, its science and research efforts were lagging somewhat behind those of the British.

Eventually, Britain and America got together and established an agreement to share atomic weapon research. It was meant to be an agreement of equals where the UK would benefit from American wealth, and America would benefit from Britain's know-how. However, looking back, some have suggested that it was America that gained most from the agreement. Furthermore, it soon became clear that the sharing partnership was beset with problems, mainly due to security concerns the Americans had about their British partners. Such was the level of distrust that in 1942 the sharing agreement was stopped, only to be restarted again in 1943 under the auspices of the Quebec Agreement.

Project Manhattan bore fruit for America in July 1945 when the country tested its first atomic bomb in the New Mexico desert. The success of this test resulted in two atomic bombs being dropped on Japan, one on Hiroshima on 6 August and one on Nagasaki on 9 August. The results were devastating and it wasn't long before Japan sued for peace. Not long afterwards, in 1946, the USA, still distrustful of the British, passed the McMahon Act that ended all atomic cooperation with Great Britain. As a result, in 1947, Britain decided to go it alone and develop its own atomic bomb. The bomb was ordered to satisfy Operational Requirement (OR) 1001 and the project was code-named Blue Danube.

Scientists estimated that Blue Danube would be an extremely large bomb measuring some 25 feet in length, weighing close to 10,000 lbs and offering an explosive yield similar to that of the American bombs dropped on Japan – close to 15 kilotons of TNT. Whilst the only practical means of delivering Blue Danube on to its target would be by air, it was also quite obvious that Britain's existing fleet of obsolescent Avro Lincoln Bombers would not be suitable for the task. This set in motion an urgent programme to develop a new jet bomber. Government scientists and other technical and operational staff, having taken due note of the distance to the most likely targets in Russia, and being cognisant of the approximate dimensions and weight of the bomb, issued Operational Requirement 229 for a new jet bomber. This led to the development and promulgation of Specification B35/46. UK aircraft companies, having been given sight of the specification, were invited to respond with their technical solutions.

It stated a requirement for the aircraft to be able to carry a single 10,000-lb weapon over a radius of action of around 1,500 nautical miles at 500 knots, and deliver the weapon from an altitude of at least 50,000 feet when overhead the target. There was, also, an additional need for it to be able to carry a 20,000-lb conventional bomb load over a shorter distance. There were many other demands included, some of which proved to be beyond the science and technology available at the time and others that were deemed to be over-ambitious given the funding available. Nevertheless, the remaining, extremely challenging set of requirements eventually drew responses from a number of aircraft manufacturers.

After careful study of all the proposals, the government focused its attention on just two companies; Avro with what would become the Vulcan, and Handley Page with what would become the Victor. While both proposals were considered to be suitably advanced, they were also seen as carrying considerable risk. To provide reassurance, the government decided to allow Vickers to develop its lower risk (and lower performance) proposal for an aircraft that would eventually become known as the Valiant. As a further backstop, Shorts of Belfast was contracted to build a basic, but functional, bomber called the Sperrin. As things turned out, the Sperrin was never developed beyond the very early prototype stage, thus leaving the Vulcan, Victor and Valiant – the V Bombers – to advance through development and into production.

The Vulcan's design offered a number of attributes that made it eminently suitable for the high-level bombing role. It had a delta-shaped wing that was derived from advanced aerodynamic research carried out in Germany during WWII and exploited by Britain and other western powers after the war ended. Avro, by basing its design on the delta-shaped wing, took on a significant level of risk, but it was seen to be a risk worth taking when set against the many clear advantages that it offered. The delta wing's swept-back leading edge delayed the onset of compressibility, a phenomenon that significantly increased an aircraft's drag when flying close to the speed of sound. Its large surface area meant that its wing loading (aircraft weight divided by its wing area) would be relatively low and this would enhance the aircraft's ability to fly and manoeuvre at transonic speeds at very high altitude. In addition, the large volume of space inside the delta wing provided ample room for the aircraft's four engines, main undercarriage structure and the large quantity of fuel needed for it to meet the specified range requirement. Last but not least, the delta wing offered simplicity of design, ease of manufacture, and excellent structural strength and stiffness; attributes that would become crucially important later in the Vulcan's service. The Vulcan B1 entered service in 1956 with the first aircraft being delivered to RAF Waddington in Lincolnshire. As deliveries accelerated, the number of in-service, combat-ready Vulcan squadrons increased significantly. With Victor and Valiant squadrons also rapidly being formed, the UK government was soon in a position to declare that the Vulcan, Victor and Valiant bombers – the V Force – was ready to serve as the UK's strategic deterrent.

In 1960, an American U-2 reconnaissance aircraft flying at 67,000 ft over Russia was shot down by a SA-2 SAM. This led the RAF to review the concept of operations which, at that time, required the V Bombers to penetrate the Soviet Union at high altitude. In light of the rapid deployment of these SAM systems around Soviet cities and military targets, it was decided that the V Bombers should switch from flying a hi-hi-hi flight profile to a hi-lo-hi profile, where the transit to and from the Union of Soviet Socialist Republics (USSR) would be carried out at high altitude, but the flight to and from the target, when close to and within Soviet airspace, would be carried out at low altitude. This, it was thought, would reduce the chance of the bombers being tracked by Soviet early warning and ground-controlled intercept (GCI) radar systems and reduce the aircraft's vulnerability to SA-2. The Valiant was the first of the V Bombers to change to hi-lo-hi mode of operations in 1961, followed in 1963 by the Vulcan and Victor bombers. Unfortunately, the Valiant proved to be insufficiently strong to withstand the stresses of low-level flight, and after a weakness was discovered in the aircraft's rear wing spar in 1964, it was decided that the aircraft should be grounded. Later, the Victor, too, proved to be insufficiently robust for operations at low level and after undergoing significant modification, it gradually replaced those Valiants that were providing the UK's air-to-air refuelling (AAR) capability. Later, a number of Victors were also modified to take over the strategic radar reconnaissance role previously carried out by the Valiants of 543 Squadron. This left the Vulcan as the only V Bomber dedicated to the low-level, sub-strategic, nuclear-strike role.

## The Vulcan B2 in Service

Each Vulcan carried a crew of five officers. This included a first pilot/captain and a co-pilot, both of whom sat on Martin-Baker ejection seats mounted side-by-side on the flight deck of the aircraft. Being an AEO, I sat with the navigator plotter (nav plotter) and navigator radar (nav radar) in the rather dark and dank cabin situated behind and

617 Squadron Vulcan B2. (Aviation Photo Company)

Nav radar and nav plotter crew positions in the Vulcan. (H. Heeley, Newark Air Museum)

below the pilots. Colloquially known as the 'rear crew' we sat side-by-side in a row of seats that were of the 'non-ejection' variety and that faced backwards towards the tail of the Vulcan. The nav radar's seat was positioned on the left of the row (facing the rear of the aircraft), I sat on the right, and the nav plotter sat in the middle – it was a tight fit. The nav radar and I had seats that could slide back and forth, and be swivelled around to simplify entry to and exit from our crew positions. Being stuck in the middle, the nav plotter's seat could not be swivelled, but it could be slid back and forward on its rails to allow the occupant to adopt a comfortable sitting position. To get into and out of his seat, the nav plotter had to rely upon either the nav radar or myself vacating our seats first – not an ideal situation. The three of us shared a common workbench that spanned the width of the cabin, and almost all the equipment needed to perform our individual duties was set out on the bulkhead facing us and on the nearby fuselage walls. This arrangement was 'cosy' but functional. It is just a pity that our seats faced backwards and not forward. Facing the 'wrong' way certainly felt a bit unnatural. Interestingly, this backward-facing arrangement held sway in the Valiant and Victor aircraft too – I wonder why?

Vulcan pilots, as you might have guessed, were primarily responsible for flying the aircraft. However, unlike on some other aircraft where a navigator or an AEO could be appointed aircraft captain, the Vulcan captain was always the first pilot and he occupied the ejector seat on the left side of the cockpit. The co-pilot sat on the right-hand ejector seat. In addition to taking his turn to fly the aircraft, the co-pilot was responsible for a number of other things including managing the aircraft's fuel and cabin conditioning systems and, if required, visually dropping the bomb.

Despite the Vulcan being in service, in one form or another, for many years, when I started flying in it in 1977, it struck me as being very old-fashioned. Very little had been done to modernise the aircraft's radar, bombing computer, navigation system and ECM equipment. Of the few changes that had been made, one of the most important was the installation of the military flight system (MFS). The MFS provided a beam compass and a director horizon to assist and simplify flight management for the pilots. Instead of trying to satisfy heading changes by reference to the compass, the pilot simply dialled the new heading into the MFS and followed the left/right commands shown on the director horizon to arrive at the correct heading. The MFS could also accept heading commands from the nav plotter and steering inputs from the aircraft's navigation and bombing system (NBS). In this latter case, pilots simply had to follow the left/right steering commands to fly towards the weapon release point.

Other important updates included the installation of both the terrain-following radar (TFR) and Mk. 7B low-level radio altimeter. The integrated output from these two systems was fed to the MFS to provide pitch demands on the director horizon display. Pilots simply followed the MFS pitch commands to maintain a constant, pilot-selectable height down to a minimum of 200 feet above the terrain over which the aircraft was being flown. The combination of MFS, the TFR and the radio altimeter significantly simplified the pilot's task of flying their aircraft to the weapon release point over undulating terrain, at low level, day or night, and in most weather conditions.

The nav plotter took care of everything to do with navigation. He had a number of systems to help him fulfil this task including an extremely accurate, gyro-based, heading reference system (HRS Mk. 2) and an electro-mechanical ground position indicator Mk. 6 (GPI Mk. 6) – surely the ultimate in precision electro-mechanical engineering at that time. The GPI Mk. 6, once initialised with the aircraft's starting position, would automatically update the aircraft's position using heading information from HRS, and ground speed and drift information from the aircraft's Decca Doppler 72 navigation radar. The nav plotter also had use of a tactical air navigation (TACAN) transceiver that provided accurate bearing and slant range to ground- and ship-based TACAN beacons. He also had access to the single AD709D radio compass receiver. Furthermore, he could update his GPI position using H2S radar-derived navigational fixes passed by the nav radar. On the deficit side, the only long-range navigation equipment available to the nav plotter was a periscope sextant that was mounted in the ceiling of the rear cabin just above and behind the AEO's seat. This could be used to take single-line sun shots during daytime or star fixes at night. Interestingly, 27 Squadron Vulcans, that took over the maritime radar reconnaissance (MRR) role from the Victor, were fitted with Loran C, a long-range hyperbolic navigation system. It's a pity that the opportunity wasn't taken to install Loran C in all the Vulcans. I am sure that nav plotters would have really appreciated the gesture.

The AEO position in the Vulcan.

The nav radar was, in effect, the radar bomb aimer. He had dedicated use of the Vulcan's rather old H2S Mk. 9 ground-mapping radar and the obsolete, but still functional, analogue-based NBS to allow him identify the target and steer the aircraft to the weapon release point. The H2S Mk. 9 was an I-Band radar that was an improved version of the H2S radar fitted to Lancaster and Halifax bombers during WWII. Many of the radar's electronic circuits and electronic components had been updated and a new five-foot-wide scanner was fitted in the nose of the Vulcan. This new scanner significantly reduced the radar's azimuthal beam width thus sharpening up the H2S display and allowing the navigator to mark landmarks more precisely and target offset structures with his bearing marker. The combination of H2S Mk. 9, NBS and inputs from other systems, allowed Vulcan crews to deliver their bombs on target with a level of accuracy compatible with the use of nuclear weapons. Although the nav radar had access to a Mk. 6 radar altimeter for use when flying at high altitudes, I don't think it found much day-to-day utility, especially after the Vulcan was assigned to the low-level strike role.

My job as AEO was to manage the Vulcan's electrical system, take care of all the HF and some V/UHF communications, and operate the Vulcan's ESM and ECM systems. The aircraft was fitted with a Collins 618T HF transceiver that allowed me to communicate over long distances using continuous wave (CW) for Morse code, as well as amplitude modulation (AM), and single-sideband (SSB) modulations for voice communications. For short-range VHF and UHF line-of-sight communications, I had control of a V/UHF PTR-175 radio. The captain had control of an AN/ARC-52 UHF radio which I could also use if so required. In terms of passive ESM, I had sole control and access to the air radio installation (ARI) 18228 RWR. This was a superb piece of equipment that gave excellent warning when being illuminated by pulse radars operating in the E through to J frequency bands (approximately equivalent to the old S through to Ku bands). It also gave warning when the Vulcan was being tracked by a CW radar, such as that used by the UK's Bloodhound SAM system, and CW transmissions associated with semi-active homing weapons. Its only deficiency, as far as I could tell, was its dubious performance against radars that operated in the Pulse Doppler (PD) mode. The Vulcan's active ESM capability included the Red Steer Mk. 2, tail warning radar. This was a simple, but reliable sector scanning I-Band radar that looked out to the rear of the aircraft allowing the AEO to search the large volume of airspace in the aircraft's rear hemisphere. It could pick up a fighter in excess of 15 miles and, interestingly, it was reputed to be able to detect an incoming air-to-air missile. I wonder what happened to the poor soul that made that discovery? A rear-viewing periscope was also installed inside the desk in front of the AEO. By lifting the small desk cover, raising the periscope and peering through the eyepiece, the AEO was able to observe the outside environment spanning from wing tip to wing tip, both above and below the aircraft – including the terrain below, he was also able to inspect most of the Vulcan's airframe located behind the crew cabin. Horizontal and vertical movement of the periscope was accomplished using a handle arrangement tucked under the AEO's desk.

In addition, the Vulcan had installed in its wings, four containers/hoppers, three of which held large quantities of chaff of varying types. This allowed the AEO to dispense the chaff type appropriate to the type of radar he wished to act against. The fourth underwing hopper contained IR decoy flares. Both the chaff and the flares were controlled from dual chaff dispenser control units mounted above the AEO's workstation. Additionally, the AEO could fire cartridges of 'rapid blooming' chaff from the Very pistol located on the upper-right side of the

Left: AEO's position with a Very pistol at the top right. (H. Heeley, Newark Air Museum)

Below: AEO's periscope stowed in a desk with its operation handle positioned beneath the desk. (H. Heeley, Newark Air Museum)

cabin wall next to his position. The chaff in these cartridges comprised a cocktail of 'metal-coated fibreglass needles' cut to various radar wavelengths to provide good reflectivity across a wide band of threat frequencies. Firing chaff from the Very pistol ensured that it would bloom very rapidly thus providing an instant false target to confuse threat radar systems.

Unfortunately, despite the increasing sophistication of radar-controlled air-defence missile and AAA systems entering service throughout the Soviet Union, the 617 Squadron Vulcans were never fitted with an up-to-date ECM deception jamming system. The only ECM fitted to the Scampton Vulcan B2s was the long-obsolescent Red Shrimp barrage noise jammer that operated in the D and E frequency bands. It was practically useless against modern radar-controlled threat systems that generally operated at much higher frequencies. Furthermore, the position of the Red Shrimp aerials on the Vulcan was sub-optimal for an aircraft operating at low level. I will cover this issue in greater detail when writing about the Vulcan's war missions. Another deficiency in the Vulcan's electronic warfare (EW) suite that emerged during my time on the squadron was the lack of some form of missile approach warning system (MAWS) to counter the wide range of man portable air defence systems (MANPADS) missiles that were being issued in large quantities to Soviet troops. MANPADS missiles could home on to infrared emissions radiating from the Vulcan's jet exhaust. As they did not rely on radar guidance or data links of any kind, their presence could not be detected via the RWR. Unfortunately, MAWS were still in development at that time, and this left the Vulcan, and other attack aircraft of that era, vulnerable to attack, particularly when getting close to the target where concentrations of MANPADS-equipped troops could be expected. So, despite having an ample supply of IR decoy flares able to counter MANPADS missiles, by not having a MAWS, the AEO had no way of knowing when a MANPADS missile was being launched in the direction of his aircraft.

Some targets, such as command and control centres, were buried underground rendering them invisible to the pilots and the Vulcan's H2S radar. To overcome this problem a rather more complicated procedure for getting aircraft to the weapon release point and placing the bomb on target was used. This procedure was called 'offset bombing'. It required the nav radar to decide upon a suitable structure or geographical feature, not too far removed from the known position of the target, that would readily show up on radar. He would then measure the differences in distance between the latitudes and longitudes of the target and the chosen feature, and enter the details into the NBS. When, during flight, the nav radar placed his range and bearing markers over the offset feature showing on his H2S display, the NBS would automatically calculate the actual position of the target and route the appropriate steering commands through to the pilot's MFS. These commands, when followed, would guide the pilots to the correct weapon release point. NBS also took account of a number of variables when calculating the weapon release point, such as the aircraft's speed, altitude, and heading, and the ballistic attributes of the bomb. Some of these variables had little impact on accuracy when bombing at low level, but they were vitally important when bombing from high altitude.

## Vulcan Crew Escape Facilities and Procedures

During the design of the Vulcan, someone must have decided to give some thought to the subject of aircraft abandonment, be it on the ground, during flight, or after ditching in the sea. There were two main methods of escaping from a Vulcan whilst it was on the ground. Should an emergency occur while the aircraft was still standing on its undercarriage, the crew simply informed ATC on the radio, stopped the engines, turned the electrics off (unless it was night-time in which case the battery switch could be left on to supply power for cabin lighting) and vacated the aircraft as quickly as possible via the entry/exit door. Should the aircraft suffer a crash landing or an emergency on the ground such that the bottom of the fuselage was resting on the ground making crew escape via the entry/exit door impossible, the pilots would jettison the aircraft canopy, make their ejector seats safe, climb out of the cockpit, drop down to the ground and make haste upwind from the aircraft. The rear crew would release themselves from their seats and clamber, one at a time, up the ladder leading to the cockpit, climb over the ejection seats, drop down from the cockpit, and run off in the same direction as the pilots.

A similar escape method would also be used if the Vulcan ditched in the sea albeit the crew would have to remember to swim rather than run. Also, they would have to remember to inflate their life jackets just prior to jumping into the water. Once 'in the drink' and having swam to a safe distance from the sinking Vulcan, they would inflate and board their single-seat dinghies and paddle away from the aircraft in a crosswind direction. An MS5 multi-seat dinghy was enclosed in the back of the cockpit behind the pilots presumably for use during ditching. However, if my memory serves me correctly, the MS5, as its name implies, was designed to hold five people, yet the Vulcan regularly flew with six or seven people on board during long overwater deployments. Ouch!

If a decision was made to abandon the Vulcan during flight, pilots would make use of their ejector seats. Operation of either one of the ejector seats would automatically cause the canopy to be jettisoned just prior to firing the cartridge that would propel the seat up its guide rails. We lesser mortals down the back remained stuck in 'manual mode'. We had to release our straps, struggle out of our seats, clamber down to the bottom of the aircraft, and then bale out, one at a time, via the aircraft's entry/exit hatch-cum-escape chute located on the aircraft's floor. This was easy to say, but it probably would have been quite difficult to do if significant G forces were being generated due to the aircraft spinning, or spiralling out of control. To help in this regard, rear crew seats were fitted with an inflatable cushion. After the nav plotter and AEO had swivelled their seats to a forward-facing direction, they could operate a toggle on the side of their seats which would inflate a cushion and this would propel them upwards and outwards from their seats towards the aircraft escape hatch. Although the nav plotter also had an inflatable cushion fitted to his seat, he would have been very reluctant to use it because his seat could not be swivelled and inflating the cushion would possibly have trapped his knees or thighs under his workstation, thus preventing his escape. Most of the nav plotters that I knew swore that they would never use the facility. In summary, the rear crew escape procedures, dreamt up when the Vulcan was assigned to the high-level strike role, were not particularly conducive to a seamless and rapid abandonment of the aircraft when it was being operated at low level. In truth, in the event of a catastrophic failure of the aircraft, or serious damage caused by enemy action when the aircraft was flying at low level, there would have been very little time for the pilots to assess the situation, give the order to abandon aircraft, and eject. The unfortunate rear crew would have had even less time to make good their manual escape. Things became even worse when attempting to abandon the Vulcan when the undercarriage was down.

As you may have noticed, the Vulcan's nose wheel is located directly behind the crew entry/exit door/escape chute. Had any rear crew member attempted to abandon aircraft in the normal fashion when the undercarriage was down, he would have found himself painfully wrapped around the nose wheel. To overcome this problem, the pilots were encouraged to make sure the undercarriage was retracted prior to giving the order to abandon aircraft. If it was not possible to raise the undercarriage – and this is the real eye opener – rear crew members were advised that, when sliding down the escape chute, they should grab hold of one of the escape chute door struts and swing themselves out sideways into the slipstream, rather like a trapeze artist, thus avoiding the nose wheel. We were all assured that a flight trial had proved that this procedure was safe and that it should result in a successful escape. No doubt the trial was conducted in ideal conditions with the aircraft flying straight and level and with no need for urgency. As I am sure you will agree, this was never likely to be a realistic scenario.

If things went seriously wrong during the take-off or landing phase of a sortie, such that the captain felt compelled to order the crew to abandon aircraft, it generally meant that he had lost, or thought he was about to lose, control of the aircraft. Given this situation, it was far from certain that the aircraft would be flying in a stable, wings level attitude. Furthermore, by the time the captain had expended all his options for controlling the aircraft and realised that the flight was doomed much of the time needed to allow the rear crew to escape would probably have been used up, thus giving the rear crew very little chance of executing a successful escape.

Examples of this include the crash of XA897 at Heathrow Airport in October 1956 and the crash of XM645 at Malta in 1975. Had the rear cabin been fitted with ejection seats, it is possible that in both these cases the whole crew would have been able to abandon the aircraft, not just the pilots. To my knowledge, no rear crew member has ever made a successful parachute escape from a crippled Vulcan during flight when the undercarriage was down. What I find particularly interesting, is that most of those that were previously associated in some way with the Vulcan and who argued against the need for rear crew ejection seats were, a) those not destined to spend a large part of their lives flying as rear crew in a Vulcan, or b) pilots who felt free to voice their opinions from the safety of their ejector seats.

I believe that the issue of rear crew escape was re-assessed when the Vulcan was first assigned to the low-level strike role. Indeed, I know that there was a cunning plan to provide some form of rear crew ejector seat facility. But, the cost of such a significant engineering undertaking when set against the short time that the aircraft was (wrongly) expected to remain in service, probably led to it being considered a poor return for investment. In any case, there would have remained a problem of how crew chiefs and other personnel riding as passengers or instructors would have been able to escape. The sad truth is that once the design of the Vulcan had been accepted, and production had started, any chance of substantially changing things to improving rear crew escape provision was lost. Some might argue that this was a marginal consideration when the Vulcan was dedicated to the high-level strategic strike role, but it certainly became more pertinent after the Vulcan was re-assigned to the low-level tactical strike role.

Although it is all water under the bridge now, I still find it perplexing that with all the consideration and thought that went into the design and development of the Vulcan including a modern escape system for the pilots, rear crew members were provided with a set of escape options that were marginally worse than those provided to crews that flew in the Lincoln bomber – one of the aircraft that the Vulcan was designed to replace. All of that said, the idea of actually having to abandon a Vulcan in peacetime was not something that seriously occupied the minds of most Vulcan rear crew members. Perhaps this was because over the years the Vulcan had proved to be an extremely safe and reliable aircraft. But then again, perhaps it was because we, rear crew types, simply lacked imagination.

# Aircraft and Weapon Development

Going back to when the Vulcan B1 was entering service, Avro continued its efforts to enhance the performance and handling qualities of the aircraft. Certain modifications were carried out on Vulcan B1s that were already in service to narrow the performance gap between the B1 and the expected final version, the Vulcan B2. These interim aircraft were called Vulcan B1As. Later, when it finally entered service, the B2 version of the Vulcan had a newly sculptured wing which increased the aircraft's wing span and total area. It also featured a significantly modified leading edge that improved the aircraft's performance and handling qualities. More powerful Olympus engines were installed, and later, a rapid start capability was provided to enable all four engines to be started simultaneously, thus allowing the Vulcan to get airborne well within the estimated four-minute warning time of a ballistic missile attack. A new 200V, 400 Hz, three-phase alternating current (AC) electrical system was installed replacing the old 112 V direct current (DC) system used in the B1. This offered a significant improvement in electrical system reliability as well as providing the additional power needed to supply the B2's new on-board systems, in particular the aircraft's power-hungry ECM equipment.

Changes to the Vulcan's pitch and roll flight control surfaces resulted in the aircraft's four elevators and four ailerons being replaced by a set of eight elevons (combined ailerons and elevators). This change, I am told, improved aircraft handling qualities when it was being flown within its normal flight envelope and it significantly reduced the impact on aircraft control caused by the loss of one or more PFCUs. However, on the debit side, it was said by some that these changes brought about an increase in the amount of adverse – out of turn – yaw induced when the aircraft was banked aggressively at low speed, thus requiring the pilots to counter by applying rather more in-to-turn rudder than would normally be required on a modern jet aircraft.[1]

During the period that the Vulcan was assigned to the nuclear deterrent role, the instrumentation, navigation, and communication, ECM and ESM systems were incrementally improved to maintain the aircraft's effectiveness and improve its survivability. However, not long after being re-assigned to the low-level tactical-strike role, this incremental upgrading process gradually slowed to a halt, possibly to release funds for the development of other, more modern, weapon systems due to enter service such as the Tornado IDS. Also, at some point in the Vulcan's career, someone decided that the aircraft's ability to top up its tanks via AAR should be allowed to lapse. Similarly, it was decided that the conventional bombing capability was no longer

1   The adverse yaw phenomenon and the pilots' mitigating use of rudder was easy to see during Vulcan displays when the aircraft was being rapidly rolled at low speed.

Blue Danube atomic bomb being fitted to a Valiant B1.

required. The enabling equipment for these two capabilities was either scrapped or no longer maintained in good working order.

Similar decisions were made to forego updating the Vulcan's ECM system. When I first arrived on 617 Squadron, I was intrigued to find that, in addition to Red Shrimp, Waddington Vulcans were also fitted with an I-Band ECM jammer. Scampton Vulcans were fitted with the Red Shrimp D/E-Band jammer only. I have no idea how good the I-Band jammer was, or why it was never fitted to the Scampton Vulcans. Whatever the reasons, the cumulative deletion of both the conventional bombing and AAR capabilities and the failure to update the Vulcan with a modern ECM suite must have been viewed with some regret when it was decided to use the Vulcan on Operation Black Buck in 1982.

The Atomic Weapons Research Establishment (AWRE) was/is responsible for the research, development and production of Britain's nuclear weapons. It worked continuously to create, modify and improve the range of weapons that were earmarked for carriage by the V Bombers and on other UK aircraft and missile systems. Some failed to achieve operational utility, but others were brought into service. Of these, only a few were produced in any significant numbers. The Blue Danube atomic (fission) bomb proved to have a rather short operational life and only around 24 examples were built. The bombs were stored at two special sites, one at RAF Faldingworth in Lincolnshire, and the other at RAF Barnham in the Thetford Forest in East Anglia. These facilities are no longer used for weapon storage, but I have been told that at some point after being decommissioned, the Barnham site was used as a mushroom farm. A quirky coincidence, don't you think, atomic bomb storage – mushroom farm?

It is difficult to set out with any certainty the dates and types of fission and fusion weapons that entered service on the Vulcan and the exact yield that they provided. Indeed, there were times during the Cold War when some V Force and tactical aircraft squadrons were armed with American weapons such as the B28 nuclear bomb. As for UK-developed weapons, the Blue Danube atomic bomb was replaced in or around 1961 with a much smaller and more modern fission bomb called Red Beard. There were two marks of Red Beard, the Mk. 1 having a yield of around 15kt and the Mk. 2 offering a yield of around 25kt. The Red Beard was earmarked for delivery by V Bombers, Canberras and some Fleet Air Arm aircraft and a number of bombs were stockpiled in Cyprus in support of the Central Treaty Organisation (CENTO) and in Singapore is support of the South East Asian Treaty Organisation (SEATO) as well in the UK.

Overlapping this, in 1959 the UK introduced into service a free-fall weapon called Yellow Sun, a name, incidentally, that referred to the bomb casing only. There were two marks of Yellow Sun. The Mk. 1 bomb was fitted with a large boosted fission warhead called Green Grass that offered a nominal yield of around 400 kt. Unfortunately, this weapon required complex and less than ideal handling and safety management due to the design of its warhead. As a result, only a small number were brought into service and they were soon replaced with the Yellow Sun Mk. 2 fitted with the Red Snow thermonuclear (fusion) warhead providing a yield of just over 1Mt. The design of the Red Snow was, I believe, based upon American W28 nuclear weapons technology re-engineered to satisfy UK safety and operational requirements. To help both Yellow Sun Mk. 1 and Mk. 2 weapons separate cleanly from their host bomber, and to limit their rate of fall, the nose of the bomb casing was designed to be perfectly flat, thus providing a similar amount of aerodynamic drag to that normally provided by a parachute retardation system. The flat nose of the weapon had another advantage. It avoided the build-up of transonic airflows over the bomb casing that complicated the placement and use of the barometric altitude sensors that were needed for the bomb to function properly.

Yellow Sun bomb casing.

A WE.177 nuclear bomb in its mobility trolley. (NELSAM)

Another major weapon enhancement took place in 1963 when a number of Victor and Vulcan squadrons – including 617 Squadron – were armed with the Blue Steel rocket-powered and nuclear-armed stand-off missile. Blue Steel had an operational range of around 150 miles when launched at high altitude and about 35 miles when launched at low altitude. When it was dropped from the aircraft, a tape attached to both the aircraft and the missile unfurled and reached tension at 100 ft at which point it pulled a switch on the missile that fired the Stentor rocket motor. The Stentor, having a thrust of around 26,000 lbs, accelerated the missile to Mach 2.5 and, if launched from low level, caused the missile to climb to around 40,000 feet. The missile's early generation inertial navigation system (INS) was sufficiently accurate to guide the missile to the target area at which point the missile would bunt over and dive onto its target. It was claimed that the missile had a circular error of probability (CEP) of hitting the target of around 600 ft.

I have no idea how reliable the weapon would have proved to be 'come the day'. Its INS largely depended on thermionic-valve technology and would not have taken kindly to the buffeting experienced during its carriage at low level. Furthermore, the rapid accelerations associated with its launch and climb to altitude and the negative G bunting manoeuvre performed when diving onto the target would have placed great stress on the weapon's systems. The missile had the additional drawback of relying upon the use of high-test peroxide (HTP) with kerosene for fuel. HTP is a very volatile substance and great care had to be taken when carrying out maintenance, refuelling and general handling of the weapon.

Nevertheless, the Vulcan B2 and Victor B2 armed with Blue Steel missiles continued to serve as the UK's nuclear deterrent until 1968–69, at which point the RN took over the role with its ship submersible ballistic nuclear (SSBN) submarines carrying nuclear-armed Polaris submarine-launched ballistic missiles (SLBM). After relinquishing the nuclear-deterrent role, the Blue Steel missile was removed from service and the Vulcans were re-armed with the WE.177 nuclear bomb configured for low-level, laydown delivery against sub-strategic targets.

The WE.177 used a UK re-engineered version of the American W59 warhead and three versions were built. The A version was a boosted fission bomb offering a choice of two yields – 0.5 kt and 10 kt; the B model was a thermonuclear bomb that provided a yield of around 450 kt, and the C model was also a thermonuclear weapon that had a yield of around 200 kt. The A version was mainly used by short- to medium-range tactical-strike aircraft such as the Jaguar and, in its depth-bomb guise, by RAF Nimrod MPAs and RN ASW helicopters. I also believe that two Vulcan B2 squadrons (9 and 35 Squadrons) were armed with the WE.177A or C as a replacement for the Red Beard weapons allocated for CENTO. Also, it is possible that some UK-based Vulcan missions could have been allocated the A or C models – for use on selective release (warning) missions – but I cannot confirm this. However, the primary armament for UK-based Vulcans was the WE.177B. Later when the Vulcan was withdrawn from service in 1981–82, the WE.177A, B and C were used to arm the UK's Tornado, Jaguar and Buccaneer tactical strike aircraft. All WE.177 weapons were removed from service after the collapse of the Soviet Union and the end of the Cold War.

# CHAPTER FIVE
# THE VULCAN OCU

I was looking forward to starting my conversion to the Vulcan B2 at No. 230 OCU, and later, joining 617 Squadron, both of which were conveniently located at Scampton. But before I could do so, I was ordered to attend a short electrical systems familiarisation course at RAF Finningley. This, I was told, would set me up nicely for managing the electrical system on the Vulcan. I can't remember much about the Finningley course except that I was given some hands-on instruction on an aircraft electrical system training rig. The odd thing about this rig was that instead of simulating an aircraft with four engines and alternators as-per the Vulcan B2, Victor Tanker and VC10 etc., it represented an aircraft with only three engines. To my knowledge no such aircraft existed on the RAF inventory at that time. So why, you may ask, would the RAF purchase a three-engine training device when, for a small extra sum, it could have bought one that was representative of all or most of the four-engine aircraft in current RAF service? I can only assume that the officer responsible for the purchase had his very own crystal ball and foresaw that in 1984, the three-engine Lockheed TriStar would enter service with the RAF in the tanker/passenger/cargo role, thus justifying his purchase. Although I did have some moderately useful training time on this device, I cannot remember learning much else at Finningley and I was more than happy when the course ended and I was allowed to make my way to Scampton to start my conversion onto the Vulcan.

Alas, once again I was stopped in my tracks and told that, prior to starting the OCU, I would have to attend an aeromedicine course at the AMTC at RAF North Luffenham. However, I cheered up when I discovered that the other four officers that would make up my first Vulcan crew were also attendees on the course. Just like crews on the Maritime Force, Vulcan crews were constituted and remained together for longish periods of time. So, the two or three days spent at North Luffenham gave the five of us time to get acquainted and to learn a bit about each other's background. I soon determined that Sqn Ldr Keith Walters (captain) and Flt Lt David Bruce (nav plotter) had previously served on the Vulcan B2, but Fg Off Bill Dart (nav radar) and Flt Lt Bob Lindo (co-pilot) were, like myself, new to the Vulcan Force. So our crew had a reasonable mix of Vulcan experience.

During the aeromedicine course we were given lectures on a wide range of physiological phenomena associated with operating aircraft at high altitude. These included being able to recognise the onset of hypoxia (lack of oxygen) and the various symptoms associated with decompression sickness; a phenomenon associated with working in a low air-pressure environment where gases that normally remain dissolved in the blood come out of solution and form bubbles inside the body. The latter could cause a number of unwelcomed symptoms ranging from mild skin and muscular irritation all the way through to complete loss of cognitive function and even death. To counter the hypoxia risk, the Vulcan was fitted out with an excellent oxygen system. This ensured that the correct amount of oxygen was provided to the crew's oxygen masks for all phases of flight.

Oxygen was routed to the crew via individual regulators located at each crew position. The regulator monitored the cabin altitude and altered the mix of air and oxygen to suit. Starting at ground level and assuming no cabin pressurisation system, the regulator would supply a mixture of air and oxygen to the individual's oxygen mask, with the amount of oxygen gradually being increased as the cabin altitude increased. At around 12,000 ft the pressure of the air/oxygen mix was, if I remember correctly, slightly increased providing a positive differential pressure compared to the ambient air pressure in the cabin – a sort of safety pressure. When the cabin altitude reached around 34,000 feet, the regulators would be supplying 100 per cent pure oxygen to the crew member, and at 39,000 feet and above, the regulator provided 100 per cent oxygen at a significantly higher pressure, forcing oxygen into the crew member's lungs. A switch on each oxygen regulator allowed crew members to select 100 per cent oxygen when certain situations demanded it, such as the presence of toxic fumes in the cockpit/cabin. Crew members could also, by operating a toggle on the mask, change the pressure that the mask was held against their faces. Prior to getting airborne crew members would adjust the attachment mechanism on their masks to provide a leak-free flow of oxygen whilst still being comfortable to wear. Moving the toggle on the mask downwards would cause the mask to be forced much tighter against the wearer's face to ensure that there was absolutely no oxygen leakage, particularly when operating under pressure-breathing conditions. Fortunately, the Vulcan had an excellent cabin pressurisation system so the need for pressure breathing was limited to exceptional circumstances such as loss of cabin pressure above 39,000 feet.

The cabin pressurisation system had two settings, 'cruise' for everyday flight, and 'combat' for operating in a combat zone. When the aircraft was climbing after take-off with cruise selected, the pressurisation system would become active at around 8,000 feet and then maintain that comfortable cabin altitude all the way up to an aircraft's cruising altitude of around 45,000 feet – an arrangement similar to that found in modern high-flying business jets. At this altitude, the maximum safe pressure differential between the inside and the outside of the cabin of 9 PSI (pounds per square inch) would be reached. If the climb was continued to an even higher altitude, then the altitude inside the cabin would be allowed to increase also to maintain the safe pressure differential limit. Alternatively, when entering an area at high altitude where enemy action was possible, the combat setting would be selected. This would reduce the maximum allowable pressure difference between the inside and the outside of the cabin to around 4 PSI thus providing a cabin altitude of around 20,000 feet when flying at 40,000 feet. Any increase in altitude would cause the cabin altitude to increase also. The reason for having the combat pressurisation option was to limit the cabin's internal-to-external pressure differential to a level that would reduce the chances of catastrophic failure of the cabin structure (rather like a balloon bursting) in the event of cabin damage due to enemy action.

During the time when the Vulcan was employed as a high-altitude strategic bomber flying at 50,000 feet and above, selecting combat pressure would have resulted in the crew being subjected to a cabin altitude in excess of 25,000 feet for an extended period of time. This could have resulted in crew members experiencing symptoms of decompression sickness. To provide protection against this, and also to protect the crew in the event of pressurisation failure and/or having to abandon the aircraft at very high altitude, crew members were issued with partial pressure jackets and anti-G pants. Upon detection of a drop in cabin pressure below a certain value the jackets would be inflated automatically by oxygen from the aircraft's oxygen supply system to maintain a required level of external pressure around the crew member's chest. The anti-G pants would also inflate to provide an external pressure around the crew member's lower abdomen and legs roughly equal to that provided by the pressure jacket, thus preventing blood from draining from the upper body and pooling in the legs. At the same time, the oxygen regulator at each rear crew position would automatically feed 100 per cent oxygen under pressure to each crew member's oxygen mask. When the Vulcan B2 was reassigned to the low-level role in 1968–69, flight above 45,000 feet became unnecessary and crews were no longer routinely equipped with pressure jackets and anti-G pants. However, the Vulcan SR2s operated by No. 27 MRR Squadron were, on certain occasions, required to operate above 45,000 feet and crews were routinely equipped with pressure jackets and G-pants.

In the event of aircraft abandonment at high altitude, an oxygen bottle fitted in the pilot's ejection seats provided emergency oxygen to the occupant until the seat/pilot combination reached 10,000 feet at which point the seat would automatically release the pilot allowing his parachute to be automatically deployed. An emergency oxygen bottle was also fitted at the top of the rear crew's parachutes that automatically fed oxygen to the wearer's mask upon exiting the aircraft. The rear crew member would be allowed to free-fall to around 10,000 feet at which point a barostat device would initiate parachute deployment. Pilots had the means to separate themselves from their seats manually if the automatic separation mechanism failed. They also had a ripcord to allow manual deployment of their parachutes once they had separated from their seats should the automatic system fail to do so. Likewise, the rear crew members had a ripcord function that allowed them to deploy their parachute manually should the barostat system fail for any reason. To make sure we could physically cope with cabin pressurisation failures at 45,000 feet, crews were subjected to the somewhat uncomfortable experience of being explosively decompressed from 25,000 feet to 45,000 feet inside the AMTC decompression chamber. None of my crew showed any detrimental symptoms from this experience and we were declared fit to fly in the Vulcan.

Whilst still at AMTC, crews were measured for and issued with a flying helmet, oxygen mask and a personal equipment connector (PEC) hose assembly. The PEC hose assemblies contained all of the wire and tubes needed to connect a crew member's oxygen mask and headset to the aircraft's oxygen and intercom systems. PECs for the pilots were arranged to work in conjunction with their ejector seats. Those provided to the rear crew included a parachute static line connector that activated the parachute immediately upon exiting the aircraft in an emergency. There was also an electrical connection that turned on a 'crew gone light' in the cockpit when a rear crew member exited the aircraft. Regarding the helmets, most crew members preferred to use the two-piece helmet arrangement that comprised a cloth, G-type inner helmet and a Mk. 1 protective helmet (bone dome). The G-type inner helmet and oxygen mask was worn continuously during flight to provide access to the intercom and the aircraft's oxygen supply. While I cannot recall what the approved protocol was for wearing bone domes, I seem to remember that they would be donned during take-offs and landings and, if time permits, during a crash landing. Most of the rear crews that I flew with preferred to use this two-piece helmet arrangement. However, I much preferred wearing the Mk. 3 'all-in-one' helmet. The reason being that the cloth G-type helmet made my head itch unbearably, whereas I found the Mk. 3 helmets to be suitably lightweight and comfortable enough to be worn for the whole duration of the Vulcan's sortie – some four to five hours.

There being no more obstacles thrown in my path, I finally found myself walking through the doors of the 230 OCU training building at Scampton in April 1977. The first thing on the agenda was a mass, extracurricular, meeting of OCU instructors with pilots, navigators and AEOs from the Waddington squadrons, all crowded into one of the lecture rooms. The meeting was to try to resolve some obscure bone of contention between the Waddington crews and the OCU staff. Being a sunny spring day, the temperature in the room soon soared making it difficult to concentrate on what was being said. Heated verbal exchanges between the opposing groups seemed to drag on for ages resulting in those not directly involved in the discussion becoming increasingly restless and fidgety. The noisy sucking of breath, shuffling of feet and scraping of chairs must have sent a subliminal message to the OCU staff telling them that those of us not au fait with the subject under discussion, or too far away to hear what was being said, badly needed to get outside into the fresh Lincolnshire air. Sensing that agreement was out of reach, the verbal combatants decided to bring the meeting to an end. This was followed by a grand dispersal of aircrew back to their squadrons leaving my crew and an assortment of instructors to mill about and engage in small talk. Eventually, one of the AEO instructors came over to where I was standing and asked if I was Fg Off Jim Walls. When I answered in the affirmative, he told me to take the rest of the day off and to make myself available in the OCU lecture room at 0900 the following day. "Excellent," I thought. "At last, someone has acknowledged my presence." The following day I was told, in general terms, what I would be doing for the next couple of months. I must admit, I was expecting most of the crew being present for the majority of the lectures. This was not to be. Instead, the pilots and navigators attended their own lectures leaving me, the sole AEO on the course, to attend the AEO-related lectures on my own.

It is a strange experience being the only pupil attending a lecture. I certainly preferred it when there were other students present to liven up discussion, ask illuminating questions and, at times, obscure my lack of attention. On one particularly hot day I was attending a lecture given by an AEO instructor called Flt Lt John Hathaway. The subject of the lecture was the vapour cycle cooling pack (VCCP). A refrigeration system designed to control the temperature of the Red Shrimp ECM system. It wasn't the most inspiring of subjects. Perhaps it was the cosy, all-enveloping comfort of the easy-chairs, coupled with the darkness of the room and the soft whirring of the projector fan, that caused me to succumb to John's hypnotic voice and fall into a rather deep sleep. I am not sure how long I remained asleep, but when I opened my eyes the curtains and windows were wide open, the overhead projector was switched off and John was no longer there. I was mortified! I slowly made my way upstairs to the instructor's office where I found John, furiously concentrating on some admin work. I caught his eye and apologised profusely – what else could I do? He rather stiffly suggested that as I had all the relevant books, I could study the subject myself. This I did, but to this day I still squirm with embarrassment when I think about the incident.

As you would expect, the AEO course covered all the actions that I would be expected to carry out during the pre-flight, in-flight and post-flight phases of a sortie. It also included instruction on the actions to be followed when abandoning the aircraft in the event of an emergency. For this, our crew assembled in a building that contained the nose section of a Vulcan fuselage forward of the engine intakes – the bit that housed the cockpit and rear crew cabin. The escape drills were fairly straight forward and we had ample time to practise the recommended aircraft escape procedures, some details of which I have covered in the previous paragraphs. Instruction about ECM and ESM and some secondary systems were also covered on the course, but only to a very basic technical level, and only to familiarise me with their controls and displays. It soon became abundantly clear that the main focus of training would concentrate on the workings of the Vulcan's electrical system and the manipulation of its controls. This, I suppose, was understandable, as the Vulcan's flight control system relied exclusively on the use of electro-hydraulic PFCUs, the function of which relied in turn upon electrical power supplied by the aircraft's four engine-driven alternators. The Vulcan B2 had a total of ten PFCUs, eight to move the elevons on the trailing edge of the wings and two (one main and one standby) to operate the rudder. There were no secondary or manual back-up systems so it was vital for the AEO to take great care when manipulating the electrical system during flight and when managing electrical malfunctions.

The Vulcan B2's electrical system was designed with lots of in-built redundancy. DC power was provided by a 24V, 40Ah nickel cadmium battery which in turn was charged by the DC output from two 28V, 7.5Kw transformer rectifier units (TRU). The aircraft's main AC power was provided by four 40KW, 200V, 400Hz three-phase alternators, each one coupled via a constant speed drive unit to each of the four engines. These alternators supplied power to four corresponding busbars, across which all of the aircraft's electrical loads were fairly equally divided. To cater for the loss of an engine or alternator, the Vulcan also had a synchronising (or sharing) busbar which could be used to route the electrical output from one of the serviceable alternators to the failed alternator's busbar to maintain power to its electrical loads.

The default system configuration was for the No. 2 alternator to automatically connect to the synchronising busbar if it sensed that there was no power already applied to it. However, the AEO could replace the No. 2 alternator with any one of the other three alternators if so desired. During high-level flight, it was normal practice to connect the No. 4 alternator to the synchronising busbar, and when at low-level flight, it was usual to connect the No. 3 alternator to the synchronising busbar. However, as a safety precaution, if the system sensed that there was no power on the synchronising busbar at any time, it would automatically re-connect the No. 2 alternator thus maintaining power on the synchronising busbar at all times. During flight at low level, if the pilots felt or sensed that the aircraft had suffered a bird strike, the AEO would start the AAPP and connect its output to the synchronising busbar so that there was always power available to feed the busbar of any engine/alternator that might have been damaged due to bird ingestion. To cater for the loss of two or more engines/alternators a red light would flash in the cockpit and the captain would operate a control that would cause the ram air turbine (RAT) to be dropped into the slipstream. The RAT would almost instantaneously achieve operating RPM causing its alternator to deliver 22kVA of 200V 400Hz AC power. When operating above 20,000 ft, the AEO would couple the output of the RAT to the synchronising busbar which, in turn, would supply power to the busbar of the failed engine/alternator thus maintaining power to its electrical loads. Deploying the RAT also caused the aircraft's non-essential electrical loads to be disconnected thus reducing the total electrical load on the electrical supply system. However, the RAT tended to lose its efficiency when the Vulcan descended through 20,000 feet. To provide emergency electrical power below that altitude, the AEO would start the AAPP. The AAPP was a small Rover gas turbine engine/alternator combination that provided 40kVa of 200V 400Hz three-phase AC electrical power. When started by the AEO, its output could be connected to the synchronising busbar to replace that provided by the RAT thus maintaining electrical power to the busbars of the failed engine/alternators all the way down to ground level. Simulated double engine/alternator failures at high level were occasionally practised and the captain and AEO would run through the sequential use of the RAT followed by the AAPP until the aircraft was safely down at low level. This and many other emergency procedures were taught on the electrical system simulator by the OCU's instructors. I have to say that the quality of instruction on the Vulcan's electrical system was first class, and having finished training on the simulator, I definitely felt ready for the real thing.

At air shows, the glamour and awe that people attributed to the Vulcan B2 was due, in no small part, to the fantastic sound made by its four Olympus engines and, perhaps even more so, to the aircraft's unique, futuristic and somewhat threatening 'bat-like' external appearance. What is absolutely certain is that it cannot have had anything whatsoever to do with the inside of the Vulcan's crew compartment! Having spent many hours flying in the lightly coloured and airy environment of the Nimrod MR1 and even the R1, I genuinely felt a pang of disappointment when I first climbed into the Vulcan. Boarding through the under-belly access hatch took you into an almost windowless, dark, and rather dismal world where everything was painted dark green, matt-black, or not painted at all.

Ram air turbine (RAT) on the Vulcan B2.

AAPP intake scoop and exhaust aperture.

The bizarre seating layout was arranged in three vertical levels. The pilots sat upstairs facing forward in their rather cramped 'penthouse' cockpit. The three rear crew members occupied the mid-level 'apartment' where they sat, side-by-side, facing the back of the aircraft on seats mounted on a mezzanine bench. Meanwhile, on the 'ground floor' crew chiefs, instructors or passengers were required to sit facing each other on what were, in essence, two wooden boxes with safety straps. At the time the Vulcan was built, and for some time later, there must have been a total ban on the use of light greys, blues and other colours regularly seen in modern cockpits.

Lacking money for modernisation over the years, and certainly before I appeared on the scene, meant that most of the instrumentation in the rear crew compartment was still of the old-fashioned black and white variety and, in some cases, the positioning of dials and switches seemed to have more to do with finding somewhere for them to go rather than offering any thought to their usage. Many of the electrical cables associated with the H2S radar and the NBS plugged on to the front of the units presented the nav radar with a rather Heath Robinson vision of clutter, make-do, and old-fashioned engineering; the use of blind electrical connectors had obviously not been considered at the time the cabin layout was designed. Electrical lighting in the rear cabin was provided by a single overhead lamp. In addition, a single semi-flexible, overhead wander-lamp was located above each of the three rear crew positions. Unfortunately, due to time in service, the overhead wander-lamps had become 'over-bent' and tended to wander on their own volition and regularly failed to maintain the position desired by the crew member. Light bulbs and their fittings were also showing their age by flickering on and off, or simply going off for good, at the slightest hint of turbulence.

I must say that it was a rather dismal sight to behold, but given the age of the aircraft and the lack of serious recapitalisation over the years, I suppose it was to be expected.

The low wing loading that allowed the Vulcan to fly and manoeuvre so magnificently at high altitude proved to be something of a disadvantage when flying in turbulent air conditions at low level as even the mildest of air disturbance outside the aircraft would induce sharp bumps or slumps inside the aircraft cabin. All of this led to a certain rear crew member announcing that, for him, "the happiest sight in the world was seeing a Vulcan flying by, because that meant I wasn't in it!" That said, there were some plus-points such as the provision of an air ventilated suits (AVS) facility. The AVS was worn under the crew members' flying suits. They were special, full-body, lightweight, nylon or cotton one-piece suits that had lots of finely perforated tubes sewn into their every extremity. These tubes all came together and joined up to a wider tube that connected the suit to the Vulcan's AVS air supply. Crew members could, if they wished, individually control the temperature of the air flowing into the suit. I must admit, climbing into the Vulcan on a hot sticky day, starting the AAPP, connecting up to the AVS system and selecting 'cool' offered a wonderful, full-body chilling and even 'erotic' sensation. On the other hand, using the AVS during the winter months, when crews were compelled to wear their water and air-tight immersion suits, had some interesting results. Turning on the AVS controls would cause the immersion suit to rapidly inflate like a balloon transforming the wearer into a replica Michelin Man, making it almost impossible for him to bend his arms and legs. Being ever resourceful, crew members would position a pencil or some other convenient object under the rubber neck band of the immersion suit to let the air escape. While this allowed us to retain our normal size and mobility, it had the unfortunate side effect of creating a noise rather similar to that heard when releasing air from a balloon which, when multiplied by the number of AVS suits in use, generated the most unedifying and somewhat embarrassing noise inside the cabin.

Another on-board 'luxury' was the provision of soup heaters. Crew members could pierce the top of a tin of soup, place it in the soup heater, switch on the power and hey presto, after a short while they had hot soup to drink. However, it was vitally important to remember to pierce the tin before putting it in the soup heater. Another luxury was the provision of a 'pee tube' or 'urinal bladder' conveniently located at each crew position. The system was simple and it worked quite well as long as each crew member remembered to empty their own urinal bladder after landing. This was the situation that existed when I first started flying the Vulcan in 1977. The aircraft, having repeatedly had its retirement date delayed whilst at the same time being deprived of funds for system upgrades and refurbishment, was very definitely at the fag-end of its career as a medium-range, low-level, nuclear-strike bomber. With that in mind, you may be compelled to ask if the Vulcan was capable of carrying out successfully its war role from 1977 through to its retirement in 1981–82.

Spadeadam Cymbeline mortar radar simulating a Soviet SAM radar during a Vulcan training exercise over Devon.

The OCU flying phase included 15 flights spread over four or five weeks. My first flight took place on 5 July 1977 and, as luck would have it, the aircraft suffered an alternator failure whilst taxiing out of dispersal. I re-set the alternator which came back online, but prudence suggested that I should allow an aircraft electrics tradesman to check the system prior to continuing the sortie. We taxied back into dispersal where the tradesman dropped the relevant underwing panel, checked some connections and, afterwards, entered the aircraft to check out a few other things before declaring that the system was serviceable – as far as he could ascertain. So off we went and spent four hours of general aircraft handling for the benefit of the pilots. My task was limited to working some of the V/UHF communications, reading the check list, and last but not least, keeping a beady eye on the suspect alternator. The flights that followed gradually became more pertinent to the Vulcan's role, and I was more frequently joined by members of my own crew. I think I experienced only one sortie where our Vulcan was flown through the Spadeadam EW Range near Carlisle thus allowing me an opportunity to note the display of threat radars on the RWR. I also flew on a number of sorties that included carrying out practice bird strike drills followed by diversions to nearby RAF airfields. One sortie of note allowed me, under supervision from the senior OCU AEO, to practise the loss of two alternators (by switching them off) at high altitude thus causing the captain and I to have a realistic run through the RAT/AAPP drill procedures mentioned previously. Apart from that, the OCU flying phase was, for me, a bit of a non-event and I was glad when our crew completed the last training sortie and we moved over to 617 Squadron.

# CHAPTER SIX
# VULCAN CREW TRAINING

## Ground-Based Training

The 617 Squadron planning team was responsible for compiling and maintaining the squadron planning board. The large Perspex-covered board, which was fixed to the wall in the squadron operations office, was drawn up in a two-dimensional, line-and-column, spreadsheet fashion. The names of the captains were listed down the left side of the board and the days – looking forward by about two weeks – were set out across the top of the columns. All flights, detachments, leave and ground-based training sessions were entered on the board such that crews could see at a glance what they were expected to do on any given day. The planning was organised to ensure that all the squadron crews had plenty of opportunity to complete their mandated air and ground basic training requirements (BTR) by the end of each training period.

Pilots were regularly scheduled to undergo flight procedural training in the Vulcan flight simulator at Waddington. Navigators had their own training regime, and AEOs were routinely scheduled to attend electrical system training sessions on the Vulcan electrics training simulator in the OCU building. Electrical training rig instructors were able to demonstrate a large number of electrical faults that could occur for real on the Vulcan and advise the trainee on the best action to take in each case. I considered these training sessions to be very useful.

There was also an electronic warfare training office in the Scampton operations building where AEOs, and other crew members, if so inclined, could read up on the latest intelligence information from a rather limited set of classified documents. Better still, the room next to the

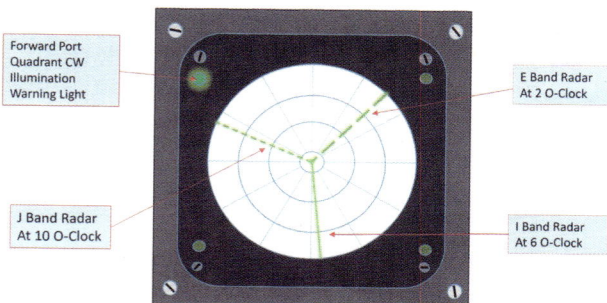

Diagram of an ARI 18228 RWR display.

ARI 18228 RWR antennas on top of the Vulcan's fin.

training office was equipped with a radar signal simulator (RSS), the signal output from which was coupled to an ARI 18228 RWR display that was installed in a small cubical designed to represent the AEO's position in the Vulcan. The RSS could be programmed by squadron and wing EW instructors to generate a large number of Soviet and NATO radar types for display on the RWR. This was a very useful familiarisation and refresher training aid for the AEOs. Unfortunately, it could also be used by the Headquarters One Group (HQ 1 Gp) standardisation team – affectionately known as the 'trappers' – who would use it to test the AEO's radar identification skills during periodic standardisation checks. Typically, the 'trapper' would feed a series of signal types through to the RWR and then ask the AEO to identify the radar, the threat it represented, the nature of its associated weapon system and the appropriate countermeasure action to be taken. Sometimes other members of the crew were invited to sit in on such events and observe the AEO's performance. Needless to say, if the AEO made a wrong identification, he would be mocked mercilessly by the rest of the crew. The RWR training cubical was not sufficiently equipped or integrated to allow airborne targets detected on the RWR to be seen on the Red Steer scope. Also, it could not simulate the use of chaff, flares and Red Shrimp jammers. So it was not possible to run a proper EW training scenario where the AEO could observe the impact of his chaff and jamming on the behaviour of the simulated threat system's radar. In fact, it was a rather hair-shirt training aid, but it was certainly better than nothing.

To maintain some semblance of purpose, crews were periodically required to make their way to the station's operations block in order to carry out periods of target study.

Target details were kept in a folder that contained all the information needed for a crew to carry out their allocated war sortie such as routeing and timing details, information on the target, communication procedures, recovery procedures, and intelligence on the threats likely to be encountered on route etc. In one of my crew's folders, I noticed that the information on a likely-to-be-encountered threat system was somewhat at variance with the personal knowledge I had acquired whilst flying on intelligence collection sorties on the Nimrod R1 of 51 Squadron a year or so earlier. I mentioned this discrepancy to one of the vault officers responsible for maintaining the folders. He advised me that folders were routinely updated and that the one in question was probably due to be updated soon. It occurred to me that it must have been a full-time and rather difficult job maintaining the currency of the folders to ensure that they

reflected the very latest disposition of Soviet radar and threat systems since many of these systems were mobile and easily moved.

Fairly realistic ground-based training could be conducted in the Vulcan full mission simulator (FMS) at Waddington. The FMS was based upon an actual Vulcan cockpit and rear crew cabin so that it faithfully represented the inside of the operational aircraft. Each FMS session gave crews an opportunity to practise most of the procedures and activities associated with planning and flying a typical wartime sortie. Crews wore their flying clothing including oxygen masks and flying helmets etc. during these sessions which helped to accentuate the feeling of realism. Unfortunately, the simulator system was old and some of the Vulcan's sub-systems lacked proper integration. It also lacked many of the modern flight simulator technologies – such as visual representation of the world outside the cockpit – that were commonplace on other simulators that existed during that period. Nevertheless, those responsible for operating the FMS did their best to make training sorties as realistic as possible, including simulating the impact of AAA rounds hitting the aircraft by banging noisily on the side of the simulator! Despite its many limitations, it did offer some reasonable operational and procedural training for the crews. In fact, the FMS must have been in almost permanent high demand because despite its importance for coordinated crew training, I can only remember my crew being scheduled to 'fly' in it once or twice during my four years on 617 Squadron.

Every so often Vulcan crews were driven in a bus up to Bridlington where they would partake in a session of sea survival training organised by the squadron rescue and survival training officer. Once there they would be ushered onto a RAF launch which would

617 Squadron crews conducting sea survival training off the coast of Bridlington.

take them out into the North Sea to a position, perhaps a mile or so, from the shore to carry out sea survival training. Whilst the launch made its way to the exercise area, crews would don their bunny suits (more on this later), immersion suits and their life jackets. They would then make themselves available on deck for a safety briefing by the captain of the launch followed by a sea survival briefing by the squadron's rescue and survival training officer. Each crew member would then take their turn at being strapped into a parachute harness that was attached to the back of the launch and then dragged along to simulate what it would be like to parachute into the sea during high wind conditions. After managing to release themselves from the parachute harness, crew members were expected to inflate and board their single-seat dinghies, activate their personal locator beacons and try to stay upright while the launch raced to-and-fro nearby in an attempt to capsize them. Later a helicopter would arrive on the scene and winch up the 'survivors' and drop them on to the deck of the launch. As well as being good fun, it was also a very worthwhile training activity.

# In-Flight Training

When I first arrived on 617 Squadron in 1976, I was keen to find out what types of sorties my crew would expect to fly on. I searched for a document that would describe the full range of Vulcan operations, and the tactics and procedures to be implemented in any given situation. My search drew a blank. I was surprised, and a bit disappointed, to find that the conventional bombing capability, with its variety of possible weapon types and attack profiles had been effectively removed from the Vulcan's offensive repertoire. What remained of the Vulcan's bombing capability was wholly centred on the carriage and delivery of a single WE.177 bomb and, of course, some 28-lb practice bombs; a rather skimpy repertoire for such a capable aircraft. This single-mission type had the effect of limiting nearly all our training sorties to flying the same hi-lo-hi flight profile. Some effort was made to introduce complications into the bombing process by pretending that equipment or information normally available to the navigator team was unavailable, thus forcing them to employ 'limited-aids' procedures to carry out an attack. This was fine as far as it went, but it was hardly mind stretching. The Nimrod MR1, on which I served for four years, was expected to conduct a wide range of complicated mission types. To provide a source of reference for these sorties, a metal box containing a comprehensive set of tactics manuals and other reference books was carried on board the aircraft. As for the Vulcan, someone must have decided that, as the aircraft had only one role to perform, it probably didn't warrant the cost and effort of developing a tactics manual for the crew. One day while I was enjoying a cup of coffee in the 617 Squadron crew room, I raised the issue with

Shackleton MR Mk. 3 (Aviation Photo Company)

120 Squadron Nimrod MR1 at CFB Greenwood.

120 Squadron Nimrod MR1. (Aviation Photo Company)

Top: Nimrod R1 at Wyton.

Above: Nimrod R1 with underwing Boz chaff and flare pods for Operation Granby.

Left: View of Vulcan rear crew positions. (H. Heeley, Newark Air Museum)

Above: Vulcans awaiting order to scramble. (IWM)

Below: Blue Steel Vulcan scramble. (IWM)

No. 15 Squadron Handley Page Victor B1. (Aviation Photo Company)

Vickers Valiant B1. (Aviation Photo Company)

Vulcan XL319 at the North East Land, Sea and Air Museum. This aircraft was the one that the author undertook his Vulcan training sortie on 22 June 1977. (NELSAM)

Right: Red Steer radome with Red Shrimp ECM bay opened and VCCP cooling duct on the side.

Below: Flt Lt John Hills (centre) and crew at USAFB Barksdale.

Bottom: The author's Vulcan at Barksdale.

Left: The author's first Vulcan crew. From left to right: the author, Sqn Ldr Keith Walters, Flt Lt David Bruce, Flt Lt Mike Hearn (who replaced Flt Lt Bob Lindo as co-pilot) and Flt Lt Bill Dart.

Below: A Vulcan snowed in at Offutt.

Bottom: Vulcan outside the RAF hangar at Goose Bay.

Top: Vulcan flying at low level near Goose Bay. (RAF HQ 1 Gp 1982)

Above: Vulcan flying at low level in Canada. (RAF HQ 1 Gp 1982)

Left: Wg Cdr Herbertson's crew at RAAF Edinburgh.

Below: Anzac Day fly-past over Adelaide on 25 April 1980.

Above: 617 Squadron (Australia) Memorial Ceremony at Adelaide in 1980.

Below left: 617 Squadron Dambuster memorial plaque at Adelaide.

Below right: MACR Steve Moore and MACR Mick Thompson (centre) and the author (right) with DSTL flight trials team at FRA Bournemouth.

Above: Author and wife, Jess, after landing at Perranporth Airfield in Cornwall.

Left: The Herbertson crew at RAAF Amberley, Australia.

Flt Lt Jamie Hamilton – a widely experienced AEO who soon became my good friend. He listened patiently to my whinge about there not being a comprehensive and well set out Vulcan tactics manual. After a short and thoughtful pause, Jamie looked me straight in the eye, and with a rather puzzled look said, "Jim, all you have to do is get airborne, fly to the target, drop the bomb, fly home, land, and try not to get shot down in the process. What else do you need to know?" Touché! Sadly, Jamie was killed in August 1978 when the Vulcan in which he was flying crashed soon after take-off from Glenview Naval Air Station (NAS) near Chicago.

## A Vulcan Training Sortie

For a typical Vulcan training sortie, our crew would assemble in the briefing room at the Scampton operations block two hours before the planned take-off time. The captain would telephone the 617 Squadron line office to be briefed on the aircraft he had been allocated, on which pan it was parked, its fuel state, and if it had any defects or limitations that could impact the sortie. In the meantime, the co-pilot would collect the latest weather details, develop his fuel plan and make sure that transport had been arranged to take the crew from the operations block to the aircraft at the appropriate time. The captain and co-pilot together would then study, in some detail, the latest meteorological data pertaining to the areas where we would be flying and scrutinise the forecast weathers for Scampton and our planned diversion airfields. While this was going on, the other crew members busied themselves collecting up-to-date documents, drawing up charts and performing other tasks required for the flight. NOTAMs were checked for any changes or restrictions to ATC procedures, navigation aids and airspace allocations etc. The nav radar and nav plotter would confer on the target to be 'bombed' and would check that they had all of the up-to-date information required for the simulated attack. The nav plotter would also submit our air traffic flight plan to wing operations for onward transmission to the appropriate agencies. I would attempt to book some high-level fighter affiliation training, perhaps with a Lightning from Binbrook. Also, if we were planning to fly through the electronic warfare training range at RAF Spadeadam, I would attempt to book some specific radar threat emitter activity. Similarly, if our flight was routed across the Western Isles of Scotland, I would book a threat-avoidance session with the threat simulator facility located at Stornoway Airport. While Vulcan B2 training sorties were focused primarily on delivering their single WE.177 nuclear bomb on target, it would seem that 617 Squadron (and perhaps other squadrons) could, on rare occasions, be ordered to fly MRR sorties, a task normally allocated to 27 Squadron. This might have been a local arrangement to provide relief for 27 Squadron during periods of high demand, or if

27 Squadron crews/aircraft were not available to be tasked. During my four years flying on the Vulcan, my crew was scheduled to fly on only one such MRR training sortie. More about that later.

Once everyone was satisfied that they had all the information they needed for the sortie, the captain would start the formal crew briefing by outlining the purpose of the sortie, and the timing and sequencing of events. He would briefly mention the weather in the areas where we planned to operate and declare the diversion airfields to be used. He would then ask each of the other crew members to chip in in turn with their specialist briefing. Once the briefing was over and there were no more questions to be answered, the crew would synchronise their watches and the captain would enter details of our sortie in the flight authorisation sheet. The crew would then retire to the aircrew restaurant where they could enjoy a meal that was freshly prepared by the duty RAF chef. After the meal, the crew would make its way to the safety equipment section, don their AVS, bunny and immersion suits, and collect their helmets, life jackets and other necessary paraphernalia from their lockers.

Wearing an AVS was not essential and the decision to do so was left up to individual crew members. However, if the sea temperature in the areas where we were planning to fly was below a certain temperature the wearing of rubberised, full-body immersion suits was mandatory. These suits were rather like the wet suits worn by surfboarders, but they were heavier, stronger, and much more difficult to get on and off. Crew members would also wear under their immersion suits, but on top of their AVS, a green-coloured thermal protection suit that was generally known as a 'bunny suit'. The bunny suit was a full body-sized, one-piece suit made from a warm, fleecy material. It was comfortable to wear and it provided superb thermal insulation. Having done quite a few sea survival drills wearing a combination of bunny suit and immersion suit, I can vouch for their potential life-saving properties. Just before departing the operations block, a crew member would pick up a box containing soft drinks and some snacks to see us through the rest of the day. We would then gather up all of the paraphernalia needed for the flight and board the vehicle to take us to our allocated aircraft.

The crew chief responsible for our aircraft would be waiting at the line hut for our transport to arrive. Once we were there, he would present the captain with the aircraft's Form 700E. Together they would go through the aircraft acceptance procedure including a check that all consumables (fuel, oil, oxygen and nitrogen etc.) had been replenished and that the pre-flight inspections carried out by airmen from the various trade groups had been done and signed for. The crew chief would verify that faults reported on previous flights had been rectified and he would make sure that the crew was aware of items listed in the acceptable/deferred defect log. After the captain accepted the aircraft, we would all make our way towards it. The crew chief would make sure that a ground power generator was plugged in to the Vulcan to provide 200V AC electrical power, and that a Palouste air-starter trolley was available for starting the engines. Simultaneously, the crew would carry out their individual external checks of the aircraft.

Being the AEO, I made sure that specified electrical circuit breakers in the nose-wheel bay were set to ON and that the various aerials and dielectric panels fitted to the aircraft were secure and undamaged. I would also check that the AAPP air intake was in the open position and that there were no bird nests or other foreign objects lodged inside. I also made sure that there were no remnants of chaff and flares from previous flights stuck in the chaff and flare dispenser chutes. Once everyone was happy with the aircraft's externals, we would all climb on board the aircraft, strap in and connect up to the various aircraft services such as intercom, oxygen and AVS etc. We would then silently run through our individual pre-start preparations.

The crew chief would assist the pilots to settle into their ejection seats then, when instructed, he would remove the ejector seat and canopy jettison pins and hand them to the pilots who would place them in the pin holders located on the side of the cockpit. The crew chief would also make sure that the aircraft's control locks, pitot-head covers, F700E and other relevant bits and pieces were stowed in one of the two locker-cum-passenger seats located either side of the entrance door. Amongst many other things, I made sure that all the switches at my location were set to their pre-start positions. I checked that my oxygen and intercom systems were working properly and that I had an adequate supply of rapid blooming chaff for use during the fighter affiliation exercise. I would also carry out a UHF radio check with the tower using the captain's AN/ARC-52 radio, followed by a VHF check using the PTR-175 radio at my position. At some point during the pre-start procedure the crew chief would clear me to start the AAPP and once running, I would connect its output to the Vulcan's synchronising busbar thus allowing the external electrical generator to be disconnected.

When we were all settled and ready to go the captain would call for the pre-start checks to be read out. It was my job to read the 'challenge' part of the checks while individual crew members would carry out the actions and, hopefully, respond with the correct reply. Once checks were complete the captain would get confirmation from the crew chief that the Palouste air-starter unit was connected and ready to deliver the low-pressure air needed to spin up the engine-starting turbine. The first engine would be started, usually number four, and when it achieved idling RPM, I would check the electrical output of its associated alternator and, if satisfactory, switch it on, thus providing dedicated power to the number four busbar. The starting process would be repeated for each engine in turn until all four engines were running at idle speed and their associated alternators were feeding their respective busbars. The captain, working in coordination with me, would then start the Vulcan's PFCUs.

Once started, he would check for full and free movement of his flying controls while the crew chief outside the aircraft, would visually confirm the correct movement of the aircraft's flying control surfaces. The operation of the airbrakes and bomb doors would also be checked. With the after-start checks complete, radios set to the required frequency and airfield information and taxi clearance obtained, the captain would thank the crew chief, ask him to confirm that all the ground equipment was clear of the aircraft, and then order him to have the chocks removed in preparation for taxiing. The crew chief, or a ground tradesman delegated by him, would then marshal the Vulcan out of the pan.

The captain, keeping a careful eye on the individual doing the marshalling, would steer the aircraft on the ground by using a combination of rudder movement and the nose-wheel steering button on his control column to hydraulically turn the nose wheel. Once safely out of dispersal, the captain would taxi the aircraft slowly towards the holding point of the active runway and, once there, ask for the pre-take-off checks to be read out. When the checks were complete and we were cleared for departure by ATC, the captain would line the Vulcan up on the runway centre line and apply take-off power. The Vulcan's four Olympus engines would quickly spool up, and when the brakes were released, we would surge forward, rapidly accelerating down the runway. At the pre-calculated take-off speed – usually between 140 and 150kts – the captain would ease back on the control column causing the Vulcan to get airborne. Interestingly, despite the howling racket heard outside of a Vulcan when take-off power was applied, the noise level in the cabin remained fairly low. Acceleration, not noise, was the most noticeable sensation for the rear crew during the take-off run, a feeling that was probably accentuated by having rearward-facing seats.

Vulcan pilots, like the pilots of all other RAF aircraft, had to demonstrate that they could handle their aircraft safely, day and night and in fair weather and foul. Regular in-flight training included day and night take-offs and landings. While some landings would be carried out using normal visual-circuit techniques, others would involve following azimuth and elevation flight instructions transmitted by the airfield's precision approach radar control officer. Pilots also had to be able to show that they could handle the aircraft and its systems correctly in the event of emergencies such as, for example, single and multiple engine failures, loss of certain fuel management facilities, and an undercarriage that failed to retract or extend, to name but a few. Pilots would practise many of these emergencies in the Vulcan simulator at RAF Waddington. However, some were also practised during flight. One training event that was practised ad nauseam was the simulated double-engine failure at take-off (SIMDEFATO).

Just after take-off the captain would announce on the intercom that the aircraft had suffered a practice double-engine failure either on the port or the starboard side.

The 'failed' engines would be throttled back and the aircraft gently turned onto the downwind leg to position for a practice overweight approach, followed by an overshoot. During this time, I would read out a seemingly endless series of checks from the FRCs and make sure that I received the correct response from the crew. Normal radio exchanges were carried out with Scampton tower and once on the final approach, the captain or co-pilot would fly the Vulcan down to the required height before applying power to the two 'good' engines and initiating an asymmetric overshoot. Flying a SIMDEFATO was very much a procedural activity that, I am told, did not require any extra-special flying skills by the pilots. However, it was an important training item for an emergency that could quite easily occur for real.

The Vulcan's four engines were mounted in pairs, one pair in the port wing root and the other pair in the starboard wing root. Each pair shared a common air intake, thus, the failure of one engine could disturb the normal flow of air through the intake and cause the adjacent engine to fail also. Likewise, if one engine suffered a catastrophic failure due to a bird strike or mechanical fault, it is possible that high velocity engine parts could enter the adjacent engine causing that to fail too. The loss of two engines during take-off, when the aircraft was full of fuel and possibly carrying a heavy load in the bomb bay, was not a desirable position for the captain to find himself in, so there was, definitely, a very good case for regularly practising SIMDEFATOs.

Having completed the after-take-off checks, we climbed rapidly to the north for our appointment with a Lightning fighter from Binbrook. It doesn't take long for a Vulcan to climb to around 40,000 feet and in no time at all we were settled at that altitude and talking with the fighter control officer at RAF Boulmer on UHF. They would monitor our work with the Lightning. Soon after entering the military restricted area to the east of Newcastle, we turned onto a southerly heading during which Bulmer informed us that our 'playmate' was just getting airborne from RAF Binbrook. Although the Vulcan could demonstrate an impressive rate of climb, it was nothing compared to the climbing performance of a Lightning which, according to its pilots, was like being strapped on top of a rocket. Within a minute or so from being told that the Lightning was airborne we were informed that its pilot had already checked in with Boulmer Radar on another frequency and was being vectored towards us. Let battle begin!

After a short pause I heard the familiar 'beep, beep, beeping' in my earphones and saw the corresponding solid flashing strobe on my RWR indicating that we were being illuminated by an I-Band, sector-scanning radar from somewhere out in our one o'clock. This, without doubt, was the Lightning's AI-23 fire-control radar. We maintained our southerly heading while noticing that the beeps in my earphones were becoming irregular and that the strobe on the RWR was slowly moving towards the three o'clock position. It looked as if he was going to approach from our starboard beam and slide in behind us for a simulated IR missile attack. I kept the pilots informed of what was happening and before long the co-pilot picked up the Lightning visually. It was important for the captain to manoeuvre the Vulcan such that the Lightning pilot could not get his aircraft into our rear hemisphere where he could simulate an attack with either a Firestreak or Red Top missile.

The Firestreak was an IR-homing missile that had to be positioned behind the Vulcan before it could reliably lock on to the aircraft's heat exhaust signature. The more modern Red Top had an improved seeker head that offered a limited 'head-on' capability against supersonic targets, where the leading edge of the target's airframe being heated by high-

No. 5 Squadron English Electric Lightning F6. (Aviation Photo Company)

speed air friction would allow the missile's IR seeker to lock on. However, against a sub-sonic target, such as the Vulcan, it was probably still compelled to be used for a rear hemisphere attack albeit it would have had a better acquisition and lock-on range than the Firestreak and would be able to acquire us from a wider range of angles.

The captain, Sqn Ldr Keith Walters, made good use of the Vulcan's superb, high-altitude and low-speed turning capability to prevent the Lightning from getting into a missile-firing position. Our cavorting about the sky went on for a while until, having spent long enough frustrating the efforts of the Lightning pilot, I asked the captain to return to straight-and-level flight in order to allow the Lightning to enter our six o'clock position. My RWR and Red Steer radar offered excellent situation awareness

and I was able to see the Lightning as it swung in behind us. I noticed on my RWR that the Lightning's radar had stopped sector scanning and was now firmly locked on to us. At that point I asked the captain to initiate a fairly tight turn to port while I fired off a cartridge of rapid blooming chaff from the Very pistol located at my position. The steady tone of the Lightning's radar slowly faded away as his radar was seduced away from our aircraft by the bigger target produced by the chaff. I fired off another chaff cartridge to provide another false target for his radar should the pilot attempt to quickly re-acquire lock on the Vulcan. After a short period of manoeuvring the captain resumed level flight to allow the Lightning to close up once more on our six o'clock position. On this occasion I fired one IR decoy flare to allow the Lightning pilot to observe the effect, if any, it would have on his missile's seeker. A few seconds later I fired off a single bundle of chaff from one of our main chaff dispensers located in the Vulcan's wings followed immediately by the captain executing another fairly tight turn. The chaff, once again, caused the Lightning's radar to lose lock, although within a few seconds the pilot had quickly re-established us on his radar. As our exercise was coming to an end, I raised the rear-viewing periscope from within my desk and took the opportunity to take a good long look at this beautiful British-built fighter as it nudged up close behind us. A Vulcan and a Lightning together; two iconic old-timers still training for an event that everyone hoped would never happen. At that point, with the Lightning probably running low on fuel, it banked sharply away from our six o'clock position and headed south, descending back towards Binbrook.

Firestreak IR-homing missile.

As we headed north towards our descent point for the low-level segment of the sortie, I felt certain that, lacking a modern jammer, the use of rapid blooming chaff and flares coupled with a sharpish manoeuvre was probably the best response we could make to ward off a fighter attack. Rapid blooming chaff needles were cut to represent a number of different wavelengths in order to produce a solid radar return over a broad band of frequencies such as those used by SAM, AAA and fighter AI radar systems. The term 'rapid blooming' reflected the very rapid dispersion of the chaff when it was fired from the Very pistol. I often wondered why the Lightning's radar (and that of some other NATO fighters) was so easily seduced by chaff. When I worked as a radar fitter on Gloster Javelin night fighters, its old-fashioned AI-17 radar had a velocity gate rejection circuit built in to its electronics. This circuit detected the sudden change in closing velocity between the fighter and its target, typical of that caused by chaff, and sensing that it was a false target, caused the radar to maintain its lock on the real target. At least that was what was supposed to happen. I never thought to ask a Javelin navigator/radar operator if it actually worked. Although conducting daytime-fighter affiliation training at high level did not represent the reality of our war role which would require us to operate at low level when close to and over Soviet territory, it did, nevertheless, reinforce my belief that the Vulcan stood some small chance of surviving an attack by fighters equipped with a conventional pulsed-radar capability; more so if the intercept took place at night and at low altitude. If my memory serves me correctly, low-level fighter affiliation at night was not a mandated training requirement. I wonder why?

During our descent I made radio contact with RAF Leuchars and requested a radar-monitoring service. Leuchars, as always, was obliging. I copied their weather, the area altimeter setting, and I set the requested squawk on our IFF/secondary surveillance radar (SSR) transponder. On this day we were going to enter the UK low-level system at a point near North Berwick, about ten miles east of Edinburgh. The weather was good and having completed our pre-low-level checks I closed down with Leuchars Approach. During low-level training sorties in the UK, we typically flew at around 500 feet above ground level – sometimes higher and sometimes a bit lower – and maintained an airspeed of around 240 to 300 knots. The route this day took us in a southerly direction over the beautiful, and visually satisfying, (for the pilots) Scottish countryside. The nav radar was busy doing his thing with his radar and NBS systems while the nav plotter was monitoring our progress along the planned route with the pilots providing visual updates on key navigation points.

As we intended to fly through the Spadeadam EW range in Cumbria I tried to make contact with the Spadeadam controller on the appropriate frequency, but didn't get a reply. When booking our EW run, I had asked Spadeadam to activate threat signals in the E and J frequency bands to simulate the older version of the SA-2 SAM Fan Song,

Mobile EW threat detachment from RAF Spadeadam.

and the Gun Dish AAA radar systems. Spadeadam was (and still is) an excellent facility that could simulate threats from a wide variety of Soviet threat systems. In addition to its main base operations, the unit was able to send out small, Land Rover-based, detachments of personnel with mobile threat emitter systems to remote areas of the country to provide realistic threat avoidance training for aircraft flying on exercises.

I tried once more to contact the EW Range on radio and this time they replied giving me a squawk to set on our IFF/SSR equipment. A minute or so later, having entered the range an E-Band threat, obvious by its dashed strobe on my RWR display, indicated that the SA-2 threat was active so I switched on the Red Shrimp jammer. The nav radar was clearly happy with the progress of the bombing run and he had already identified on radar his planned target offset feature. The NBS was now guiding our Vulcan to the weapon release point for our chosen target. We approached the initial point (IP) for our target and the captain reduced our height and advanced the Vulcan's throttles to give us the required attack speed of 300 knots. The co-pilot made preparations to drop the bomb visually, if so required, using the SFOM attack sight mounted on the cockpit coaming just in front of his windscreen. The SFOM (Société Française d'Optique Mécanique) attack sight was a French-manufactured, low-cost, weapon-aiming device that some pilots regarded as being marginally better than trying to 'eye-ball' the target using the refuelling probe or the lower part of the cockpit for reference. As we raced towards our target the J-Band Gun Dish AAA threat transmission became active and both threat radars were screaming in my ears. In reality, I would have been using chaff to try to defeat the tracking radars, but dropping chaff at Spadeadam had been disallowed due to farmers complaining that their sheep were eating the stuff. This was a valid restriction in my opinion, as no one, especially Vulcan aircrews, wanted to find bits of chaff in their lamb kebab. We passed the IP and were now firmly established on the final run to the target. Any threat-avoidance manoeuvre would be detrimental to getting the bomb on target, so there was little else I could do. This was the time when, for real, the crew would have to remain steadfastly on course and carry on regardless of hostile fire. Our chosen target was some small building within the Spadeadam Range area and with bomb doors open we bore down towards the weapon release point. "Do you have the target visual?" the captain asked the co-pilot. "Can't see a bloody thing," replied the co-pilot, then, a few seconds later the nav radar announced, "weapon gone". Bomb doors were closed and we started a gentle climb to a more comfortable height. I was about to transmit a quick thank you to Spadeadam, but before I could utter a word the captain called: "Practice, practice, bird strike, climbing out."

I immediately started the AAPP, checked its output and connected it to the synchronising busbar. I quickly closed down with Spadeadam and then made a practice PAN call to Newcastle Radar advising them that we were climbing out of the Spadeadam Range with a simulated bird strike. Newcastle acknowledged my call and gave me a squawk to set on our IFF/SSR transponder. By that time the captain was demanding that I read out the required action items from the FRCs. Once the checks were complete, he stated that we would carry out a practice diversion to RAF Leeming in North Yorkshire. I was about to advise Newcastle Radar of our intention to divert to Leeming, when the civilian controller at Newcastle beat me to it. "I am experiencing some interference on my radar from your direction, could you please check that your EW equipment has been switched off!" "Bloody hell!" I said to myself. I looked down and saw that my Red Shrimp jammers were still transmitting. I must have omitted to turn them off when the captain announced his practice bird strike. I quickly turned them off and issued a curt apology to Newcastle Radar. I swear I could almost hear the word 'prat' from those inside the Vulcan as well as from the controllers in the Newcastle radar room. This reminds me to mention that another great advantage of the Mk. 3 flying helmet and oxygen mask combination was that no one could see you blushing when you made a cock-up. However, I did select the cool setting on my AVS to lower my temperature and quash my embarrassment. Doing my best to sound calm and collected, I advised Newcastle Radar of our intention to divert to Leeming. A minute or so later Newcastle advised me that Leeming were aware of our intention and that I should contact Leeming Approach for further service. This I did. I couldn't get off the Newcastle frequency fast enough!

In 1960, RAF Leeming was home to No. 228 OCU. Its task was to train new and converting pilots and navigators to operate the Gloster Javelin night fighter. In addition to being the station where I served my first tour as an air radar mechanic, it was also the allocated dispersal base for 617 Squadron Vulcans during periods of increased threat levels. Several times a year an exercise would be called that required us to fly our Vulcans to Leeming to prevent them being 'destroyed' on the ground at Scampton by an ICBM attack. It was usual for the squadron to deploy four Vulcans and they were normally parked on a hard standing on the west side of the airfield near to the village of Londonderry. Once there, we would be placed on QRA training meaning we had to be ready to scramble in very short order. We worked, slept and played cards in the nearby hutted accommodation whilst remaining dressed in our flying garb and nuclear, biological and chemical (NBC) protection suits for periods of time that sometimes lasted several days. Occasionally, we would be brought up to cockpit readiness, rush to our aircraft, then wait for further instructions. Usually, after 15 minutes or so, we would be stood back down to accommodation readiness. This 'rush-to-wait' activity would be rehearsed several times. It was an extremely tedious pastime and everyone was happy when the order to scramble was finally given and we could all rush out to our Vulcans and get airborne. One day, whilst waiting to be scrambled, the squadron senior engineering officer walked over to me and told me that when we were eventually ordered to scramble, he would wander out onto the grass area between the dispersal and the runway to watch 'his' four Vulcans roaring past and climbing away. I once asked him why he didn't come along for a ride with us one day. He just gave me a rather bemused look and said: "You must be bloody joking!"

Getting back to our training flight, we overshot from our approach to Leeming and climbed out, heading south towards Scampton. I called Waddington Approach on UHF, passed our intentions and obtained the Scampton weather. Waddington Radar provided the airfield approach service for both Scampton and Waddington. When nearing Scampton I closed down with Waddington and changed frequency to Scampton Tower. I advised the ATC officer that we intended to enter the circuit for a touch-and-go followed by a full stop landing. Having completed the touch-and-go, we landed at Scampton and the captain streamed the Vulcan's brake parachute, the retardation effect of which was very noticeable indeed. Once we had slowed to a walking pace the captain jettisoned the parachute, cleared the runway and taxied our Vulcan back to the 617 Squadron dispersal.

Safely in dispersal, we shut down the aircraft, handed it back to its 'rightful owner', then made our way over to the line office where we briefed senior ground tradesmen on any snags that had occurred during flight. With the technical debrief complete, we boarded the transport that took us back to the operations building where we talked about the sortie to tease out any learning points. We then made our way to the relevant section and handed back our safety equipment to the on-duty staff members for checking and stowing back into the respective lockers.

After the crew had dispersed to carry out other duties, I took the opportunity to phone Newcastle Radar and apologise for unintentionally causing interference on their airfield radar. The controller was quite light hearted about it and told me that the effect was minimal and that, anyway, it was not an uncommon occurrence. That took the sting out of things a bit, but I was still cursing myself for failing to switch off the Red Shrimp before climbing out from Spadeadam. To err is human, but it is still damn annoying!

# Memorable Training Flights

Training flights within the UK allowed us to utilise any part of the official low-level route around the UK. However, at night, the EW ranges were normally closed and, as everyone knows, fighter pilots tend to 'knock off' at tea time, so this left me with little to do during these night flights other than carry out routine system checks every 15 minutes. On one occasion when flying at night and at low level over Devon towards Wales I decided to transmit an 'operations normal' message for relay to Scampton via the military HF facility, call sign 'Architect'. But instead of using the normal SSB voice channel, I decided to take the opportunity to get some practice at using Morse code. I dialled in the required frequency and selected CW on the Collins HF set and opened up with Architect. My tapping on the Morse key immediately caught the attention of the nav plotter (Dave Bruce) and the nav radar (Bill Dart). Like cats spotting a mouse, they immediately stopped what they were doing and gazed, eyes wide open, in my direction. "What the hell are you doing? asked Dave. "I am sending an operations normal message via Architect to Scampton Operations using HF Morse," I said. Architect, not being used to receiving Morse messages from Vulcans, was a bit hesitant in replying, so I initiated the call again, banging away on the Morse key. This unusual activity clearly fascinated and for some reason delighted the nav team. Architect was now replying to my call in slow, but perfect, Morse asking me to pass my message. As I started bashing out the message on the Morse key, Dave and Bill, always game for a jolly jape, mischievously started banging the lids of their desks up and down to try to interrupt the flow of my Morse. It took all of my concentration to suppress my laughter and complete my message successfully with Architect. Bloody navigators!

We sometimes flew at low level from Mull all the way up and over the numerous islands and lochs on the west side of Scotland towards Stornoway. This offered beautiful scenery for the pilots to enjoy. The low-level run up Scotland's west coast would culminate in an avoidance manoeuvre to dodge the threat signals being transmitted by the RAF Signals Unit at Stornoway Airfield. The standard threat avoidance manoeuvre was called 'Veronica', possibly due to the curvaceous flight path that the manoeuvre entailed. Essentially, when a threat was detected ahead of the aircraft on the RWR, the captain would initiate a turn to port or starboard, whichever one offered the best terrain screening, fly for a set time then turn back onto the previous heading to fly parallel to our original track, but well outside the range of the threat. Once clear, we would recover to our original track. It was a basic manoeuvre designed to keep us out of a threat system's engagement zone and it seemed to work.

One day, having completed our threat avoidance run at Stornoway I picked up an E-Band radar signal to the south-west of Lewis on my RWR. Being enthusiastic about all things to do with radar I asked the captain if we had time to have a look at what it might be. "Affirmative," he said. Having conferred with the nav plotter, I passed him a heading that placed the radar directly ahead of the aircraft. Someone on the crew asked what I thought it might be. I replied that it was probably a ship navigation radar, and as it was transmitting on E-Band, I guessed the ship would be medium-to-large in size; possibly a tanker, large cargo ship, a cruise liner or, if we were lucky, a warship. I continued to pass "left a bit, right a bit" corrections to the captain and after a short while he said that he was visual with the vessel dead-ahead and, a short while later as we passed overhead, the captain announced that he thought it was a tanker. I thoroughly enjoyed my four minutes pretending I was back in the Nimrod MR1 prosecuting an ESM target, albeit in a Vulcan using a basic RWR.

On 15 December 1977 we were returning to Scampton after a night sortie when we were advised that the weather at Scampton and Waddington had deteriorated to such an extent that we would have to divert to the RAF master diversion airfield at RAF Valley in Anglesey, Wales. We didn't have a crew chief on board and the ground crew at Valley would not be available for several hours to carry out aircraft fuel and oil replenishment, so we decided to carry out the servicing ourselves. We were certainly keen to do so because the weather at Scampton was expected to improve within a few hours and we wanted to get home. The single sodium light on the pan at RAF Valley cast a dim and somewhat eerie yellow hue across the top of our Vulcan while offering little or no light on the Vulcan's underside. Also, there was a chilly drizzle in progress that made climbing steps and ladders etc. rather slippery and hazardous, but we got stuck in.

The co-pilot and I took care of the refuelling which went remarkably well thanks to the Vulcan's superb refuelling system. Basically, it entailed connecting the earth lead and refuelling hose from the fuel bowser to the Vulcan, dialling up the percentage of fuel required on the Vulcan's external refuelling panel, telling the bowser driver to start the fuel flow, then letting the Vulcan's in-built automation take care of sharing out the fuel in the correct quantities to all of the Vulcan's fuel tanks. While I monitored events outside the aircraft, the co-pilot sat in the cockpit to watch the refuelling process and ensure that the fuel system's centre of gravity remained within safe limits.

In the meantime, despite the captain reminding us that it was not strictly necessary on this occasion for the aircraft's engine oil reservoirs to be topped up, the nav radar seemed to be determined to do so. It would appear that he wanted to practise the duty that had been allocated to him during his aircraft-turnaround servicing training at the squadron. He grabbed his torch, climbed the wobbling ladder, lowered the appropriate underwing panels and had a peer inside. Satisfied that he knew what he was doing, he came down from the ladder and extracted an oil container and a re-oiling pump and hose assembly from its stowage in the aircraft. Meanwhile the co-pilot and I had finished the refuelling task, so I offered to give the nav radar a hand. He gladly accepted my offer and set about removing the cap from what I think was a five-litre (or bigger) can of engine oil into which he inserted the pipe of the manual pump and hose assembly. He suggested that I should operate the pump and he would take the nozzle end of the hose and do the re-oiling. "Fair enough," I said. He then made his way back up the wobbling ladder towards the dark underside of the Vulcan's wing and started to grope around to find the oil refilling point. Having only two hands – one to carry the torch and one to hold on to the wobbling ladder – he had obviously decided that it would be a good idea to tuck the nozzle of the oil hose in his pocket, gun-in-holster fashion, prior to climbing the ladder.

After a short spell of muttering to himself, he shouted for me to start pumping, which I did. A short while later he shouted down to ask me if I was pumping. I told him I was. It could only have been ten or 20 seconds later that, under the dim yellow glow of the sodium lamps, I noticed a liquid substance running down the ladder. I immediately stopped pumping and asked him if he had inserted the nozzle properly into the filling aperture. There was a long pause followed by a slow "Oh my god!" It would seem that having taken great delight in locating the oil filling point, he had completely forgotten to insert the nozzle of the filling hose into the engine's oil tank. In fact, the nozzle was still in his pocket. The oil had filled his pocket, ran down the leg of his flying suit, over his boots, down the steps of the ladder, rung by rung, and was now settling in an ever-expanding puddle on the ground. What a mess he was in, but none of us could stop laughing. Needless to say, we got a grip on the situation, managed to re-oil all the engines, sign off the paperwork and clean up the mess as best we could with several large rolls of blue paper. Then, having been advised that Scampton was now open for business, we started our engines, and while trying not to look too impatient, got airborne and headed back home.

The poor nav radar had to remove his flying suit and fly back to Scampton in his green long johns and vest while reeking to high heaven of engine oil. It is at moments such as these that you appreciate how important it is to have a crew chief on board whenever possible to make sure that things on the ground are done properly. It also explains why crew chiefs are reluctant to lend their aircraft to aircrew.

As mentioned earlier in the chapter, it would seem that 617 Squadron had some undeclared commitment to fly MRR sorties. Training for this never featured as part of our formal OCU, ground or airborne BTRs. Nevertheless, on one occasion our crew was tasked to carry out a radar reconnaissance and strike-support mission against an American aircraft carrier task force that was exercising in the Bay of Biscay. The job required us to fly out towards the last known position of the carrier strike group, find it on radar, and then, while remaining at a safe distance from its surface-to-air weaponry, transmit information about its location back to the MHQ at Plymouth. Plymouth would then task an attack/reconnaissance fast jet to 'probe' the group in order to identify the disposition of its major elements and then report the information to the Vulcan on UHF. I would then relay this information on HF back to MHQ at Plymouth. It would also form the basis of my HF broadcast to a flight of four Buccaneer bombers that would soon afterwards carry out a simulated attack on the carrier strike group.

We got airborne, climbed to altitude and made our way down towards Land's End at the south-westerly tip of England before heading out across the South West Approaches towards the Bay of Biscay. As the Vulcan had no useful long-range navigation aids, our nav plotter was keen to keep his TACAN system locked on to the beacon at Land's End for as long as possible before we flew out of range. A short while later the nav radar picked up on his radar a set of echoes that had all the hallmarks of the carrier strike group. He compiled the appropriate disposition matrix and passed the information to me and I immediately sent it to MHQ at Plymouth. A short while later I received a message from MHQ informing me that a Dassault Étendard reconnaissance/strike fighter of the French navy was being launched from Landivisiau in France to carry out a probe operation against the carrier group, and that upon receipt of the pilot's disposition report, we were to start broadcasting the carrier strike group's position on HF and UHF. A short time later the Étendard pilot checked in with us on UHF. Later, having completed his probe/reconnaissance of the group, the Étendard pilot transmitted an updated position for the task force and then described the disposition of the major vessels within the group. We knew that the Étendard had an INS and that the position he sent to us would probably be very accurate.

With this new information, I started to broadcast the target's disposition report on HF and UHF. Between broadcasts MHQ came up on HF to advise me that an attack formation of four Buccaneers had just taken off from St Mawgan and would be entering the area soon. The nav radar continued to update the position of the task force using his radar while I continued the broadcasts. Whilst doing this, I noticed that one of the CW illumination warning lights on my RWR had come on for about 30 seconds or so. My guess was that we had probably been intercepted by a United States Navy (USN) fighter, probably an F-14 Tomcat, and that the crew had just carried out a simulated AAM attack on us. I noted the time and position for the debrief, then carried

Fitting the brake parachute in a Vulcan. (IWM)

on broadcasting. About 15 minutes or so later one of the Buccaneers transmitted what sounded like "Bananas. Bananas" on UHF. This meant nothing to me, but it must have meant something to the Buccaneer crews. Some short time later, one of the Buccaneer crews transmitted a post-strike report to me on UHF which I duly relayed to MHQ. Job done, we turned north back to Scampton. My captain later told me that he had spoken with the CO of the Buccaneer squadron that had taken part in the attack and it would seem that he was pleased with the service we had provided. While such a sortie would have probably been better carried out by a No. 27 MRR Squadron crew, it was nevertheless refreshing and interesting to be tasked to do something completely different from practising the delivery of WE.177 nuclear bombs.

Vulcan crews were occasionally sent on detachment to places overseas to give them experience at operating from foreign airfields and flying over different types of terrain. The most regular detachments took Vulcans to CFB Goose Bay in Canada and Offutt AFB in Nebraska, USA, more on which follows later. However, crews were also sent on detachment to European countries such as Cyprus, Malta and Italy. These were mostly routine training flights that, apart from one, offer little or no reason for comment.

The one exception was when we were flying to Malta on 18 September 1978. The captain, or perhaps it was the co-pilot, noticed that we were losing hydraulic pressure. I had a look outside under the wings using my periscope and sure enough, there was fluid streaming back from under the port wing. The captain decided to ask Malta for permission to land the Vulcan on the airfield's newly built and suitably long runway, instead of landing on the shorter runway normally used by the RAF. Our request was denied by a rather imperious Maltese ATC controller. We informed him that we had a problem with our hydraulics system which could compromise our braking performance and would prefer to use the long runway. He responded that if we wanted to land on his shiny new runway, we would have to declare an emergency. The captain, getting a bit fed up with this R/T exchange, declared an emergency and hey presto we were cleared to land on Malta's new runway.

The captain advised the Maltese controller that he would be streaming a brake parachute and that he would appreciate it if he could arrange for the local RAF ground personnel to collect the parachute when it was jettisoned after landing. It was normal, when landing at any airfield other than Scampton and Waddington, to refrain from streaming the brake parachute as there would be no one there qualified to safely recover it. Also, it meant that the spare brake parachute carried on board the Vulcan during detachments would have to be fitted. This could be quite an onerous and sometimes dangerous task for the crew chief, even with – or because of – help from the aircrew. I once had a go at helping some squadron NCOs to fit a brake parachute on the brake parachute training rig in the OCU building, so I knew just how difficult and potentially dangerous it could be for those not familiar with the task.

As we descended towards Malta the captain briefed the crew on what he wanted us to do in the event that the Vulcan's brakes failed completely causing us to run off the end of the runway. Having done all the necessary checks we carried out a visual approach to land on Malta's new runway. After touchdown, the captain streamed the brake parachute and applied the brakes which, despite the loss of hydraulic oil, still seemed to work. Maltese fire engines and an ambulance followed us down the runway as the captain slowed the Vulcan to a walking pace and jettisoned the brake parachute near the runway exit point. He then very slowly taxied clear of the runway, shut down the Vulcan's engines and handed the aircraft over to our crew chief who subsequently arranged for it to be towed to the RAF dispersal. Although the incident was rather low key compared to some of the other things that could go wrong on detachment, it must have raised a bit of excitement amongst the many holidaymakers watching from Malta's civilian air terminal, because that evening when we were down in Valetta enjoying a beer or three, we heard a group of young ladies talking rather excitedly about how they saw a big green aeroplane coming down on a parachute at Malta's airport.

# CHAPTER SEVEN
# CANADA, AMERICA AND A TRIP DOWN UNDER

## Canada

Vulcan crews were regularly sent to Goose Bay in Canada to fly training routes over the Canadian tundra; terrain quite similar to that found in the northern regions of the Soviet Union. Goose Bay is situated near Happy Valley, a village located at the western end of Lake Melville in the provinces of Newfoundland and Labrador. The terrain at and to the south of Goose Bay is well forested with lots of small lakes, rivers and some hills and mountains. Flying north from Goose Bay, the terrain is still peppered and streaked with small lakes and rivers, but it becomes less forested, more desolate and seriously uninviting. In winter, snow and ice can conceal some of the smaller lakes and rivers making it a bit more awkward for the nav radar to cross reference what he sees on his radar with the detail shown on his maps, thus making the identification of geographical features that could be used for navigation and as offset features a little more difficult. The freezing over of lakes and rivers also makes it more difficult for the

617 Squadron Vulcan at Goose Bay.

pilots to offer reliable, visual navigation assistance to the nav plotter. In other words, it was a good training experience for the pilots and navigation team. Unfortunately, it provided very little training value for the AEO.

When on detachment at Goose Bay during the winter months, crews were occasionally scheduled to take part in winter survival training which, in addition to being educational, was also fun, as it usually ended up with a good old-fashioned snowball fight. The RAF detachment at Goose Bay also ran a nice little officers' mess where crews could relax in the evenings. Unfortunately, I managed to make myself *persona non grata* on one detachment when, after the day's flying was over, I decided to do some personal laundry. I tossed my olive-green long johns, woollen socks and vest into one of the mess's washing machines and set it going. A few hours later while relaxing with other crew members in the mess bar and sipping on a bottle of Moose Head beer, the entrance door banged open and in stormed a red-faced WRAF officer holding aloft a once white, olive-green bra and a small pair of olive-green knickers. She demanded to know which of us had washed their smelly green flying clothing in the mess washing machine without checking to see if it was empty. It took less than a second for me to realise that I was the culprit. I blushingly and profusely apologised offering to pay for the damage done to her underwear. She rejected my offer, called me a few interesting, but unprintable, names and stormed back out of the mess bar. Needless to say, I was the butt of many jokes for the next few days and I was glad when it was time to fly back home to Scampton.

There were a number of training routes that could be flown from Goose Bay. Some required us to remain at low level from take-off to landing (lo-lo-lo), and others involved a lengthy period of high-level navigation. Two of the low-level routes could be flown in one day; one in the morning, and then after a burger lunch, another in the afternoon. Each low-level sortie lasted just over two hours, whereas the high-level sorties tended to last about four. These sorties provided excellent training for the pilots and navigators, but, as previously mentioned, they offered very little in the way of training for the AEO. In fact, short of doing my quarter-hour systems checks and scouting around on HF to obtain weather updates for Goose Bay and our diversion airfield, I had very little to do. It is a pity the RAF hadn't established a small fighter or EW detachment at Goose Bay where they could have offered some fairly realistic low-level fighter affiliation and threat-avoidance training for Vulcan crews. Some Vulcan crews had, in the past, managed to arrange some high-level fighter affiliation training with the Canadian air force F-101 Voodoo squadron that was based at Bagotville near Saguenay, Quebec, some 400 miles south-west of Goose Bay, but it wasn't something that could be arranged with any regularity. Despite the lack of training value for AEOs, the regular detachments to Goose Bay did offer a welcomed change from Scampton and an opportunity to experience operating the Vulcan away from home base. It

Sqn Ldr Walters briefing his crew at Goose Bay.

also gave me a chance to view the rugged, but beautiful Canadian landscape at close quarters (sometimes too close) through my periscope.

Flying from Scampton to Goose Bay involved crossing the Atlantic Ocean at the normal Vulcan cruising altitude of around 43,000 and 45,000 feet. Our transit flight would typically route from Scampton to the Prestwick TACAN beacon in Scotland, then we would head out over the ocean passing 200 miles or more to the south of Iceland, then onwards past the southerly tip of Greenland, towards the Labrador coast and Goose Bay. The westbound transit normally took between four and five hours, but the homeward-bound transit took rather less time due to prevailing west-to-east jet streams over the North Atlantic. Voice communication with the Shanwick, Iceland and Gander Oceanic Control

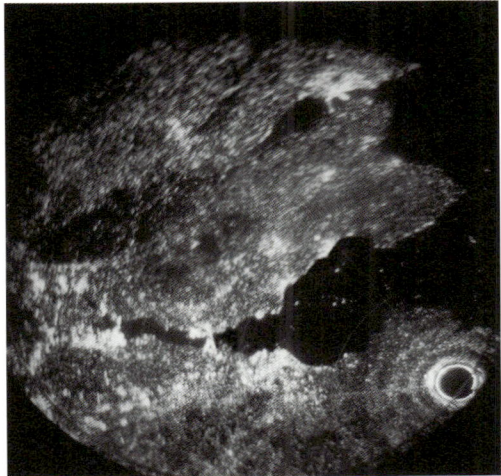

View of Edinburgh and Fife using H2S Mk. 9A from 43,000 feet.

agencies was carried out on VHF when possible, and HF/SSB when out of VHF range. As previously mentioned, Vulcans assigned to the strike role did not have any long-range navigation aids, other than the sextant periscope. So the nav plotter would dutifully take some sun shots and cross reference the results with his chart and GPI position. The nav radar, using his H2S Mk. 9A radar, would also help by providing radar fixes on prominent coastal features such as, for example, the southerly tip of Greenland. However, any degradation of the aircraft's navigation capability such as loss of the GPI Mk. 6, H2S radar or the Decca Doppler navigation radar, could result in some interesting moments for the nav plotter. Although, to my knowledge, none of our Vulcans ever got lost, I think there were a few occasions when Vulcans approached landfall in Canada on a rather different heading to that which was planned. Obviously, the transit home involved similar concerns and nav plotters were always pleased when their TACAN equipment locked on to the beacon at Tiree in Scotland and displayed a range and bearing that confirmed the accuracy of their navigation.

# America

In addition to flying training sorties from Goose Bay, crews were also scheduled to fly them from the United States Air Force (USAF) base at Offutt, Nebraska, where the central American terrain offered a landscape not too dissimilar to that found in eastern Europe and western Russia. When flying to Offutt from Scampton we would stage through Goose Bay. There, we would take the opportunity to fly one or two low-level sorties before continuing our transit to Offutt. During the four-hour, high-level transit flight to Offutt, our crew would execute a practice high-level bomb attack on a target located close to Fort Drum, a military establishment about ten miles east of Lake Ontario. Fort Drum hosted a radar bomb scoring unit (RBSU) so our attacks could be scored. On our arrival at Offutt, we would be met by members of the RAF's permanent detachment who would marshal us into our parking spot. Detachment personnel were also available to assist our crew chief with any rectifications that may be required. For accommodation, crews were checked into, what was then, the Ramada Inn, a hotel located in the nearby village of Bellevue. It was an excellent home from home that served good food, had a lively bar and offered regular entertainment.

Training flights out of Offutt followed the hi-lo-hi profile and were given an OB number such as, for example, OB-53. I can't remember what the official meaning of OB was. Perhaps it was olive branch, but it didn't really matter because crews simply referred to them as oil burners. On 28 February 1977, we were transiting at high level back to Offutt having completed a hi-lo-hi sortie on training route OB-53. The countryside below us was covered in deep snow, and we were aware that the weather at Offutt was due to take a turn for the worse later that day. So it didn't come as too much of a surprise when the ATCC relayed to us a message from the RAF operations officer at Offutt telling us that the weather at Offutt had suddenly deteriorated and that we were to execute a diversion to Grand Forks.

My first thought was "where the hell is Grand Forks?" While the nav plotter rummaged through his bag to find the required charts I asked the ATCC to give us an initial steer towards Grand Forks to help get us on our way. This they did and we were soon heading north towards the state of North Dakota. The cruise and descent were uneventful and when we got close to the airfield the radar controller positioned us on what seemed to be a rather long and extended approach to the runway, perhaps typical of that practised by B-52s. My captain, Sqn Ldr Keith Walters, having caught sight of a runway ahead, advised the radar controller that he wished to terminate the radar service and continue for a visual approach to land. "Roger, contact the tower on 234.56," said the radar controller. Established on finals, Keith mentioned that there seemed to be quite a few other airfields in the area. After landing and having slowed to a walking pace, I keyed the radio: "Grand Forks Tower this is RAFAIR 123 request taxi instructions." Back came the reply: "RAFAIR 123 this is Red River Tower. Welcome!" A stunned silence filled the Vulcan before someone blurted out on intercom "Red River? We were supposed to land at Grand Forks, what the hell have we done?" It was a few long seconds before I noticed in my en route book for US and Canada that Red River was the correct call sign for the Grand Forks ATC Tower. Relieved, we continued to taxi off the runway.

There had been a few incidents where Vulcan captains flying OB routes had failed to inform RAF operations at Offutt when, for whatever reason, they had felt compelled to land at some other airfield instead of returning to Offutt. This resulted in 'overdue' action being taken by the RAF operations officer to try to establish where the aircraft was. Therefore, I decided to ask the ATC controller in the Red River Tower if she could inform RAF operations at Offutt that we had landed safely at Grand Forks. She came back with a strong American twang: "Could you repeat that message honey? I didn't catch what you said." I adjusted my mask and, taking care to speak slowly, I repeated the request. "It's no use honey, I can't understand what you are trying to say." At this point my skipper having deciding that it was probably my indecipherable Scottish accent that was causing the confusion, called her himself in his best, authoritative, English tone. "Red River Tower this is RAFAIR 123 please contact the duty RAF operations officer at Offutt to let him know that we have landed safely at Grand Forks." Longish pause. "No…it's no use sir, I cannot understand what you are trying to say!" He tried again, but to no avail. Giving vent to his frustration, Keith impatiently keyed the radio and said, "Forget it Red River, I'll send you a letter!" At which point, the pilot of a B-52 that had been pounding the Grand Forks circuit came booming over the airwaves in a deep Southern accent, "You know, Limey, up here at Grand Forks sending a letter seems to be the only way it works!"

Having parked the Vulcan, we climbed down the stairs and into the fresh, but bitterly cold, air of North Dakota. Almost immediately I felt the need to blow my nose and, having done so, I noticed that my handkerchief was covered in blood. The temperature was so low that the hairs in my nose had instantly frozen and had acted like little daggers, perforating the lining of my nostrils. So we were all rather glad when the transport arrived to take us to the warmth of the operations building and later, to our hotel. The next morning, having been advised that Offutt was open for business and ready for our return, we went to operations to pick up the latest meteorological information. The young USAF airman behind the desk seemed to be quite excited about the whole thing and told us that we were lucky because their new weather forecasting system was being used for the first time that day and that we would be the first recipients of its output. While the captain and co-pilot perused the weather print-out, I happened to notice that the charts were dated 29 February 1978. I asked the navigators if 1978 was a leap year, but their impatient look said "don't know, don't care, go and work it out for yourself!" I turned to the airman behind the desk and asked him what date it was. "It's the first of March, sir" he replied. I then pointed out to him that the date on the weather charts read 29 February 1978. "Goddamn! How has that happened?" I laughed and suggested that he should tell his boss that the software in his shiny new weather computer must have been infested with a 'leap year bug'.

When we arrived at the aircraft there was a small gathering of aircraft aficionados that wanted to know everything about the Vulcan. We answered their questions as best we could, but it was freezing cold and we advised them that we really had to get going. They enthusiastically told us that they were going to head off in their cars down to the far end of the 12,000-ft runway, and asked if it would be okay if they took some photographs as we flew overhead. Our captain told them they could take as many photographs as they liked, and off they went in their cars. The flight back to Offutt would only last about one hour and our planned diversion was Lincoln, a city not far from Offutt, so our fuel uptake had been quite small. That, coupled with having almost nothing in the bomb bay, a very cold outside air temperature, and a moderate head wind blowing down the runway meant that our take-off was going to look quite sporty. And so it proved to be. The captain advanced the throttles and our four Olympus 201 engines howled in obedience. A short pause, brakes off, and our Vulcan rapidly accelerated from its standing start and before I could catch my breath, Keith had rotated the aircraft into a steep climb. As I looked out behind the Vulcan through my periscope, I could see the runway steadily getting smaller and smaller beneath us as we powered skywards. I hoped that the keen bunch of aircraft observers waiting with cameras at the end of the runway had remembered to fit their telephoto lenses, otherwise, when viewing us through their SLR cameras all they would see was a very small, light-coloured triangle disappearing upwards into the North Dakota sky.

In July 1979 our crew was transiting between Offutt and Loring, Maine at our usual 40,000 feet plus. I had decided to work the ATCC using a VHF frequency instead of the more usual UHF frequency so that I could listen in to the chat from the pilots of commercial airliners operating some 10,000 ft below. At around this period a NOTAM had been promulgated pointing out that the NASA Skylab Space Station was soon to re-enter the atmosphere, but no one was sure of exactly where or when. It amazed me to think that despite the great care that had been taken to get Skylab into orbit, no one seemed to have bothered to think about how and where it was going to come down. I must confess, I had no idea what the NOTAM writers expected pilots to do if they found themselves on a collision course with a white-hot, Mach 8 +, re-entering Skylab. About halfway through the transit flight I heard a Trans World Airlines pilot calling the ATCC to ask what it was that had just crossed above his aircraft. The ATCC controller said, "Standby sir and I will check." Followed by, "Sir, the object that just passed above you is a British Vulcan bomber." "Thaaank Yooou Gawd," said the Trans World pilot, "I thought it was Skylab!" This was followed by much laughing, joking, and amusing comments from other pilots on the same frequency.

On another day my crew had just settled into the cruise at FL450 on the high-level leg of an oil-burner flight when there was a loud bang followed by popping ears and an instant misting up inside the Vulcan. We had obviously suffered some form of pressurisation failure and the aircraft's oxygen system was now, as designed, force-feeding 100 per cent oxygen into my lungs. The captain closed the throttles, announced the pressurisation failure and started a rapid descent. I immediately clamped my mask down tight and declared an emergency on the ATCC frequency. I then advised the controller about our predicament and told him that we were carrying out a rapid descent to a lower altitude. This was my first and only in-flight experiencing of trying to talk on radio against the pressure of oxygen being forced into my lungs – an interesting experience. The ATCC controller's response was brilliant. He acknowledged my call, cleared our descent and started issuing new diversionary headings to the commercial air traffic flying below to create a clear space for us to descend through. Once down at a safe altitude we set course back to Offutt and landed about one hour after we had taken off. We were ordered to undergo a medical examination by the base surgeon who, having given us the all-clear, advised us that we shouldn't fly for the next three or four days – big smiles all round! Later, our crew chief advised us that the Vulcan's door seal had failed causing the rapid loss of pressurisation. He also informed us that he had already ordered a replacement door seal to be sent over from the UK. This little incident justified the training, and advice that we had received on the AMTC course prior to starting the OCU. Being grounded for three days meant that our crew, including our crew chief, had plenty of time to stroll around the nearby Strategic Air Command (SAC) Museum, do some shopping in the base exchange store and visit the nearby city of Omaha. All very pleasant.

# Red Flag

In late 1978 our crew was lucky enough to be selected, along with three other Vulcan crews, to take part in Exercise Red Flag 1979 at Nellis AFB, near Las Vegas, Nevada. Exercise Red Flag allows intensive, multi-disciplined, air-combat training to take place within a large range area of land and airspace located to the north of Las Vegas. The exercise is run by the USAF, and aircrew from other NATO and some non-NATO countries are occasionally invited to take part. The huge Nellis Air Base houses a number of fighter squadrons that act as enemy aggressors or defenders, depending upon the training scenario being run. The range area also plays host to a number of AAA and SAM radar threat simulator systems. Futhermore, the whole area is kept under close surveillance by a suite of radar and video sensors that collect high-fidelity information for use during post-exercise debriefing sessions. The size and scope of the exercises allows for simultaneous participation by a wide range of combat aircraft types including fighter, bomber, ground-attack and SAM suppression aircraft. Other participants sometimes include AAR tankers, SIGINT collection platforms and even rescue helicopters, to name but some.

During Red Flag 79 our Vulcans mainly flew night-time TFR sorties. Routeing generally required us to enter the range from the east, make our way westwards at low level to the target, and then climb out of the range somewhere to the north-west of Las Vegas. To prepare for Red Flag our crew was sent to Goose Bay to conduct refresher night TFR training. On one such training sortie, we were cruising along at low level, probably around 500 feet, and I took the opportunity to leave my seat and venture up the steps between the pilots to have a look at the TFR in operation and to compare its demands against what I could observe visually ahead of the aircraft. With very little outside ambient light, all I could see ahead of us was the black silhouette of hills and mountains, the tops of which were certainly above the height that we were flying. At the same time, I noticed that the TFR was giving a 'fly-down' command inviting us to descend into a black abyss below. Meanwhile, the nav team was giving a very good running commentary regarding the terrain ahead of the aircraft. The nav plotter mentioned that there was a wide valley just ahead of us and about three miles beyond

*Opposite: TFR radar radome on the nose of a Vulcan.*

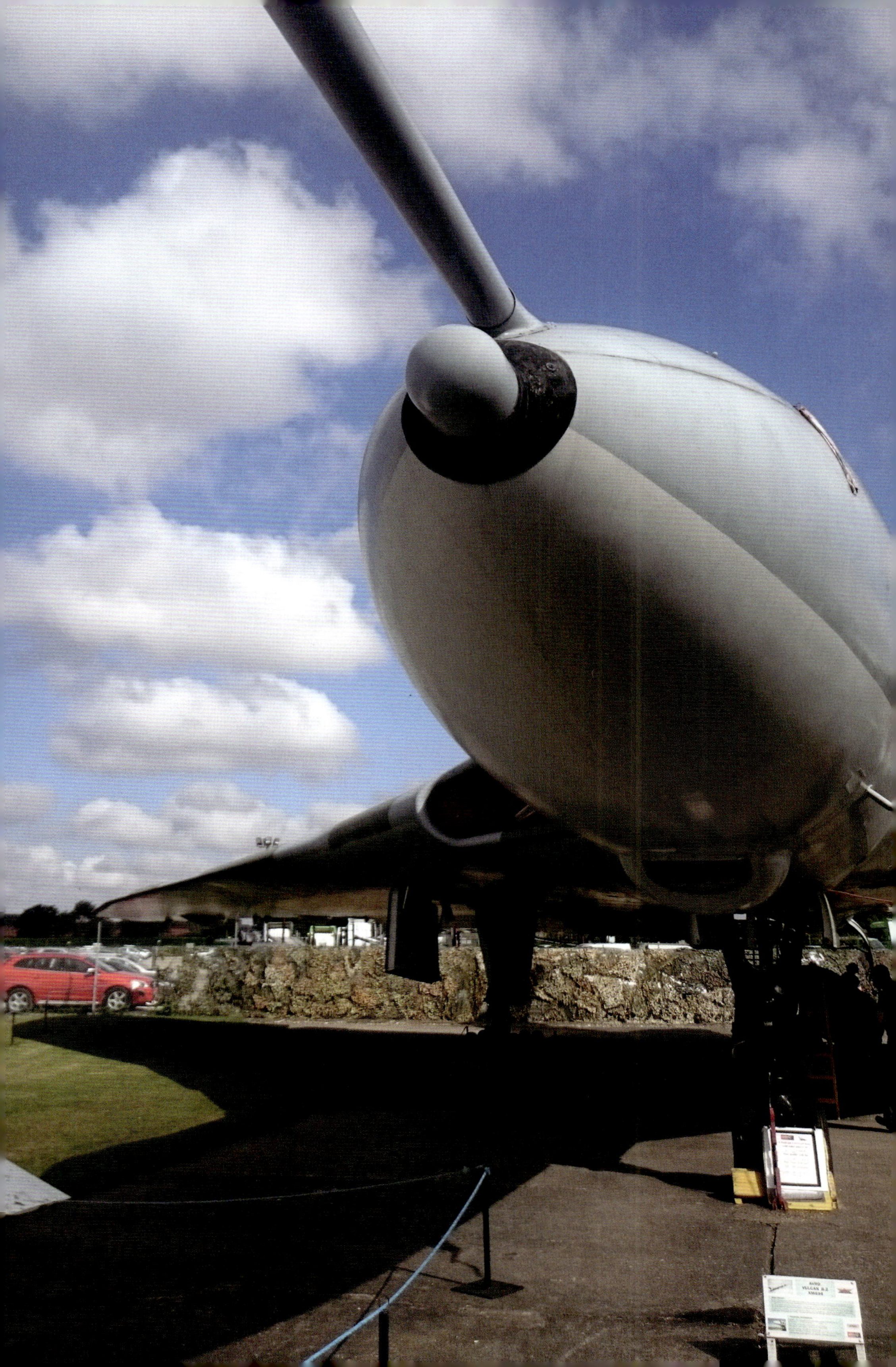
AVRO
VULCAN B.2

that was the mountains. This explained the initial TFR fly-down demands. However, it occurred to me that it must have taken some nerve for the pilots to put their faith in a system that was telling them to fly down when all their natural instincts must have been urging them to climb. I decided that it would be better if I returned to my seat rather than frighten myself witless staring at the hills and mountains out the front of the Vulcan. After a couple of training sorties at Goose Bay, we returned to the UK where we flew another couple of shake-down TFR sorties over Wales and the Lake District. Then on 23 November, we took off from Scampton to fly back to Goose Bay, where we spent a relaxing night before flying on to Nellis AFB via Offutt.

Red Flag briefings and debriefings were carried out in the purpose-built Building 201, the Red Flag HQ. During our initial briefing we were warned not to fly over 'Area 51' a highly restricted area within the Nellis range complex. Overflight of this area, we were told, would result in the offending crew being immediately sent back to the UK. Later I would learn that research aircraft being used to develop stealth technologies were based there. Warnings accepted and preparations complete, we were ready to start flying.

The Nellis Range allows plenty of room for threat avoidance and other vertical and lateral manoeuvres without having to worry about overflying towns and villages etc. However, the range area is dotted with mountains, butte hills and mesa landforms, some of which have very narrow structures and almost vertical sides. Therefore, great care had to be taken, particularly since most of our flying was going to be done at low level and at night. Crews had to take careful note of the weather on the range as any significant crosswind could lead to the Vulcan flying a track that was well to the left or right of the aircraft's heading, and possibly outside the limited azimuthal view of the TFR system. This, in extreme cases, could lead to Vulcans being inadvertently flown into high ground. So great care was always taken to watch for any significant divergence between the aircraft's heading and its track. Furthermore, crews taking evasive action at low level and at night had to be aware of exactly where their aircraft was in relation to the terrain on each side of the aircraft. It would have been so easy, while turning to evade a fighter, SAM or AAA threat, to inadvertently fly into high ground. For this reason, the navigation team closely monitored our position and, if necessary, countermanded my threat avoidance advice to the captain.

Red Flag 79 permitted some fairly liberal use of chaff, but the use of IR decoys during our visit was prohibited due to the risk of setting fire to the dry autumn grass and weeds that were scattered all over the range. Also of note was the warning given to FB-111 crews to avoid going supersonic at low level as the shock waves and sonic booms from their aircraft was scaring the hell out of the small number of civilians that worked on the land, including small-time miners that scraped a living working underground in search of gold, semi-precious stones and ancient artefacts. Our first flight was a daytime range familiarisation sortie that gave crews (the pilots) a chance to see for themselves the layout and nature of the terrain. It also exposed our aircraft to some of the radar-controlled threat systems that we could expect to come across during the night-time sorties. With the familiarisation sortie in the bag, it was time for the real thing and on the night of 30 November, we were ready for our first Red Flag night sortie.

Earlier generation fighters, such as the Lightning, Mirage III and American Century Series fighters (F-101, F-102, F-104 etc.) were fitted with pulse-modulated radar systems for target acquisition and tracking. When conducting a medium-level CAP and searching ahead and downwards with their radar for low-level intruders, the pilots found it very difficult, if not impossible, to distinguish low-flying aircraft from the mass of radar reflections from the ground. This limitation was largely overcome in the latest generation of American fighters, such as the F-15, that, at that time, was equipped with the AN/APG-63 Pulse Doppler (PD) radar. As I understood it, the AN/APG-63's highly stable transmitter circuits and its advanced electronics and Doppler frequency filters enabled the fighter to acquire and track targets flying at low level by detecting the small differences in frequency within the radar returns from the ground and those reflected from moving targets such as our Vulcan. As long as the relative radial velocity between us and the fighter was sufficiently different to that between the fighter and the ground, then the F-15 could detect and track our aircraft and carry out a 'look-down-shoot-down' attack using the AIM-7 Sparrow, semi-active homing missile. It is worth mentioning that the USN F-14A fighters had a similar, if not better, capability than the F-15A. The F-14A radar intercept officer could detect targets at ranges of around 100 miles using the aircraft's AN/AWG-9 radar, and carry out attacks on six targets simultaneously with AIM-54 Phoenix missiles. However, our principal fighter opponent during Red Flag was the F-15, and knowing the basic operating features of its PD radar, we endeavoured to make life as difficult as possible for its pilots. When flying our Vulcan at low level and being prosecuted by an F-15, our tactic was to turn our aircraft such that we provided a beam-on view to the fighter. This would result in the Doppler frequency content of our radar reflection being the same, or close to being the same, as those from the ground over which we were flying, thus making it difficult for the fighter's radar system to differentiate our Vulcan from the mass of ground returns. Things were probably a bit more complicated that, but that was our tactic of choice at the time.

We took off from Nellis on time and transited up the entry corridor on the easterly side of the range at medium altitude before descending down to our planned low-level height of around 500 feet and taking up a westerly heading towards our designated target. It wasn't long before we encountered our first threat. An F-15A pilot flying CAP above and ahead of us must have picked us up on his AN/APG-

63 thus affording him a look-down-shoot-down opportunity. The Vulcan's version of the ARI 18228 RWR, for reasons that are obscure to me, was unable to reliably detect and display the F-15's PD transmissions, but it did pick up the fighter radar's CW illuminator transmission that indicated he was in our forward port quarter and that he had taken, or was about to take a simulated AIM-7 Sparrow missile shot against us. I quickly informed the captain and suggested a 45-degree starboard turn in order to place the F-15 firmly on our port beam. With luck, our radar return would be rejected along with the ground returns. We continued to make fine adjustments to our heading to keep the fighter on our beam. Eventually, the CW illuminator light went off and we quickly resumed our race to the target. A short while later the CW light came on again and, once more, the captain taking advice from me and the navigators, manoeuvred our Vulcan onto a heading that placed us beam-on to the fighter. This time the F-15 pilot came up on the designated range frequency inviting us to "come up and fight!" An invitation that our captain had no intention of accepting. The F-15 pilot too must have had some natural regard for his physical well-being, as he chose not to descend from his medium-level CAP in order to chase us around the desert at low level in the dark.

Having, hopefully, managed to avoid being 'shot down' by the F-15 we were now getting close to our IP and our dash to the target. The captain eased forward on the throttles to accelerate the Vulcan to attack speed and we flew hell for leather (or as hell for leather as our Vulcan was allowed to go) towards the target. By now multiple threat radars were illuminating us, including an SA-2 operating at E-Band which gave me an opportunity to activate the Red Shrimp. Being on the attack heading, manoeuvre was out of the question, but I did dispense chaff as I would for real. A few seconds later, with our simulated weapon delivered, the captain closed the bomb doors and we started to climb out of the range area. While climbing to medium altitude and on course for Nellis, the pilots commented enthusiastically about the glittering display of brightly coloured lights emanating from Las Vegas – like a huge sparkling diamond surrounded by the jet-black night-time Nevada desert.

Our crew flew five other night TFR sorties during our time at Red Flag. The flying time on each sortie was short, but the activity was intense, and it almost always resulted in a sizeable array of aircraft converging on the target area over a very short space of time. I noticed that on some of the later sorties, instead of being confronted by a single F-15, the fighters were now flying in widely separated pairs, so whichever way we turned to nullify our Doppler signature for one F-15, we immediately found ourselves flying head-on towards the second F-15 – tricky! On another sortie we had the additional complication of having F-105, Republic Thunderchief 'Wild Weasel' SAM suppression aircraft operating around the target area. If, when listening in on the combat net, one heard the call "Shotgun Echo" or "Shotgun India" it meant that a simulated-Shrike ARM attack was about to be launched against a radar operating in the E or I frequency bands. Had this occurred in a real-life scenario, it would have been a good idea for crews to make sure that their radar and jammers were not transmitting on the announced frequency bands otherwise they could find themselves acting as host to a surprise visit from a Shrike ARM.

The last flight on the range was a daytime, anything goes, sortie. As we made our way to the target at low level we were overtaken by a near-supersonic FB-111 emanating shock waves as it streaked, wings back, across the desert hotly pursued by an F-15. Needless to say, our turn to be executed soon came and we were unceremoniously 'shot down' by an F-15 that had dropped down behind us. However, to our surprise, the fighter pilot then manoeuvred his F-15 alongside us and called on the combat net to tell us that he wasn't going to shoot us again, he just wanted to take a photograph of our Vulcan.

As we flew closer to the target area it was obvious from the spokes on my RWR and the racket in my headset that there was SA-2 and SA-8 SAM activity in progress along with some intermittent Flap Wheel and Gun Dish AAA activity around the target area. Furthermore, the pilots informed me that the sky above the target area was buzzing with fighters. During our run-in to the target from the IP a Northrop F-5E Tiger dived down behind us and closed in on our six o'clock position. His radar, (I think it was an AN/APG-69), was firmly locked on to our Vulcan as he steadied behind us for what I guess would be an IR missile or gun shot. In a final act of defiance, I poured out a good stream of I-Band chaff from one of our chaff dispensers and, upon doing so, the F-5E Tiger immediately broke off his attack. Our Vulcan, meanwhile, sped on towards the target, the crew serenely unaware that we had probably been 'shot down'. Having delivered our final simulated bomb at Red Flag we climbed out of the range and took up a heading for Nellis. I must say, I was glad when we left the range area as the level of air activity around the target was, according to the pilots, uncomfortably high. How all the aircraft got through these sorties and back to Nellis without bumping into each other was a miracle.

Debriefing sessions in the Red Flag building were noisy affairs, with lots of laughing, braggadocio, needle-matching, and as you would expect, some serious disagreements. But it was all for a good purpose. Many lessons were learned and a lot of practical experience gained. I managed to meet up with the Aggressor Squadron F-5E pilot who had converged on our Vulcan just before weapon release on the last sortie. He commented on the amount of crap (his words) that I had dispensed back towards his fighter during his attack. I asked him, half-joking, if it had put him off taking a shot at us. "It sure as hell did," he said, "if that stuff had gone down my intake it would have ground my engine's compressor blades down to the core and Uncle Sam would be chasing me for ten million dollars!" I also managed to talk with one of the F-15 pilots that flew on night-time medium-level CAPs, but he seemed rather reluctant to talk about his fighter's capabilities – details about the F-15A were quite hush-hush at that time. Also, I knew that the F-15A was having some niggling technical issues at around that period so I didn't press him further. On the 16th and 17th of December we flew back to the UK via Goose Bay. Red Flag over and back to reality.

# UK and US Navigation & Bombing Competitions

Vulcan crews from Scampton and Waddington frequently took part in Headquarters Strike Command bombing competitions that were held in the UK. This engendered a competitive spirit and helped to hone the navigation and bombing skills of the crews. The competition included both high-level and low-level simulated-bombing runs against targets chosen for their obscurity. This was not, as you might think, an unrealistic scenario, it was indicative of some of the targets that the Vulcans were likely to be tasked to destroy in times of war. The method used to compensate for a target's lack of visual and/or radar cues was to employ the offset bombing procedure described earlier in Chapter Four.

Bombing accuracy during competitions was determined by RBSUs. The RBSU radar would detect and lock on to the Vulcan just before it reached the published IP for its run to the target. Data derived from the RBSU radar was used to graphically plot the progress of the Vulcan on the RBSU plotting table. At or soon after reaching the IP, Vulcan crews would configure their system to transmit a continuous tone on a prescribed UHF frequency. The transmitted tone would automatically stop at weapon release causing the exact position of the aircraft at that instant to be marked on the RBSU plot. Knowing the exact position of the target, and the precise position, track, altitude and speed of the Vulcan at weapon release, plus other information such as the ballistics of the simulated bomb, and wind velocity etc., the RBSU was able to accurately calculate the likely impact point of the simulated bomb and, thus, award a score. High-level bombs were normally delivered after a prolonged transit over the North Sea, sometimes with limited navigation aids, thus challenging the nav plotter to get the aircraft to the IP at exactly the right time. Missing the IP by a significant distance or time could prevent the aircraft being picked up by the RBSU and result in a no-score. The low-level bomb was usually delivered at the culmination of a low-level sortie, perhaps flown from North Berwick in Scotland to somewhere around Boston in Lincolnshire. Umpires were carried on board flights to make sure that things were done in accordance with the rules, and after analysis of the results, scores were awarded. Some of the crews that achieved high scores would be selected to partake in the USAF Giant Voice navigation and bombing competition in America.

In August 1979, OC 617 Squadron ordered Flt Lt John Hills, the captain of one of his high-scoring crews, to prepare his crew to take part in the USAF Giant Voice competition at Barksdale AFB in Louisiana, USA. As it happened, the wife of the selected crew's AEO was expecting a baby and was due to give birth during the period of the competition. Being a staunch family man, John M asked to be taken off the detachment and I was ordered to take his place. I knew that it must have been a great disappointment for John not to be able to go with his crew and I hoped that I would prove to be a worthy replacement. I was very much aware that his crew was a tightly knit bunch and I was a bit worried about fitting in at such short notice and being accepted as a trusted part of the team. However, the crew was welcoming and my concerns were soon dispelled.

Vulcan B2 XM571 was selected to be our trusty steed for the competition. Although normally based at Scampton, it was flown over to Waddington to join three other aircraft from other Vulcan squadrons that had been selected to take part in the competition. Our Vulcan remained there for the duration of training phase and was placed under the watchful care of a selected group of ground maintenance personnel. All four Vulcans were adorned with a HQ Strike Command 'Black Panther' logo and a Union Jack flag on both sides of the tail fin. Even the crew members' bone domes were painted blue with a Union Jack flag superimposed. August saw the start of intensive training that involved flying 13 sorties in just over three weeks. Good aircraft serviceability, precise navigation and accurate bombing were essential requisites to achieving good competition scores. I am pleased to say our Vulcan performed superbly throughout the training and competition phases, thanks in no small measure to the pampering it received from the maintenance team. As one would expect, the Vulcan offered a bombing accuracy significantly better than that supplied by Lancaster and Halifax bombers in WWII. This was due to extensive post-war improvements made to the H2S radar, the development and installation of NBS, and the addition of modern airborne navigation systems including the Green Satin Doppler navigation radar (later Decca Doppler 72) and the gyro-based HRS. That said, bombing errors of around 800–1,200 yards were not uncommon. Indeed, some considered this to be par for the course and acceptable for nuclear weapon delivery. All, or most, of the flying was done in daytime, but as most of the targets were simply points on a map, they were not conducive to visual bomb aiming by the co-pilot. So, once again, it would be very much down to the navigation team to get the bomb on target. My contribution to the bombing process was to keep a stopwatch check when flying from the IP to the weapon-release point. The idea was that if the pilots flew an accurate heading and speed from the IP, we should arrive at the weapon-release point after a set time. So in the event of a total NBS failure or some other technical catastrophe during the final run from the IP, we would maintain the last known heading and speed and drop the bomb on my call. It was a small part to play but at least it allowed me to provide some back-up for the main players. Of course, my main task, in addition to doing most of the communications, was to make sure there was always 'sufficient coins in the Vulcan's electricity meter'.

Training lasted most of September, and on 15 October 1979 we departed Waddington for Barksdale AFB routeing via Goose Bay. As we approached Barksdale, we were informed that some USAF and local civilian news teams were out in force, and we were asked by an RAF officer in the ATC tower to perform an 'energetic fly-past' prior to landing. Our captain, perhaps being concerned that he might be accused of doing an airfield 'beat-up', and also not wanting to 'bend' his aircraft prior to the competition, decided to compromise and flew a not-too-energetic and perfectly safe run and break into the circuit to land. The domestic arrangements at Barksdale were first class, with our crew allocated accommodation in the base's visiting officers' quarters, which was only a short walk away from the lively officers' club. After taking a few days to settle in, we were ready to fly our first Giant Voice competition route on 19 October.

Giant Voice competition flying was always a standard hi-lo-hi profile with targets spread around the USA. There was a bit of 'shock horror' at the start of one of the competition sorties when our H2S radar failed just as we started to taxi for take-off. Our ground crew proved to be really on the ball and a senior radar tradesman came rushing up the steps and into the cabin clutching some tools and other bits and pieces that he hoped would allow him to cure the problem. To prevent us from missing our take-off time and thus being disqualified, he suggested that we continue to taxi to the runway while he tried to fix the radar. He said that he would get a lift back to the technical site in the detachment vehicle that would follow us along the taxiway. Just in time, when our Vulcan reached the runway holding point, the tradesman declared the H2S serviceable and slid out of the door which was immediately closed by the nav radar. Before you could blink, we had rolled onto the runway, opened the throttles and we were airborne with seconds to spare. It pleases me immensely when I look back on this little incident because it not only demonstrated the level of dedication and involvement of all ranks and trades in the competition, but the senior radar tradesman who fixed the radar just happened to be an old colleague of mine from the time when we were both junior radar technicians at RAF Leeming. Brian S, thank you once again. You saved the day.

Competition routes resulted in our Vulcan criss-crossing the USA many times as we made our way to and from the low-level portion of the sorties. On the sortie scheduled for 7 November, we were tasked to carry out a refuelling stop at McConnell AFB near Wichita in Kansas. As we approached the airfield, ATC told us that the local press had been informed about our visit and would be in attendance when we landed. After landing, we taxied to our allocated parking spot where a welcoming party awaited us.

Our nav plotter, always keen for a bit of free public relations, carefully combed his hair using my Red Steer radar scope as a mirror and then put on his sunglasses. As soon as the door was open, he intended to slide down the door, grab one of the door struts and swing out and round to land neatly on his feet in front of the awaiting throng – so cool! Well, it would have been cool had the back of his flying suit not caught on some small protrusion on the door. The net result was that he toppled forward, flew head first out of the hatch, and banged his head on the nose wheel, breaking his sunglasses and sustained a small, but blooded, swelling bump on his nose. Being the sort of chap he was, he put a brave face on it, got up as quickly as he could and went over to engage in conversation with the press, some of whom were doing their best not to laugh. Meanwhile, the remainder of the crew took time to fit the door ladder and exit the aircraft by the standard method. Despite our nav plotter's little nose-diving stunt, the PR visit went well and featured in one of the Wichita newspapers the following day with the headline: 'Top Secret British Bat-Like Bomber visits Wichita!'

I will refrain from writing about every sortie as, honestly, they all tend to follow a similar script. Suffice to say the RAF crews did their utmost to win, but stood little

Giant Voice crew at Barksdale with radar expert (Brian S) in the light shirt.

or no chance against the advanced navigation and bombing aiming systems carried on USAF bombers such as the FB-111 and B-52s. Furthermore, our particular Vulcan stood absolutely no chance of winning the ECM trophy as we did not carry the equipment needed to compete. During the scheduled ECM run, aircraft were tracked by an E-Band radar for scoring purposes, while the threat radars operated in other parts of the frequency spectrum. The only jammer we carried was the Red Shrimp that, as previously mentioned, operated in the D and E-Bands. So the only radar we could jam was the tracking radar. When establishing two-way radio contact with the ECM threat site, the operator would implore us not to jam his tracking radar. Interestingly though, the rules were such that if the ECM scoring unit failed to track our aircraft for any reason, we would be awarded an average score, despite the fact that we had no jamming capability against the threat radar. The temptation to unleash the Red Shrimp to see if we could jam the tracking radar and thus wangle us an unwarranted, underhand, but possible competition-winning average score was considered, but being British etc., we declined the temptation.

On one, or perhaps two, of the sorties we were confronted with a fighter threat that comprised a flight of F-106 Delta Dart fighters. Once again, our Vulcan had no jammer capable of countering the fighters' AI radar, and with the use of chaff and flares strictly forbidden, we just flew on ignoring the Delta Darts that were queuing up to shoot us down. While it was interesting to watch the fighters taking turns to shoot us down through my periscope, I actually found the experience rather depressing.

There are a large number of trophies awarded at the end of each Giant Voice competition. The much-coveted Fairchild Trophy was taken by the 509th Bomb Wing from Pease AFB. This was the fifth time in a row that the award has been won by an FB-111 crew. However, as General R H Ellis, Commander-in-Chief, Strategic Air Command put it: "Having spent so much of the nation's wealth on the FB-111, I would definitely have had some serious questions to ask if the FB-111 had not won the Fairchild Trophy." Other trophies were awarded for best ECM performance, best in-flight refuelling, best navigation, best B-52, best interceptor etc. Our crew was proclaimed the second-best Vulcan (out of four), a modest

Red Steer display and chaff and flare dispenser control units. (H. Heeley, Newark Air Museum)

achievement, but certainly 'no cigar'. To be brutally honest, I sometimes wonder how we managed to do as well as we did on these competitions. While the USAF B-52s and F-111s were regularly being upgraded with new radar and navigation systems and other capabilities aimed at improving their performance, the Vulcan had to soldier on with its obsolete radar, electromechanical bombing computer, 1960s' navigation gear and, again, no ECM-jamming capability worth talking about. I can only put our modest successes down to the quality of our pilot and navigator bombing teams and their professional dedication to the task. Equally important in my view, was the dedication and unfailing zeal of our ground crews. Somehow they managed to keep the old cogs and wheels turning.

# A Trip Down Under

In early 1980, OC 617 Squadron, Wg Cdr John Herbertson, was ordered to take a Vulcan to Adelaide in Australia to perform a joint fly-past with two Royal Australian Air Force (RAAF) Mirage fighters over the city's cathedral. The purpose of the fly-past was to commemorate the Australian and New Zealand Army Corps (Anzac) Day Memorial Service scheduled for 25 April. The trip also coincided with a No. 617 Squadron – Australia Branch – Reunion and Memorial Service. Later, on 27 April, our crew was invited to attend the laying down of a memorial stone dedicated to the Australian wartime veterans from 617 Dam Buster Squadron. I was the lucky AEO on the CO's crew.

During our stay in Australia, the Vulcan was based at RAAF Edinburgh, just outside Adelaide city. To get there, the captain and navigators planned a route that took us from RAF Scampton, onward via CFB Goose Bay, Offutt AFB near Nebraska, McClellan AFB near Sacramento, Hickam AFB in Honolulu, NAS Midway Island in the Pacific Ocean, Andersen AFB in Guam, RAAF Darwin in the Australian Northern Territories, and on to RAAF Edinburgh in South Australia. There was a fair amount of pre-detachment preparation that had to be carried out, particularly for the nav plotter who relished the challenge of navigating the Vulcan halfway around the world and back again. Of course, he was ably assisted by the nav radar. The captain and co-pilot had their own preparation to carry out with regards to arrangements for aircraft handling, crew accommodation at the various night stopovers and making sure that the essential diplomatic clearances etc. were in place. For my part, I studied the communication requirements for all stages of the trip and made sure that I had in my possession all the required, up-to-date charts and communication-related documentation.

Our crew was fortunate to be taking along two very experienced crew chiefs. They made sure that our Vulcan was in tip-top condition and ready to undertake every stage of the long haul out to Australia and back. They also checked that all the aircraft documentation was up-to-date and that all the portable servicing equipment, small consumables and spares parts that would, or could, be needed to maintain the Vulcan in good working order were loaded into the bomb-bay pannier. As it turns out, the Vulcan allocated to us for the detachment was XM571, the same aircraft that I flew on during the Giant Voice competition at Barksdale in October 1979. The aircraft had served us very well on that occasion so the omens for the trip to Australia were good. Last of all, the crew made up a pack of 617 Squadron stickers, ties, Vulcan prints and other PR paraphernalia required to spread goodwill and bonhomie during all stages of the trip.

We set off from Scampton on 15 April and arrived at Goose Bay after a transit flight of just over five hours. A good meal chased down with a couple of beers in the mess followed by a good night's sleep set us up nicely for the transit to McClellan AFB via Offutt the next day. Located about eight miles north-east of Sacramento, McClellan AFB was a fairly busy air logistics command base at the time of our visit, but it has long since closed and is now a business park. We were housed for the night in downtown Sacramento, a charming city that also happens to be the capital of California. Sacramento found fame in the late 19th century when it became the most westerly stopping point for the Pony Express postal service. I don't suppose our Vulcan's one-night stop would feature as another claim to fame for Sacramento, but we did enjoy the evening there, walking the boardwalks and generally appreciating its well-preserved Western culture.

The next stage of the trip was an over-water flight to Hickam AFB in Hawaii. Working HF communications across that sector of the Pacific Ocean was a delight. I have never experienced such good HF propagation conditions. I could hear aircraft conducting two-way voice traffic with almost every HF station on the Pacific littoral including Elmendorf in Alaska, Honolulu in Hawaii and Yokota in Japan. About halfway to Hawaii I was surprised to pick up a sector scanning I-Band transmission on the RWR. It gradually got stronger and then suddenly it stopped scanning and became steady, indicating a lock-on. It was showing in our eight o'clock position and, when cross-referring to the Red Steer, I noticed a single contact about three miles away and closing. The contact flew to within quarter of a mile from us in our seven o'clock position, then suddenly the radar went off and the contact dived away. I guessed that our IFF Mode 1 squawk, that identified us as a British bomber, must have attracted the attention of the US Navy. My assumption was that there must have been an aircraft carrier somewhere in the ocean below and one of its fighters had been sent up on a training sortie to identify us. We were too far from both the Continental United States and Hawaii for it to have been a land-based fighter. As we neared the Hawaiian islands, our nav radar began searching on his H2S radar, hoping to pick up and obtain a fix on one of the islands to the east of Honolulu for navigation refinement purposes. Sure enough, after a few minutes of searching, the islands started to show up on his radar screen and a fix was duly taken. Some minor heading adjustments were made to establish ourselves on the required track and within no time we were exchanging radio calls with Honolulu ATCC on UHF and descending to land at Hickam AFB.

Hickam is a huge base. So much so, that at that time it operated different ground movements frequencies depending upon which part of the airfield you were taxiing on. So, as we taxied around the base to our allocated parking position, we were being handed off from one ground control frequency to the next – most unusual. Once parked, the captain shut the Vulcan down and we were all able to get outside into the sunlight and stretch our legs. The crew chiefs, keen to get the aircraft turned around for the next leg of our journey to NAS Midway two days later, were already doing their after-flight checks and liaising with the captain about fuel uptake etc.

We had to hang about on the scorching dispersal pan for quite a long time waiting for the RAF liaison officer (RAFLO) to arrive and our impatience was beginning to show. However, after a number of phone calls by USAF base personnel on our behalf, the RAFLO finally arrived in his private transport. He was dressed rather nattily and had a colourful Hawaiian garland around his neck. "Aloha!" he proclaimed. I wasn't sure if our captain, who by then was getting a bit hot under the collar, appreciated the carefree Hawaiian greeting. Perhaps he would have preferred a smart salute and an apology for not being there on time to meet us. However, things did start to look up when the RAFLO reached into the cabin of his car and produced a crate of cold beer, but just as we were about to tell him what a grand chap he was, he spoiled the moment by demanding hard cash up front. The crew was not impressed. Having groped around in our flying suits we managed to club together the dollars needed to pay for the beer, and after a short delay, our crew transport arrived and whisked us off to our appointed hotel which, I was delighted to discover, overlooked Waikiki Beach.

We had two days to spend in Honolulu and I made the most of it. I went on the almost compulsory cruise around Pearl Harbor and visited the USS *Arizona* memorial viewing platform located on top of the wreck of the battleship. I also did some paddle boarding in the sea near to our hotel and, later, relaxed on the hot sands of Waikiki Beach. Two days doesn't offer much time to take in all that Honolulu has to offer and after what seemed no time at all, we were back at the aircraft loading our personal possessions and generally preparing for the three-hour transit flight to Midway Island.

NAS Midway Island, when we arrived on 19 April, was no longer a fully functioning naval base. In fact, it was minimally manned and was obviously being kept under some form of care and maintenance. In short, the base was almost deserted. We were allocated accommodation in what, at one time, must have been an officer's MQ. It was basic, but comfortable enough, and we were served a very satisfactory evening meal

The author with albatrosses at Midway Island.

in a small club-cum-mess used by the small number of resident military and civilian personnel. However, the most memorable thing about Midway was the vast number of albatross birds flying around the island and waddling about on the ground. Their nests, which were dotted all over the island including on the disused aircraft pans, runways and taxiways, are very basic in construction, comprising an 18-inch-high mound of straw, twigs and mud. I have since found out that Midway is now a national wildlife refuge and conservation area and it is one of the main albatross breeding grounds for the Pacific Oceanic area.

The adult albatross didn't seem to mind when I inspected their nests and viewed their chicks, it was all very calm. In fact, the biggest danger to life and limb at Midway was finding yourself in the path of an albatross during its take-off run, an event closely resembling the take-off run of a fully loaded B-52. The only warning you got that you were about to be run over was the sound of rapidly approaching webbed feet slapping on the ground and the powerful sighing sound from its slowly flapping wings. As the birds spend most of their life on the wing their legs are rather weak and lack the strength and agility required to execute smooth take-offs and landings; they are even ungainly when simply trying to walk. In the high temperature and nil-wind conditions that prevailed when we were there, the birds that wanted to get airborne were making take-off runs of up to 100 yards or more. Even then, not all take-offs were successful and I was amazed to see some birds giving up halfway through their run, fold their wings, then nonchalantly wander back for another go. Landings, thanks to the nil-wind conditions, were best described as controlled crashes. Although not quite as calamitous as the Kamikaze-style landings of the Wake Island gooney birds, each albatross would glide down and round out just above the ground, close to stalling speed. When their webbed feet made contact with the ground, they would do their best to run along the ground whilst trying to slow to a stop. This procedure generally failed, and for most of the landings that I watched, the poor birds ended up nose-diving on to the ground as their legs failed to keep pace with their bodies. But this didn't seem to worry the birds unduly. I really felt privileged to have had the opportunity to observe so many albatrosses in their natural environment. That said, I sincerely hoped that none of them would come into contact with our Vulcan when the time came to depart the airfield. Having received our oceanic flight clearance and departure authority for our flight to Guam from the young enlisted man working in the operations block, we took off, soaring upwards above the turquoise-coloured sea, leaving the tiny Midway Atoll and its massive albatross population behind.

The flight from Midway to Andersen AFB in Guam lasted about five hours and 30 minutes and involved us crossing the International Date Line (IDL). Interestingly, the design of the Vulcan's electro-mechanical GPI Mk. 6 navigation computer prevented it from seamlessly tracking the Vulcan's transit across the IDL. It would seem that the mechanical cogs and levers inside the unit achieved the end of their travel when reaching either 180 degrees east or 180 degrees west. So the nav plotter had to do some very rapid knob turning to wind the knobs and dials all the way back around the world from 180 degrees west to 180 degrees east just as we crossed the IDL, or at least that is how I understood it at the time. Whatever he did, he did it with remarkable aplomb because as far as I am aware it did not introduce any significant errors in our ongoing navigation.

Andersen AFB is mainly used as a bomber base for B-52s and KC-135 refuelling tankers. It certainly isn't short of real estate, sporting two 11,000-ft runways and a myriad of bomber servicing pans. When we landed there, we were taken to a rather nice, but unbelievably quiet, hotel that overlooked 'a beach to die for'. Lush green palm trees and brightly coloured and flowering bushes covered the small hillocks that dropped down from the hotel to a beach that boasted the whitest natural sands I have ever seen and which bordered the light turquoise-coloured sea. What also amazed me was the silence; no man-made sounds whatsoever. If fact all I could hear was the soft lapping sounds of small wavelets collapsing on the shore. Alas, we were only there for one night so we didn't have time to explore the surrounding country or swim in the inviting sea. Also, as the hotel bar was shut, most of us decided to have an early night in preparation for the next leg of our journey to Darwin in Australia. The following morning, we had breakfast in the hotel restaurant and then boarded the transport to take us to the airfield. Without much ado, we fired up the Vulcan and in no time at all we were airborne again, leaving Guam behind. We headed south across Papua

Herbertson's crew relaxing in Darwin.

New Guinea in the direction of Thursday Island located at the north-eastern point of Australia. Just before getting there, we turned onto a westerly heading towards Darwin where we landed almost exactly five hours after take-off from Guam.

At Darwin we were housed in a comfortable motel for the night. It had a nice sitting-out area where our team of pilots, navigators, crew chiefs and I enjoyed the evening sun while sipping on cool Australian beer. We were told that the temperature was really going to soar the following day so, come morning, we were keen to get going as early as possible on the final leg of the journey to RAAF Edinburgh. After an early breakfast we caught the transport to the aircraft only to find when we arrived there that one of the wheels on the Vulcan's port-side undercarriage bogie had a flat tyre. Fortunately, the crew chiefs had included a spare wheel in their pack-up, but we would have to jack the aircraft up to facilitate the wheel change. I was hoping that the crew chiefs would have an electrically powered hydraulic jack or some other gizmo to do the hard work, but it was not to be. Instead, the crew's collective jaws dropped when one of our crew chiefs produced a smallish cube-shaped steel box that had a rather long handle. We were all going to have to take turns pumping the lever of the little hydraulic jack to manually raise the port side of our fully fuelled Vulcan. I have no idea what the ratio of pumping motions to millimetres raised was, but it took ages with everyone having a go on the pump. A passing Ansett crew made some joking remark as they sauntered towards their pre-cooled DC-9 airliner, but no one was in the mood to laugh. After what seemed like ages, our crew chiefs announced that we had reached the required elevation and they quickly changed the wheel. Letting the hydraulic jack down was infinitely easier than raising it and, with all of our gear loaded into the aircraft, we quickly got airborne on the last leg of the journey to Adelaide.

At that time there was very little required in the way of communications when flying over central Australia. Nevertheless, for something to do, I decided to give Alice Springs a call. It took a while to elicit an answer but when they did reply, all they wanted to know was the name of the AEO on board our aircraft, so I told them my name. I am told that back in the 1960s, when Australia was developing its ATC provision, there were regular advertisements in the UK press for people to travel to Australia and work there as ATC tradesmen and controllers. Many RAF wireless and radar tradesmen and some air signallers, who were about to leave the RAF, applied and were accepted. So, on the rare occasion when a RAF aircraft overflew some of the quieter regions of Australia, ex-British ATC controllers, perhaps feeling a bit homesick, were keen to know if there was anyone on board that they knew. Having passed them my name, I waited several minutes for a response. When it came it was in the usual no-nonsense Australian vernacular: "Nobody here's ever heard of you mate. Give the Edinburgh folks a call when you get within range, G'day!" A few hours later we landed at RAAF Edinburgh.

In Adelaide, our crew was housed in a rather nice hotel that overlooked the city's cricket ground. We had plenty of free time so we were able to wander around the town, take in the sights and do a bit of shopping. Just for something different to do,

Author with a koala bear at Adelaide Zoo.

I paid a visit to the city's zoological park. One of the attendants there was allowing visitors to hold a young koala bear while their families and friends took photographs. Thinking it might be a nice photograph to show my children when I got home, I decided to have a go at holding the small bear. It soon became obvious that the koala was not very keen on being manhandled by a Scotsman and it decided to demonstrate this by using its claw to gouge a 12-inch long, triple fingered scratch across my back. It was deep enough to rip my shirt and draw blood, but not so deep that I felt the need for it to be looked at by a doctor or nurse. With hindsight, I suppose I should have arranged to have a tetanus jab. But the real problem manifested itself when I got home to Scampton. My wife Jessie, hands on hips, demanded to know how I got the scratch marks on my back. When I told her that I had been scratched by a koala bear she just stared at me with a look of utter disbelief and subjected me to a rather severe bout of the 'silent treatment'. It was many days before normal services were resumed.

Our crew was invited to attend an Edinburgh officers' mess dining-in night that was being held in honour of 617 Squadron. I seem to remember that the presiding officer was Air Cdre L R Klaffer AFC. Copious quantities of beer and wine were made available and the food was outstanding, allowing me to sample for the first time some beautifully cooked and presented barramundi fish – absolutely delicious! We all tucked in to the food and the flow of excellent Barossa Valley wine never stopped. So much so, that by the time we got to the speeches, things were becoming rather more exciting, verging on raucous, and sometimes outrightly mutinous. The presiding officer didn't seem to mind the verbal brick-bats being aimed in his direction, taking them all on the chin. It certainly reinforced my previous perceptions of Australian officers, that they do not hold back when it comes to making full and uninhibited use of their rights to 'free speech', even when addressing a senior officer. Being invited guests, we, of course, behaved impeccably, and tried not to get involved in the red-blooded banter.

On 23 April we were scheduled to fly a practice Anzac Day fly-past over the city with a RAAF Mirage fighter tucked in close on each wing tip. It all went very well with no apparent complications, although it did seem strange flying at such a low height over the city, albeit I was viewing it through my periscope. I was green with envy when I found out that our nav plotter had managed to cadge a ride in the back of one of the Mirage jets during the fly-past rehearsal. He had convinced our captain that the nav radar could easily take his place at the nav plotter's position for the practice sortie. You will fully appreciate by now that, when flying in a Vulcan, the rear crew don't get much of a chance to view and admire the passing scenery. This is particularly frustrating when flying over areas of natural beauty or performing fly-pasts over city centres etc. So I thought I would have a go at taking a photograph of Adelaide from the Vulcan's, no-longer-used, bomb-aiming position. I also took a couple of practice shots of the shadow of our Vulcan and fighter escort as we flew over the red-coloured desert just outside the city. As it turns out, turbulence completely spoiled the photo taken over the city, but the shots I took of our shadow on the desert were marginally passible.

During our time in Adelaide, our crew was invited to join wartime 617 Squadron members for a meal and a few drinks in a restaurant called 'The Jolly Swagman' somewhere up in the hills on the outskirts of the city. It was a most enjoyable night with lots of banter and interesting talk, accompanied with lots of typical Aussie food and plenty of beer to wash it down. On another day we attended the unveiling of a 617 Squadron memorial plaque to honour those members of the squadron that had laid down their lives in WWII. Gp Capt Leonard Cheshire VC was in attendance with some surviving Australian air and ground crews. It would probably be the last time that such an esteemed gathering of surviving 617 Squadron war heroes would take place. Meeting and conversing with the 617 Squadron veterans was a humbling and, at times, quite emotional experience for me. It really was an honour for the crew to be invited to the ceremony. On 25 April our Vulcan, with its two Mirage fighter escorts, performed the Anzac Day fly-past. Everything went as planned and there were numerous photographs of the formation in the following day's newspapers. Formalities and social gatherings over, it would soon be time to return to the UK.

Shadows of Vulcan and escorting Mirages on the desert landscape. The photograph was taken during practice runs for the Anzac Day fly-past.

Anzac Day fly-past Vulcan and Mirage crews.

The routeing for the return trip entailed: RAAF Edinburgh to RAAF Amberley near Brisbane, then on to Andersen AFB; NAS Midway Island; Hickam AFB; McClellan AFB; Loring AFB in Maine then on to Scampton. On our way to RAAF Amberley, we did a fly-past over the UK governor's house in Canberra before continuing on route. When we landed at RAAF Amberley, the crew received an especially warm welcome from the CO and his staff and many photographs were taken. In particular, the CO allowed one of his female staff – I believe she was a dental hygienist – to pose with the crew for photographs. One of the photographs required all of us to squeeze into the Vulcan's intake. The RAAF airwoman was a lovely young lady who was quite prepared to climb up a ladder and perch precariously on the edge of the Vulcan's starboard intake with the rest of the crew while the photographer snapped away.

The journey home passed without incident and we landed back at Scampton on 8 May. Apart from the flat tyre at Darwin, our Vulcan behaved impeccably throughout. For this, credit must go our crew chiefs who, as well as starting work early every morning to prepare the Vulcan for flight, also spent many hours after we landed making sure that all the consumables had been replenished, the paperwork was properly completed and the aircraft secured. When I asked if they were becoming increasingly tired during the detachment, they told me that they were okay as long as they could catch up with sleep when we were airborne. Seated, as they were, on the wooden boxes that served as passenger seats on the Vulcan, I didn't fancy their chances of actually getting some serious shut-eye.

# CHAPTER EIGHT
# THE VULCAN'S WAR MISSION

During my time serving on 617 Squadron (1976–1981), I was often asked if the Vulcan was still capable of successfully penetrating Soviet airspace in order to deliver its nuclear weapons. It was a good question and one that regularly crossed my mind. RN submariners used to call our planned war sorties 'suicide missions'. They were probably right about that. But if the Vulcans had been scrambled for real, it probably meant that the UK, and/or its NATO allies, were under some form of attack from the USSR and that, in all likelihood, other retaliatory nuclear forces were being launched too. Given such a scenario very few of us, whether strapped in the back of a Vulcan or tucked up in our beds at home, would have been safe from the dire consequences that were about to unfold. That said, RN submariners were also convinced that the safest place to be in the event of nuclear war was on board their patrolling SSBN. They were probably right about that too!

Being a very junior aircrew officer at the time, I was not gifted with the right to discuss or question UK planning assumptions for nuclear war. Nor did I have sight of NATO's and the UK's national strategy for war, and the sub-strategic/tactical targeting it involved. Therefore, I must impress upon you, the reader, that what follows reflects my own personal thoughts, assumptions and opinions on the matter as I viewed it from my rather low-ranking level.

Like most of the people I talked with, it was generally assumed that the trigger for nuclear war would come from some destabilising geopolitical event involving the Soviet Union and one or more NATO member countries. If handled carelessly or if left unresolved, the resulting increase in political tension could possibly escalate into a conventional confrontation. If things escalated even further, an exchange of nuclear weapons became a distinct possibility. But I also believed that during the build-up of tension and the conventional warfare phases, NATO politicians and military commanders would have been trying very hard to resolve their differences with their opposite numbers in Russia by taking part in serious negotiation coupled, if necessary, with the delivery of dire warnings. If that failed to achieve results, then it was possible that a further, more emphatic warning, reinforced by the delivery of one or more low-yield nuclear weapons on sub-strategic – low value – targets might help to get the message through. My thought was that such a demonstration of NATO or national resolve would perhaps give the Soviets reason to pause and reassess the situation before allowing events to spiral out of control.

However, as you might expect, there were many who considered this approach to be pie in the sky. They were convinced that once the nuclear genie was let out of the bottle, the momentum towards all-out nuclear war would become unstoppable. Perhaps they were right. But it had to be acknowledged that misunderstandings, misjudgements and mistakes, particularly during periods of high political tension, could easily be made by both sides. It was vital, therefore, that every effort should be made to reduce tensions and prevent the march towards nuclear war. In an attempt to support this approach, direct lines of communication linking, in the first instance, the capitals of the USA and Russia, were installed. It was thought that this 'hotline' would allow last-minute dialogue to take place to prevent the risk of nuclear conflict. However, simultaneously and as a precaution, NATO leadership in America planned for the worst case by maintaining a cadre of senior civilian and military officials whose job it was to produce and maintain a comprehensive plan for nuclear war. This plan found credence in a document called the single integrated operational plan (SIOP).

I have never set eyes on the SIOP, so I can only assume that it would have contained a comprehensive list of targets to be struck, weapons to be used and details regarding the sequencing of inter-continental ballistic missile (ICBM) and bomber strikes. I also think that it must have included options to determine which of the WP countries should be included or excluded from attack plans and which categories of targets (military bases, command and control centres, cities, industrial complexes etc.) should be attacked and in what order. Furthermore, I would have expected it to include a list of those high-priority targets earmarked for multiple nuclear strikes in order to make absolutely certain that they were destroyed. I further assume that the SIOP would be regularly updated to take account of changes in national leadership, the development of new weapons, modified attack procedures and changes in political alliances. I believe it would also have been periodically amended to embrace the evolution of new nuclear war-fighting strategies.

Apparently, one such strategy – the counterforce strategy – was intended to avoid excessive civilian casualties by limiting nuclear strikes to military targets only. However, it was soon realised that the proximity of military bases to cities, towns and other concentrations of civilian personnel rendered this strategy difficult, if not impossible, to implement. Another idea was to deliberately (and horrifically) focus nuclear strikes upon enemy centres of population and industrial might. I believe this was called 'the countervalue strategy'. While this plan would allow the enemy to retain some or most of its offensive nuclear assets, it would, hopefully, cause the enemy to think twice before using them because of the huge and perhaps irrecoverable damage and destruction that would be inflicted on their own country and its people. Crazy as it may sound, some 'strategists' even thought that both sides could perhaps agree to limit the ferocity of any first strike to allow the other side to survive and strike back thus maintaining some balance of threat. This last, rather unbelievable option, would surely have resulted in both east and west building ever more nuclear weapons and delivery platforms to guarantee the availability of second and third strike options. In my view all of these strategies and options were fanciful, if not totally ridiculous. Trying to finesse the scope and intensity of nuclear war to make it more manageable, survivable, and recoverable would simply have served to reduce the potency of deterrence and make nuclear war more likely. In my view, the only reliable defence strategy was (and still is) the one offered by mutually assured destruction (MAD); a statement of intent that any nuclear strike on NATO countries by an aggressor would trigger a full-scale nuclear response such that the act of initiating the first strike would be tantamount to committing national suicide.

Today, the ownership of nuclear weapons by countries such as India, Pakistan, North Korea, Israel and perhaps some others is upending global stability. This means that important discussions will have to be had and decisions made about how NATO and/or individual nuclear-armed nations should, or could, best respond to acts of aggression and threats from any one of these countries. But looking back at the Cold War period and the stand-off between NATO and the USSR, any thought of fine-tuning or micro-managing nuclear war was, as I have said, manifestly unworkable. In my opinion, the implementation of MAD via the SIOP was the only plan that made perfect, but terrifying, sense. It spelt out clearly and unambiguously what the Soviet Union could expect if it ever crossed the line. It was, in my view, the only realistic plan in town. However, there was another fear that lurked in the back of NATO minds during the dark days of the Cold War. What if there was no political build-up of tension? What if the Soviet Union decided to launch a surprise attack and unleashed its full arsenal of weapons against NATO without warning? Would NATO's retaliatory forces have been able to respond as planned, or would they have been destroyed or otherwise rendered unusable? Would there have been time to prepare and fly Vulcans on their pre-planned missions? Would NATO's command and control system have survived such an attack? Would plans documented in the SIOP still be relevant? Such thoughts occupied and worried the minds of many senior people at that time.

Most sane people will agree that starting an all-out nuclear war was, and still is, unthinkable because no one could ever hope to gain from such a cataclysmic event. MAD would have ensured that there could be no winners and that everybody, and I mean the total population of the world, would lose out in some form or other. Indeed, it was possible that planet earth, itself, would be rendered partially, or wholly uninhabitable. With that in mind, what could have motivated me and many others to volunteer to be part of such a catastrophic folly? What could have compelled crews to climb on board their Vulcan bombers and do their level best to deliver nuclear weapons onto military, and perhaps civilian, targets with the obvious consequences for the world? Could I, personally, have gone through with it? My answer now is the same as my answer was back then, and it is a resounding yes.

During my time on the V Force the prevailing position was that nuclear weapons, having been invented, could not be un-invented or wished away. The only way to ensure that such weapons were never used against the UK was to maintain a credible deterrent; a retaliatory force that would make the cost of any nuclear adventurism against us by an opponent so appallingly expensive for them in terms of property, treasure and lives, that no sane leader would ever seriously contemplate such an action. But for this retaliatory posture to work, it had to be believed beyond any doubt. Indeed, it had to be guaranteed. With this in mind, I remember finding it somewhat dispiriting when I heard politicians humming and hawing on radio and television, about whether or not they would give the order to retaliate in the event of a Soviet nuclear attack. One very senior politician went so far as to state that if he had been elected prime minister of the UK, and if Soviet nuclear missiles had started to rain down on Great Britain, he would have concluded that the UK's deterrent had failed and, for the sake of humanity, he would have stood down our own nuclear forces. At the time, some may have considered this to be an altruistic and perhaps even understandable position to adopt. But in my opinion, it was a totally irresponsible thing for a potential national leader to say. Would-be aggressors must never be allowed to believe that they will get away with employing nuclear, or mass conventional, weapons against our country, or other countries within NATO, without suffering catastrophic consequences in return. It was the UK's strategic deterrent acting both nationally and as part of NATO that would ultimately protect our people from large-scale conventional and/or nuclear attack. It was the maintenance of reliable nuclear-armed forces that ensured that the USSR and other potential aggressor nations, would have to think very carefully before taking a bite out of NATO's protected territories. For this reason, our strike assets had to be both capable and credible, and ready to carry out their missions should the order to attack be given. This, therefore, conveniently takes me back to the first paragraph in this chapter: if during my time serving on 617 Squadron our Vulcans had been ordered to scramble on a nuclear strike mission, could they have survived their flight to the target to deliver their WE.177 nuclear bombs?

The answer to this question, as you have probably guessed, is rather complicated, as it would have depended upon a number of important political considerations and operational discriminators extant at the time. Some within and outside the V Force fraternity have tried to quantify the effectiveness of the V Force by conducting an in-depth analysis of the Vulcan's capabilities and those of the opposing forces, and by allocating figures of reliability and effectiveness against the whole range of weapon systems. In my view such mathematical calculations and other highfalutin analyses are completely without merit because no one could know with any certainty how reliable and capable weapon systems and their operators would be on any given day, or know the political and environmental conditions extant at the time of the conflict. Results of similar studies carried out prior to other wars have proven to be very wide of the mark, mainly because the analysts have either over or under-estimated the capabilities of enemy and allied forces, or they have failed to foresee political constraints and the operational and environmental circumstances that would be extant during the period under study. One only has to compare the prognosis and the reality of the Vietnam and Korean conflicts to appreciate that mathematical and logic-based analysis alone cannot provide valid answers to many of the questions posed prior to a conflict. However, one political consideration that I think would have made a significant difference as to whether or not the Vulcans could have reached their targets was whether the strikes were part of an independent UK national response, or part of a NATO-wide, SIOP-controlled response. Another political consideration would have been whether the attack was a selective release 'warning' mission, or whether it was part of an all-out, no-hold barred onslaught against the aggressor. Over and above these considerations, a number of important operational discriminators would have effect, such as for example: the planned sequence of offensive events, the position and nature of the target, the time of day, the weather, the serviceability of the Vulcans and the experience and aggressiveness of their crews. There was also, that all-important, but arbitrary discriminator, Lady Luck! Finally, and on a rather minor technical point, there was a question about whether use of the Vulcan's Red Shrimp ECM would have helped, or hindered, a crew's chance of reaching its target during the 1977–81 period in question.

# The UK's Independent National Nuclear Deterrent

The reason for retaining an option to conduct a national-only nuclear operation was to let it be known that any attack focused primarily upon the UK and its dependencies would, or could, incur for the aggressor a cost out of all proportion to any advantage it hoped to gain. Furthermore, an aggressor could not be absolutely certain that calls for restraint from the UK's NATO allies would be sufficient to prevent the UK from enacting its independent nuclear option. I believe that this posture, or something similar, still holds true today. Consider, for example, a hypothetical scenario where, in response to some form of Soviet aggression, the UK had decided to launch its independent retaliatory strike force. It is reasonable to assume that UK SLBMs, with their multiple re-entry vehicles/warheads, would be launched from the on-station SSBN and would speed towards their targets in Russia. The Vulcans, having been scrambled, would have set course eastwards towards the Soviet Union where they would have had to face the full focus and weight of the WP air defence forces on their own. This, as you can imagine, would have made it significantly more difficult for them to survive their flight, both to and from their targets. But it almost goes without saying that such independent nuclear action would also have had potentially disastrous consequences for NATO and for the rest of the world.

A decision by the UK to retaliate against some form of hypothetical Soviet aggression by activating its independent nuclear option would have given rise to a number of serious problems. How, for example, were the Soviets to know – or believe – that the approaching SLBMs had been launched from a UK SSBN and not an American or French SSBN? All they would know for certain was that a number of missiles, coming from somewhere at sea, were heading their way. Would the Soviets have believed American and French denials of responsibility? With such a highly charged level of confusion and distrust, how could anyone know what the Soviet response would have been? Would they have limited their answer to making further attacks against the UK, or would they have covered all of their options by launching an all-out strike against other SSBN-capable NATO countries? No one can be sure what the answer to these questions would have been. But what would have been certain, is that the launch of the UK's nuclear forces would have created the potential for the crisis to escalate beyond being solely a Soviet and British problem. Britain, by responding to an attack on its own with its nuclear weapons, would possibly have set in motion an unstoppable string of events leading towards all-out global war. For this reason, I am certain that other NATO nations, particularly America, would have been very nervous indeed of any sign that the UK was contemplating unilateral nuclear action, and they would have been very forceful in advising the UK against doing so. However, as things stood then (and now?), the UK retained the right to respond to any form of aggression in a manner of its own choosing. Furthermore, no one, other than a few very senior UK individuals charged with considering such things, could possibly have any idea of what the UK national response would be for any given scenario. Would the UK really have unleashed some or all of its nuclear assets against the enemy, or would it have opted for a graduated response by launching a small number of SLBMs and/or Vulcan strikes to attack sub-strategic targets? I don't know. But down at squadron level, I can certainly imagine the dark thoughts going through the minds of the 'lucky' Vulcan crews chosen to fly on such missions.

I honestly find it almost impossible to think of a real-life situation where the UK would have felt compelled to carry out independent nuclear action against the USSR. The main reason for this is the guarantee provided in Article 5 of the NATO agreement which states that an attack on one member of the alliance will be considered an attack on all NATO member countries. Surely, therefore, the threat of an attack, or an actual attack, on the UK would have triggered a NATO-wide response? One would certainly have expected this to be the case. But then again, perhaps UK leaders had, and still have, a healthy degree of scepticism regarding the veracity of America's commitment to Article 5. Perhaps there was, and still is, some lingering doubt within the British hierarchy as to whether America really would partake in a nuclear exchange with the Soviet Union on account of some parochial argument between the Soviets and the British? All of this, of course, is pure conjecture on my part. However, for the sake of this book, let us assume a scenario where the UK has come under attack from the Soviet Union and has decided to retaliate with nuclear weapons. How do I imagine our nuclear forces would have been targeted and what would have been their chances of success – if indeed there can be such a thing as 'success' when it involves the use of nuclear weapons?

To guarantee the UK's promise to inflict a very high cost on any aggressor – in this hypothetical case, the Soviet Union – I would have thought that the majority of RN SLBM warheads would have been targeted against Soviet cities and/or industrial complexes, with only a few being aimed against major centres of political/military control. The UK would not have had sufficient missiles/re-entry vehicles to comprehensively damage or destroy the bulk of Soviet strategic and important sub-strategic targets. Perhaps if there was a protracted political build-up prior to the outbreak of hostilities, then it is possible that Britain could have generated a second RN SSBN to contribute towards its national response; although I have no idea how many additional missiles we would have had to arm the vessel. As for the Vulcans, I would have expected their attacks to be focused on the same types of targets as those suggested for SLBMs. Any thought of using Vulcans to destroy or impair the enemy's sub-strategic targets such as bomber airfields and intermediate range ballistic missile (IRBM) sites would not only have been a diversion from the promise to inflict the highest possible cost on the enemy. It would also have been rather pointless, as most, if not all, of the missile and bombers earmarked for striking the UK would have already flown. Indeed, by the time the Vulcans arrived over the Soviet Union, a second strike would probably have already been launched. Also, the very large number of Soviet mobile and fixed-ICBM sites, bomber bases, command and control centres and other military targets would have comprehensively outnumbered the limited number of 'surviving' Vulcans available to attack them. By attacking such targets, we would not only have reduced, or diluted, the cost impact of our attacks on the enemy, it is possible that the enemy would see such attacks as being 'bearable'. In a similar vein, launching Vulcan strikes against Soviet air defence forces would have been like poking a hornet's nest with a stick and hoping to escape without being stung. Such attacks would have been completely pointless as they would have had almost zero-cost impact upon the Soviet Union as well as offering absolutely no strategic value.

To be effective in national retaliation terms, Britain's independent nuclear strike forces would have had to be concentrated on imposing the maximum damage and cost on the USSR by wreaking havoc and destruction on its civilian, industrial and political infrastructure. In my opinion, any attempt at counterforce action by our very limited number of nuclear assets would have been completely futile.

To continue with this make-believe scenario, Vulcans, having been launched on national strike missions would have entered Soviet airspace within one hour from being launched. They would be facing an air-defence system that was largely unimpaired, at a high state of readiness and focused totally upon repelling UK air assets. It almost goes without saying that this would have guaranteed a torrid time for Vulcan crews. But depending upon the discriminators that I write about later in this chapter, I am convinced that a number of Vulcan attacks would have been successful. However, on the other side of the coin, if the UK had chosen to act independently of NATO and strike against the USSR with nuclear weapons, then this not only would have resulted in the total destruction of the UK, it would possibly have led to a much wider, possibly global, nuclear conflict.

## Vulcans Operating as Part of a NATO Nuclear Response

A more believable scenario is one where the Vulcans would be launched as part of a NATO-wide response to Soviet aggression. Vulcans placed under control of NATO's SACEUR would have been tasked in accordance with the SIOP. With Russian ICBM launch sites being geographically closer to the UK than America, it is possible that, depending upon the Soviet's own launch plan, missiles aimed against the UK would have reached their targets some time before those aimed at targets in America. To ensure survival, Vulcan squadrons would have had to fly to their dispersal airfields very early on during the pre-conflict phase. Not only would this early dispersal have protected our Vulcans from being destroyed en masse at their home bases, it would have seriously complicated Soviet targeting plans. Having landed at their dispersal airfields, Vulcans would have been refuelled, primed and placed on readiness to get airborne at very short notice to fly their war mission. It was estimated that no more than four minutes would elapse between the ballistic missile early warning radar at RAF Fylingdales detecting an incoming ICBM attack, and the missiles impacting on UK soil. It was vital, therefore, for the Vulcans to be able to get airborne within that four-minute warning time.

In the event of an incoming Soviet ICBM strike being detected by the radar at RAF Fylingdales, the Vulcans would have been ordered to scramble and set out on their eastward flight towards the Soviet Union. There was a line of longitude in close proximity to Scandinavia beyond which the recall of the Vulcans could not/would not have been possible; a sort of point of no return. Before reaching that line of longitude, RAF commanders could, if so ordered, recall part or all of the Vulcan Force. To ensure reliable reception of recall orders, messages authorised by the UK's Bomber Controller would have been broadcast on a wide range of frequencies including HF, UHF and possibly British Broadcasting Company and other commercial broadcast channels. In addition, Dominie T1 training aircraft from RAF Finningley would have been launched to carry out their war mission of patrolling at high altitude over the North Sea and re-broadcasting Bomber Controller UHF messages to the Vulcans as they flew eastwards. The absence of a recall message and passing the go/no-go line, would have meant that there would be no turning back. The Vulcans would have already started their descent down towards their low-level start point, ready to fight their way across Soviet territory and deliver their bombs on their assigned targets.

At the time, or perhaps just before the Vulcans penetrated Soviet airspace at low level, it is likely that a number of American and British SLBMs and other missiles, would have already started raining down on Soviet targets. Hopefully, some of these missiles would be targeted against early warning and GCI radar sites, command and control centres, SAM sites and AD bases, thus easing the way for the Vulcans, and later, American B-1 and B-52 bombers, to penetrate towards their designated targets. However, the near simultaneous arrival of missiles and Vulcans over the Soviet Union would have posed an interesting problem. In addition to working hard to avoid the plethora of Soviet fighters, SAM and AAA units, Vulcan pilots would have risked having their aircraft damaged, or even destroyed, by the intense shock waves and thermal blasts from ballistic missile warheads exploding on targets close to their planned routes. There was also a possibility that the pilots could be blinded or at least have their sight damaged by the intense light given off by the same nuclear detonations. In an effort to cater for this eye damage, Vulcan pilots were each issued with a black eyepatch to be worn over one eye during the strike mission. The idea was that if their 'looking eye' was damaged or rendered blind, pilots could simply swap the eyepatches over and continue their flight to their targets using their other eye – such was the world-beating technology employed by the V Force during the seventies. During this same period, the USAF was developing a Plexiglass visor for strike crews that would instantly turn black when exposed to extreme light. I have no idea how well this technology performed or, indeed, if it actually entered service. To mitigate the effects of this 'blue missile on blue bomber' attrition, routeing and timing constraints within the SIOP would have had to be meticulously planned and closely adhered to in the hope that, as far as possible, there would be adequate geographical and/or chronological separation between missile and bomber strikes. There was another, perhaps lesser, risk for any Vulcan crew that chose not to pay close adherence to route-timing constraints and mission abort criteria. In order to compensate for the possible failure of some of NATO's missiles and bombers to reach their allocated targets, a number of the more important targets would have been scheduled for attack by two or more, time separated, missile and/or bomber attacks. It would have been a cruel irony indeed for any Vulcan crew that had slipped back on its flight schedule and arrived over its target at the same time as a planned second strike. In theory, such things were not supposed to happen, but there is always the fog of war. In overall terms, the high number of missiles that would have been raining down on the USSR, and the large number of attacks being mounted from other NATO nations would have had the effect of reducing the Soviet air-defence capability, and what was left would have been required to operate over a much broader front. This dilution effect would, in my opinion, have offered Vulcan crews a much better chance of completing their missions when compared to their chances of survival on a national-only missions.

When taking part in a NATO strike against the WP in accordance with the SIOP, I always assumed that American ICBMs would have been targeted against high-value targets such as mobile and fixed Soviet ICBM sites, nuclear-bomber bases and centres of military and political power, most of which would be in Russia. Vulcans, I think, would have been best targeted against sub-strategic targets such as EW and GCI radar sites, SAM sites, command and control centres and hardened military fighter bases etc. The reason being that due to our previously mentioned proximity to the Soviet Union, our bombers would have probably arrived over the USSR some time before the majority of American airborne assets and it would have made some sense for them to be used to help supress the Soviet air-defence forces in order to ease the path for the B-52 and B-1 bombers that would follow soon after. NATO tactical air assets, such as those in Western Europe would, I think, have been focused on WP targets in Eastern Europe such as nearby airfields, concentrations of troops and armour, dispersed fuel and ammunition dumps and transport choke point such as bridges, tunnels, and railway junctions. At around that period, USAF B-52 crews had an improved chance of reaching their targets by firing ahead of their aircraft, multiple nuclear-tipped short-range attack missiles (SRAM) aimed at those Soviet airfields radar stations and air-defence centres located close to their intended routes. Vulcans did not have anything resembling a SRAM capability, but it was hoped that the effectiveness of Russian air-defence systems would have been significantly reduced by the earlier arrival of SLBM and perhaps some other ballistic missiles. Although I believe that the USSR would have come off worst in a nuclear clash with NATO, the point is somewhat academic, because the massive level of destruction and loss of lives on both sides would have rendered terms such as winners and losers completely without meaning.

# Discriminators

The nature and type of target allocated to each Vulcan would have been an important discriminator when considering whether or not its crew could have successfully completed its mission. It is said that the most dangerous part of any attack occurs within the last five miles or so to the target. This is particularly true of high-value military targets. It was there that short-range radar and visually directed SAMs and AAA systems were most likely to be concentrated. It is reasonable to expect, therefore, that a Vulcan, on its final run to an above-ground military target such as a bomber or fighter base would have been met with a fairly high concentration of defensive fire. On the other hand, a Vulcan tasked to attack a well-hidden underground HQ or some form of civilian military/industrial target would possibly be met with less resistance. Targets that cover large geographical areas are much more difficult to effectively defend against low-level attack. It stands to reason, therefore, that Vulcans tasked to bomb targets spread over a wide geographical area would have stood a better chance of surviving than those tasked against more concentrated high-value military installations.

Another discriminator would have been the geographical location of the target. It is reasonable to assume that a Vulcan, allocated a target just a few miles inside Russia would have stood a much better chance of reaching its target, delivering its weapon, and escaping, than one that first had to fight its way to and from its target across hundreds of miles of enemy territory.

The time of day that the strike was launched would have been a very significant discriminator. It was always accepted that the Vulcan would struggle to survive a daytime low-level penetration of Russia. Being a fairly large aircraft, it would have been relatively easy to detect if it ventured close to GCI and EW radar systems and, thanks to daylight, fairly easy to spot visually. Despite being able to fly at transonic speeds at high altitude, the Vulcan's speed when flying at low level was a rather modest 240 to 350kts. Furthermore, its large delta-shaped wing and rather low G limitations would have rendered the pilot's ability to employ very rapid high-energy avoidance manoeuvres at low level difficult, if not impossible, to accomplish. I think it is fair to say that, in daytime, Vulcans would have proved easy prey for the full gambit of WP fighters including the then modern Foxbats, Flagons and Floggers, all the way down to the old, but abundantly available, MiG-21s of that era. Even older combat types and some sub-sonic training machines armed only with cannon, could have unzipped a Vulcan from nose to tail with relative ease during a daytime attack. Soviet SAM and AAA systems, in addition to employing their radar to acquire and track the Vulcans, would have been able to make good use of direct-visual and electro-optical tracking options. Point defence SAMs and visually aimed AAA located in the vicinity of the target area would have had a field day too. In such a scenario, what means the Vulcan had to defend itself would have been of very limited value; chaff and flares offer absolutely zero defence against visually aimed cannon shells. Furthermore, what little jamming capability the Scampton Vulcan had would have been largely ineffective against the modern radar-guided air-defence threats in service at that time. Chaff could have had some beneficial effect against tracking radars and flares could have countered MANPAD IR-homing missiles assuming, of course, that the pilots saw the missiles coming; visual detection was the only way of knowing that an IR-homing MANPADS missile was on its way. Conducting a daytime attack in a Vulcan would definitely have been a rather gruesome undertaking. However, just like bombing operations during WWII, things looked a lot more doable when they were carried out at night, particularly during zero moon conditions.

Night-time was the Vulcan's friend, and it would have been an important discriminator when assessing if it could have survived its journey to the target. The risk posed by visually aimed threats would have been significantly reduced. Flying at low level, using the terrain for shielding and by making maximum use of TFR would have helped Vulcan crews remain below the majority of early warning and GCI-radar coverage. It would also have limited the acquisition coverage of many of the Soviet's radar and electro-optical-based weapon systems. In the event of being illuminated by a radar-controlled threat system, the AEO could have made careful and measured use of the Vulcan's abundant supply of chaff whilst recommending an appropriate turning manoeuvre to the captain. The threat from obsolescent fighters and non-radar-equipped training aircraft, would have been significantly reduced at night. Even modern radar-equipped fighters would have been reluctant to operate at low level at night, particularly over land. Some of the newer WP fighters of that era, such as the Foxbat and Flogger B, were credited with having a limited look-down-shoot-down capability. But the Soviet Union covers a large geographical area and these aircraft would have been spread out rather thinly. Even so, the threat they posed could possibly have been countered by the use of manoeuvre to help to defeat the fighter's limited semi-active fire-control system (see the Red Flag section in Chapter Seven). Short-range SAM and AAA systems, no longer having the luxury of daylight-visual aiming, would have had to rely totally upon their radar and night-vision systems to obtain a firing solution. In these circumstances, chaff and manoeuvre would have been a useful countermeasure. If confronted by visually aimed AAA during the final run to the target, the judicious and intermittent use of IR flares could, perhaps, have temporarily degraded the night vision of their operators. Flares could also have been used to seduce any IR-homing MANPADS missiles being launched against the Vulcan. However, as previously mentioned in an earlier chapter, the lack of MAWS equipment at that time meant that the AEO had no way of detecting the approach of such missiles. Nevertheless, in overall terms, the Vulcan stood a fighting chance of reaching its target at night.

All the advantages of mounting an attack at night would have been improved even further if the weather was poor. Not necessarily lashing with rain or snow, but with solid cloud cover reaching down to between 500 to 1,000 feet above ground level, complemented with moderately poor visibility. Such a combination of conditions, night-time and poor weather/visibility, would have significantly limited the effectiveness of visually aimed SAM and AAA systems as well as reducing, by a large margin, the capability of the Soviet air-defence fighters. There is little doubt that night-time and poor weather offered Vulcan crews the very best chance of surviving the flight to the target and mounting a successful attack.

Another potential discriminator was the serviceability of the aircraft allocated to each crew. It was not guaranteed that crews about to fly on a wartime mission would be allocated an aircraft that was fully serviceable. For every Vulcan there was a list of acceptable defects that crews would have to accept in time of war. Most were minor in nature, but some were faults that would not normally be accepted by a crew during peacetime, such as a faulty engine-driven alternator. This fault, on its own, would not pose a serious problem for the Vulcan as the aircraft had an abundance of electrical power that could easily be shared to keep all systems working. However, it would have eaten into the aircraft reserves such that in the event of losing another alternator, perhaps due to equipment failure or enemy action, things would have become much more serious and, depending upon the actions of the captain and AEO, could potentially have resulted in mission failure. Whilst ground crews would have done their utmost to provide every crew with a fully functioning aircraft, there would have been a limit to what could be achieved depending upon the warning time given prior to aircraft dispersal and the subsequent scramble. So it was almost guaranteed that one or more crews would find themselves being allocated an aircraft that was deficient in some way or other. You can perhaps imagine the gut-wrenching depression felt by the crew that was last in the queue for aircraft allocation. No one would want to be given the 'Hangar Queen' for their first, and probably only wartime mission.

Achieving a successful attack would have been determined, to some degree, by the crew's experience and aggressiveness. I am absolutely certain that if the balloon had gone up, all Vulcan crews would have carried out their missions to the best of their ability. There are, nevertheless, some fairly significant factors that separate one crew from another. In my short time flying on Vulcans, it was noticeable that some crews seemed to have to work a lot harder than others to achieve, and keep on achieving, good bombing results. I am not sure why, or what the magic sauce was, but one could feel it; it was tangible. This difference in performance also manifested itself during bombing competitions. A similar example of crew effectiveness could be seen during simple training exercises like high-level fighter affiliation. When the fighter pilot requested evasive manoeuvres, most AEOs and pilots would do their best to make life difficult for the fighter while some other crews seemed to be content to bumble along in a straight line, perhaps throwing in a gentle turn or two, and then allow the fighter to line up for an easy attack. This minimised the training value for both the fighter pilot and the bomber crew. During my time flying on Vulcans, and also Nimrods, I served on crews where each crew member instinctively knew what the others were thinking and acted without a word passing between them; they were performing on a higher plane, and somehow it brought forth results. But there were also crews that were not able to perform in this manner, or as our American friends would put it, "they couldn't get their act together". Interestingly, I also found that some of the most experienced crews seemed to be the least aggressive.

During WWII, some bomber crews worked well together, felt lucky, and somehow survived a tour, or at least an above-average number of sorties. This feeling of 'luck' was very important to those crews endowed with it and they would go to extraordinary lengths to keep it that way by jealously fending off any potential changes to their tightly knit crew. On the other hand, there were some crews that admitted to feeling dysfunctional and, for some reason, unlucky. They were convinced that their time would soon run out, and on many occasions, it did. What was 'luck' and what was it that seemed to make crews who 'had it' perform better and, dare I say it, feel invincible? At the end of the day, would a Vulcan crew's chance of surviving the flight to their target simply have boiled down to luck. Would Lady Luck have proven to be the ultimate discriminator?

# Red Shrimp's Contribution to Mission Success – or Otherwise

The retention and use of the Red Shrimp ECM system after around 1970 and during the period that the aircraft was assigned to the low-level strike role has always been a good subject for discussion. The Red Shrimp, as previously mentioned, was a barrage noise jammer that used a carcinotron microwave component to generate and transmit white noise across the D and E frequency bands. This was the region of the radio frequency (RF) spectrum where a number of Soviet early warning and GCI radars operated. It also covered the frequency bands of some radars associated with obsolescent, and no longer widely used, AAA systems and the early versions of SA-2 Guideline SAM systems. However, most Soviet AI radars and the acquisition and tracking radars associated with the more modern Soviet SAM and AAA systems of that period operated at frequencies well outside the coverage of Red Shrimp. To counter these systems, Scampton Vulcan crews could rely only on chaff, terrain concealment and manoeuvre.

The electronic technologies available when Red Shrimp was designed and built resulted in a very large portion of the electrical power allocated to the jammer ending up, not as RF-jamming power, but as unwanted heat. In fact, so much heat was generated by Red Shrimp that a VCCP had to be installed in an effort to keep the system cool. Furthermore, the amount of RF-jamming energy that was eventually transmitted was spread over such a wide frequency spectrum that the portion of jamming power actually captured by individual radar systems, working within their own narrow band of frequencies, was quite low. So much so, that the net effect of using the Red Shrimp jammer while at moderate or long range from the Soviet Union was to produce a fairly weak and narrow strobe line of interference on the ground radar operator's plan position indicator (PPI) display, and this line of interference pointed straight towards the Vulcan that was attempting the jamming. So instead of offering protection to the Vulcan, switching on the Red Shrimp simply highlighted the Vulcan's presence to Soviet radar controllers. To effectively jam a single GCI radar, it would have been better if all of the jamming power could have been concentrated at the frequency

Left: Red Shrimp transmitters.
Below: Red Shrimp control unit. (H. Heeley, Newark Air Museum)

or frequencies used by that particular radar. However, given that most radars of that era could switch operating frequencies, and that a large number of different D and E-Band early warning and GCI radars were operated by the Soviet Union at that time, such an individually tailored approach was deemed not to be practical.

Radar aerials/dishes/scanners call them what you will, are generally designed to beam the RF energy generated by a radar transmitter in one direction only – this is called the radar's main beam or main lobe. Likewise, most of the reflected radar energy collected by the aerial is via the main lobe. In conventional early warning and GCI radars, this directional aerial system is continuously rotated through 360 degrees to provide an all-round, periodic search or illumination of the area under surveillance. However, due to design and construction constrains, aerials tend to have, in addition to the main lobe, multiple minor lobes that project out to the side and even behind the radar's intended direction of stare. So, while the majority of a radar's transmitted power is focused in the direction of the main lobe, small amounts of transmitted power can 'leak' out via the side and back lobes. Likewise, while the majority of RF energy that is reflected back to the radar from mountains, clouds and aircraft enter the receiver via the aerial's main lobe, some small amounts of energy reflected back from nearby objects can also gain entry to the radar receiver via the aerial's side and back lobes. This unwanted interference is usually quite easily seen as dense clutter close to and around the centre of the radar system's PPI display. Designers of radar aerials make great efforts to minimise these secondary lobes, but they can't eradicate them entirely. For a noise-jamming system to be really effective, it has to be able to transmit enough power to not only enter the radar receiver via the main lobe, but also gain access to the radar's receiver via its much less sensitive side and back lobes, thus causing interference across the whole, or at least a very large segment, of the radar operator's display. Red Shrimp would only have been able to achieve this level of interference when it was very close to the target radar. For Vulcans operating at distance from search radars, jamming power entering receivers of the target radar systems would only have been detected via the radar's highly sensitive main lobe and this, as previously mentioned, would have manifested itself on the Soviet GCI display as a noise strobe pointing directly at the Vulcan doing the jamming – not a healthy situation. For this reason, in the early days when the Vulcan (and the Victor which also used Red Shrimp) flew a hi-hi-hi flight profile, the thinking was that the V Bombers would be approaching the Soviet Union at approximately the same time and they would be spread out across a fairly wide front. If they all switched their Red Shrimp jammers on at approximately the same time, or when crossing a pre-determined line of longitude, and then left them on, the early warning and GCI radars would be subjected to noise jamming coming from many different directions simultaneously resulting in multiple interference spokes being displayed on their

Red Shrimp aerials under the Vulcan's starboard wing.

screens. This jamming would become more effective as the bombers got closer to the radar systems due to the jamming power starting to penetrate into the radar's side and back lobes. This mutual support jamming method was a reasonable proposition when the V Bombers operated at high altitude. But when the bombers were consigned to the low-level strike role due to the widespread deployment of SA-2 missile systems throughout the USSR, this tactic was no longer valid and the efficacy and relevance of the Red Shrimp jammer was very much diminished.

Due to the curvature of the earth, the distance that early warning and GCI radars can 'see' an attacking aircraft is significantly reduced when the aircraft is flying at low level. Likewise, the distance from which a jammer can seriously interfere with a radar is limited for the same reason. When operating at low level, noise jamming is only useful when the aircraft is operating very close to the target radar and when the jamming power is sufficient to swamp the radar receiver. Red Shrimp could possibly have achieved this if its aerial system had been optimised for use at low level. As things stood, the Vulcan's Red Shrimp aerials were attached to the underside of the Vulcan's starboard wing root resulting in a radiation pattern rather like an inverted cone fanning down below the aircraft. This was considered to be reasonable when the Vulcan was jamming from high level as most of the jamming power would be radiated downwards and outwards towards the target radar systems. But it was of very little use when the Vulcan was operating at low level as most of the jamming power was tightly contained within the very short distance between the Vulcan and the terrain below, and almost none of it was transmitted forward and sideways from the aircraft where it stood a chance of being effective against some of the older threat radars. For Red Shrimp to retain some minimal usefulness at low level, it would have needed a new, designed-for-purpose, aerial system. But even then, the amount of protection it would have offered would have been very low as most of the serious threat systems operated well outside the frequency coverage of the jammer. Therefore, given the limitations of the Red Shrimp jammer/aerial combination and taking in to account the height the Vulcan was being flown, the nature of the surrounding terrain, and distance between the Vulcan and the radar to be jammed, switching on the Red Shrimp would, in all likelihood, have had no serious effect whatsoever on enemy early warning, GCI and missile acquisition radar systems. But worse than having no effect, if by chance a small amount of Red Shrimp jamming power was detected by a radar's main lobe as it swept across the Vulcan's position, it would have, as previously mentioned, resulted in a weak noise strobe showing on the GCI radar screen, and that strobe would have been pointing directly towards the Vulcan. This would be rather like the Vulcan crew waving their hands and shouting, "look we're over here" to the radar controller. Again, not a good idea. So, in my opinion, the use of the Red Shrimp during the Vulcan's ingress to and egress from a target was likely to be detrimental, rather than helpful to the survival of the aircraft. In my opinion, the best thing a Vulcan crew could do when penetrating towards the Soviet Union at low level was to leave the Red Shrimp switched off, fly as low as they could, use terrain to best advantage, and fly as fast as possible within the constraints imposed by aircraft limitations and the mandatory route timings imposed by the strike plan. With hindsight, it seems unbelievable that Vulcans were required to haul this heavy, obsolete and mostly useless ECM system, plus its associated VCCP, all over the world after the mid-1970s. If the 'thinkers' in Ministry of Defence (MoD) could not bring themselves to install a suitable aerial array to allow the system to offer some useful jamming capability, or better still, replace Red Shrimp with an entirely new jamming system then, at the very least, they could have stripped the system out of the Vulcan altogether. This would have significantly reduced the aircraft's weight. It would also have saved a lot of needless spending on Red Shrimp maintenance and support.

As mentioned earlier in the book, an oddity of the Vulcan Force, was that the aircraft based at Waddington had an I-Band jammer fitted in addition to Red Shrimp. Scampton-based Vulcans had to do without. This was possibly because at the time Scampton Vulcans carried the Blue Steel stand-off missile and therefore had less need to fly the last and most dangerous five miles to the target. But there may have been other reasons. Perhaps there were some physical/structural/safety constraints imposed when the Vulcan was carrying the Blue Steel missile that prevented the Scampton-based Vulcans from being fitted with an I-Band jammer. If this is the case, it does beg the question why, having given up the Blue Steel missile and changed to the lay-down WE.177 bombing option in 1969–70, the Scampton Vulcans were not then fitted with the I-Band jammer. As it is, I have no idea how useful or useless the I-Band jammer

Blue Steel missile at Newark Air Museum.

on the Waddington Vulcans was and whether it would have made much difference to the Vulcan's ability to survive its flight to the target.

Another curiosity regarding the Vulcan was that, in the event of war, it was likely to spend more time over hostile territory than any other RAF strike/attack aircraft of that era, such as the Buccaneer and Jaguar. Yet while senior officers in MoD thought it was vital to equip the Buccaneer and Jaguar with the, then modern, AN/ALQ-101 deception jamming pods, it chose not to consider something similar for the Vulcan. A modern deception jammer, with a similar capability to that of the AN/ALQ-101 would have been a great addition to the Vulcan's EW suite. But it was not to be. It would seem that having been relieved of its nuclear deterrent role in 1969, the Vulcan was no longer deemed worthy of further investment, even if it meant offering enhanced protection to the crew and improving the chance of mission success. Thank you, MoD!

## Post-Strike Action

The next most popular question I was asked was what was a Vulcan crew supposed to do after it had delivered its weapon? The answer, as I am sure you can imagine, was to exit the scene as fast as possible. Despite the short delay built into the WE.177 trigger mechanism to give the Vulcans time to vacate the target area before the explosion took place, the supersonic shock wave from the explosion would almost certainly have caught up with the Vulcan. This could possibly have inflicted some damage to rear of the aircraft, in particular to its fragile flying control surfaces. However, with luck (that word again!) it would be minor in nature and still leave the Vulcan able to proceed to its post-strike recovery airfield. Some surviving Vulcans were expected to return to the UK, others were expected to land elsewhere. Those that were ordered to return to the UK would have attempted to make radio contact with surviving ATC agencies in order to receive routeing instructions towards a suitable airfield. One must assume that most if not all of the UK's air-defence radar systems would have been damaged or destroyed by the time the surviving Vulcans came limping home, therefore special procedures would have/might have been in place to allow returning Vulcans to make their way safely through surviving UK fighter defences. Furthermore, lacking target direction from the EW/GCI radar sites, Bloodhound SAM batteries positioned in and around the east of England at that time, would have had to operate in 'autonomous mode' when the surviving Vulcans returned. This would have posed a problem for the Vulcan crews because the Bloodhound SAM system did not have an integrated IFF interrogation capability and could not, therefore, positively identify aircraft approaching the UK as being a friend or a foe. Therefore, to avoid the possibility of being shot down by a Bloodhound missile, returning crews were advised to follow a cunning pre-briefed flight procedure that, we were told, would be 'instantly recognisable' by the Bloodhound operators. Good luck with that!

# CHAPTER NINE
# OPERATION BLACK BUCK

One cannot avoid the irony, that having spent such a vast amount of national wealth developing the Avro Vulcan, first as a high-level bomber and later as a low-level bomber, optimised in both cases to deliver nuclear weapons against the Soviet Union, when it was eventually used in anger by the UK, it was to deliver conventional 1,000-lb bombs and Shrike ARMs from medium altitude onto the small airfield at Port Stanley in the Falkland Islands.

I was employed in the Vulcan Office in HQ 1 Group at RAF Bawtry in 1982 when Argentina invaded the Falkland Islands and I soon became aware that a small team of Vulcan and Victor specialist officers were working on secret plans that I guessed were associated with the recovery of the islands – Operation Corporate. However, I neither asked for nor received any information regarding their activities; the need-to-know principle was watertight. It was only much later that I found out that the team had been planning Operation Black Buck, a series of Vulcan attacks against Port Stanley airfield. Like most other people, I obtained my information about the attacks from the national press, television news bulletins and later, from reports, articles and books published long after the conflict was over. Today, most people are aware of the geopolitical events leading up to and following the Argentinian capture of the Falkland Islands, and why the decision was made to mount Vulcan bomber attacks on Port Stanley airfield. But for those that missed out on all of this, I will briefly describe the run of events as I saw them at the time. I will also discuss some points of contention raised by military and civilian commentators on the wisdom of mounting the operation, the efficacy of the attacks, and their contribution to Britain's re-possession of the Falkland Islands.

Argentinians have always claimed that the Falkland Islands, or *Islas Malvinas* as they prefer to call them, rightfully belong to them and they reject the UK's claim of sovereignty over the archipelago. In early 1982, a series of minor, and seemingly disparate geopolitical events took place within the Argentinian mainland and, to a lesser, but nevertheless important extent, at South Georgia Island – one of many islands forming the British overseas territory of the Sandwich Islands located 800 miles south-east of the Falklands. These events were deliberately exaggerated and hyped up by Argentinian nationalists who called for the Falkland and Sandwich Islands to be handed back to Argentinian ownership. The UK government rejected the claims. Things came to a head on 2 April 1982 when Argentinian forces, operating under Operation Rosario, invaded and occupied the Falkland Islands. The British prime minister, Margaret Thatcher, was taken aback by this hostile move, and furious at being caught unawares, ordered her ministers and military leaders to develop a plan to recover the islands. The plan, when it was announced, was called Operation Corporate. It involved sending a RN aircraft carrier Task Force, along with requisitioned commercial shipping, able or modified to carry the bulk of UK ground forces and their equipment, 8,000 miles south across the Atlantic Ocean to re-claim the islands. With few other options to choose from, Ascension Island, which lies some 3,000 miles north of the Falkland Islands, was chosen to be the forward operating base (FOB) for the operation.

Although Operation Corporate was primarily considered to be a naval and army operation, RAF commanders were determined to get involved. RAF Air Support Command helped to move large volumes of personnel and equipment from the UK to the FOB. Harrier GR3s from 1 Squadron were embarked on the civilian cargo ships, *Atlantic Conveyor* and *Atlantic Causeway*, for transportation to a point close to the Falklands, at which the plan was to transfer them to the RN aircraft carrier, HMS *Hermes*, in preparation for ground-attack operations. RAF Chinook helicopters were also embarked on the cargo ships. RN Sea Harrier FRS1s flying from both HMS *Ark Royal* and HMS *Hermes*, plus a number of RN warships optimised for the air-defence role, were tasked to provide air cover for the Task Force during its transit south to the Falklands via Ascension Island. Once in the vicinity of the Falklands, their responsibility was widened to providing air cover for UK land forces put ashore to retake the islands.

As the Task Force sailed south, the Task Force commander, Admiral Sir John 'Sandy' Woodward, became increasingly concerned that the small airfield at Port Stanley on the Falklands could be used by Argentinian fighter-bombers, and that they could pose a significant threat to his ships as they drew closer to the area of operations. It was also clear that there was nothing of any consequence that the RN and army could do to dispel his concerns. RAF commanders, having focused their attention on the problem, considered a range of bombing options that could, perhaps, render Port Stanley airfield unusable. After much discussion and head scratching a plan was hatched that involved using the only aircraft that, with sufficient AAR support, could deliver the required weight of bombs onto Port Stanley airfield, the soon-to-be-retired, Vulcan B2. Operation Black Buck was born.

Early Black Buck sorties were runway denial missions. Each attack required a single Vulcan B2 armed with 21 x 1,000-lb high explosive bombs to carry out a night-time H2S/NBS attack on the airfield from medium altitude on a heading that was offset by 35 degrees from the runway centre line. Statistical analysis during the planning stage showed that, taking everything into account, this attack profile offered the best, albeit still only moderate, chance of getting at least one bomb onto the runway. Also, remaining at medium altitude would keep the Vulcan outside the accurate engagement zones of Argentinian Roland SAM and Oerlikon Skyguard AAA systems. In addition, dropping the bombs from medium level would allow them to accelerate to near supersonic speed, thus imparting maximum kinetic energy onto the runway and the airfield's surrounding equipment and infrastructure. Although the chosen attack profile offered the best, but still only moderate, chance of detonating a bomb on the Port Stanley runway, practical experience gained by crews over many years of conducting radar offset bombing suggested that, in reality, there was a distinct possibility that none of the bombs would hit their target.

The distance involved, plus the fact that the Vulcan would be heavily laden with bombs on its outwards journey, meant that the amount of AAR support required from the fleet of Victor K2 tanker aircraft would be much greater than anything that had previously been attempted. It ultimately required 11 Victor tankers plus a few reserves to support one Black Buck Vulcan. This, on its own, significantly increased the risk of mission failure. Furthermore, decisions made much earlier in the Vulcan's service, to remove or disable the aircraft's conventional bombing and in-flight refuelling capabilities, had to be reversed and the crews re-trained to perform these tasks. Upgrades deemed to be essential for mission success included the fitting of a Delco Carousel INS to allow the navigators to more accurately guide the aircraft over the long distances to be flown, and an AN/ALQ-101 ECM deception jamming pod to help protect the Vulcan from the Roland and Skyguard air-defence systems that were dotted around the vicinity of the airfield. Despite this intense preparation, some senior members in the government and in the MoD thought the attack plan was too complicated and risked failure. They were also afraid that if a Vulcan was lost, it would provide Argentina with a public relations coup. There was further concern that, even with the best possible bombing results, the anticipated weapons effect would be too limited to warrant the massive effort required to mount the attacks. However, the doubters were overruled and the order was given to proceed. The Task Force headed south and the Black Buck bombing missions were flown. Troops were eventually put ashore and, and after some fierce fighting, the Falkland Islands were retaken.

Of the three Black Buck Vulcans tasked to bomb the runway at Port Stanley, only Black Buck 1, flown by the reserve crew on 30 April, managed to get one of its 21 bombs onto the runway, with a second bomb landing close to the runway's edge. The remaining 19 bombs landed elsewhere causing some minor and secondary damage to nearby buildings and parked aircraft. Despite this being the best result that could possibly be expected from a single attack, its effect on Argentinian aircraft operations was minimal and after a pause of around 36 hours Argentinian C-130s, I-58 Pucará, and possibly some Aermacchi MB-339 light-trainer/ground-attack aircraft were observed using the airfield. Three days later, Black Buck 2, flying slightly higher at 18,000 feet, carried out another runway denial attack, but all of its bombs missed the runway. However, perhaps by chance, some of the bombs did land on an area of open ground at the end of the runway which, if the Argentinians had got their act together soon after taking control of the islands, could have been used to extend the runway and render it more suitable for fast-attack aircraft such as the A-4 Skyhawk and Dassault Étendard. However, the enemy clearly lacked the intention and/or the foresight to do so. Black Buck 3, which was scheduled to fly later in the month, was cancelled due to bad weather. To the surprise of many, this marked the end of the runway denial operations against Port Stanley airfield. But what shocked commentators even more was the claim that the single crater inflicted on the runway by Black Buck 1 was sufficient to rule out the airfield being used by Argentinian A-4 Skyhawks. The runway, prior to Black Buck 1, was already deemed generally unsuitable for use by fuelled and weaponised Argentinian Dagger and Étendard aircraft. Ex-military critics took very little time to remind everyone that during the Cold War, it was always assumed that our fast jets based in Germany would have to operate from damaged runways. They would do this by marking off the damaged parts of the runway to make it clear to pilots which parts were to be avoided, and/or by using perimeter taxiways as runways, and/or by executing fast and effective repairs. Knowing this, some ex-RAF's fast-jet operators and runway repair specialists must have sucked hard on their teeth at the claim that one bomb crater on a runway was sufficient to render the Port Stanley runway completely unusable for fighter-bomber operations. Furthermore, and for reasons that escape me, the RAF's claim of mission success seemed to raise the hackles of some members of the RN. They protested that the RAF's claim of mission success was nothing more than hyperbole, and that the attack actually amounted to an extravagant air-power demonstration designed to beam sunshine on the RAF while contributing nothing of substance to the re-taking of the Falkland Islands. Those of us outside the 'inner circle of all knowledge' could only speculate as to whether that single bomb crater would have prevented the airfield being used for fast-jet operations should the Argentinians have decided to do so. Some say it would have, others say it wouldn't. All I can say for certain is that it did not prevent the airfield being used by Argentinian C-130 and Pucará light-attack aircraft.

Black Buck 4, 5 and 6 were suppression of enemy air defence (SEAD) missions carried out by Vulcans armed with AGM-45 Shrike ARMs. The Task Force commander was particularly keen to see the AN/TPS-43, long-range surveillance radar located at Port Stanley airfield, disabled or destroyed. He was concerned that Argentinian radar operators, in addition to warning their commanders of imminent Harrier attacks, would also be able to establish the location of the Task Force by monitoring and analysing the flight paths of the Harriers as they flew to and from the Task Force carriers. Unfortunately, Black Buck 4 which flew on 28 May was unable to complete its mission due to a technical problem with one of the Victor tankers. However, three days later, Black Buck 5 managed to fire two Shrike missiles at the AN/TPS-43 radar. One of the missiles landed close enough to the radar to inflict some minor damage which, I am told, temporarily degraded the performance of the radar by some small measure, but not enough to negate the risk that the radar posed. The second missile missed the radar completely. On 3 June, Black Buck 6 was unable to launch any of its Shrikes against the AN/TPS-43 because the radar was switched off during the period that the Vulcan was in the vicinity, thus denying the missiles a signal source to home on to. However, the Vulcan AEO did manage to fire two Shrike ARMs at a Skyguard AAA radar resulting in its destruction and the death of some of its operators. During the execution of a scheduled AAR event on this Vulcan's return journey to Ascension Island, the aircraft's refuelling probe snapped. This prevented the aircraft from taking on the extra fuel needed to reach the FOB. Being left with no other choice other than ditching his aircraft into the sea, the captain decided to divert his aircraft to Rio de Janeiro Airport in Brazil. Like the runway denial operation, the radar denial operation ended before the task was comprehensively accomplished.

On the 12th of June, Black Buck 7 was ordered to carry out an anti-personnel bombing attack against Argentinian troops tented around Port Stanley airfield. Unfortunately, all of the bombs dropped by this mission landed wide of the intended target area. But even if the bombs had landed on their intended target, they would not have caused the anti-personnel effects required because the bombs' fuses had been set incorrectly. This mission ended Vulcan operations in support of Operation Corporate.

To summarise, in very stark terms, the runway denial missions failed to prevent the Argentinian light-attack aircraft from continuing to use Port Stanley airfield. Whether it would have prevented the airfield being used by A-4 Skyhawks, if the Argentinians had chosen to do so, is still an unanswered question. The three SEAD missions too were only partially successful causing the destruction of one Skyguard AAA system and some minor damage to the AN/TPS-43 radar – the primary target. Finally, the mission to bomb Argentinian troops concentrations around Port Stanley airfield failed. This set of results must have been quite disappointing to those that sanctioned the missions. Senior officers from the three services working within and outside of the MoD asked why so little was achieved by the Vulcan raids, particularly given the vast effort and resources spent mounting the operations. They wanted to know why senior RAF officers decided to take on the airfield denial task when they must have known that such operations were devilishly difficult to carry out at the best of times, let alone at a distance of around 3,000 miles from the FOB and without the benefit of laser-guided bombs or purpose-built runway denial weapons. Mission planners must also have known that given the small number of planned airfield denial sorties, and with each sortie capable, at best, of placing only one bomb on the runway, the damage inflicted would, in all probability, be insufficient to render the runway unusable for long. This, in fact, proved to be the case and the airfield continued to be used by Argentinian aircraft throughout most of the Black Buck period.

Some have questioned the wisdom of bombing from medium altitude when Vulcan crews were well-rehearsed in the tactic of bombing from low level. Whilst conceding that bombs dropped from medium level imparted higher destructive power than those dropped from low level, the potential effect of this was significantly diluted by the statistical analysis that showed that getting just one or two bombs on to the runway per sortie was likely to be the very best result that could be achieved. Doubters argued that, at least for the first raid, conducting a low-level attack with pilots using night-vision goggles to allow visual aiming, and flying a track slightly offset from the runway centre line offered a substantially better chance of getting more bombs onto the runway. This, despite each bomb having lower kinetic energy at impact, plus the possibility that some bombs could 'skip' off the runway due to their shallow grazing angle at impact. They argued that the cumulative effect of getting multiple bombs onto the runway would have spread the damage across a much larger area and caused more disruption to airfield operation than one high-velocity bomb dropped from medium level. They did concede, however, that flying such an attack profile would have placed the Vulcan well inside the engagement zones of the highly effective Roland SAMs and Skyguard AAA systems. There was also some criticism about the low tempo of the runway denial operations. Some insist that the bombing sorties should have been flown with sufficient frequency to dash any hope the Argentinians may have had of conducting runway repairs (assuming that such repairs were ever intended or even possible). They further claim that if RAF commanders knew that the required high tempo of operations was not going to be possible, then this should have been taken into account before ordering the missions to proceed.

There were, also, some who harboured serious doubts about the perceived risk to the Task Force from Argentinian fast-attack jets flying from Port Stanley. Naysayers claim that the airport was never ideally, or even marginally, suitable for weaponised fast-jet operations due to the short length of its runway, its low load-bearing properties and the poor condition of the airfield in general. Although there is some evidence to show that such thoughts did cross the minds of the Argentinian leaders, the serious work required to turn the idea into reality never took place. The doubters also claim, this time with some compelling logic, that if the Argentinians had intended to base fast jets at Port Stanley, they would have started preparations to do so immediately after taking over the island, or at least as soon as they knew that a UK Task Force was on its way. The fact that the Argentinians chose not to do so, suggests that the Task

Force commander's concerns were unfounded. Furthermore, they claim that even if the Argentinians had decided at the last minute to operate some A-4 Skyhawk fighter bombers from Port Stanley, it is unlikely that the single bomb dropped by Black Buck 1 would have prevented them from doing so.

Finally, air-power aficionados, both military and civilian, claim that Black Buck flew in the face of three important tenets of warfare; it failed to provide sufficient concentration of force, it failed to maintain the aim (or in this case aims), and it paid scant regard to economy of effort. They claim that three runway denial sorties spread over two weeks was never going to provide sufficient concentration of force to shut down Argentinian air operations at Port Stanley. In addition, they question why, after only three planned runway denial missions, there was a mysterious loss of interest in doing further damage to the runway. Some have suggested that this was to preserve the runway for use by UK F-4 Phantom aircraft that would arrive after the islands were re-taken. I must confess, this explanation sounds rather contrived to me. Nevertheless, the runway denial operation was halted and the focus of effort was turned towards disabling or destroying the AN/TPS-43 radar. But before this task could be accomplished, the focus of the raids changed yet again, when Black Buck 7 was tasked to bomb Argentinian troops and their equipment located around Port Stanley airfield. After just one failed attempt, this last objective, too, was dropped. So there does seem to be some validity in the accusation that the concentration of force and maintenance of the primary aim, and the other aims, was inadequate thus allowing the runway to remain in 'limited' service, the AN/TPS-43 to remain working albeit possibly in a degraded fashion, and the troops around Port Stanley to enjoy threat-free, peace and quiet around their campsite at night. As for economy of effort, detractors insist that the massive, and almost all-consuming, effort required to mount Black Buck was out of all proportion to what was, or could be, achieved in military terms. They claim that the missions were contrived and launched on a 'wing and a prayer' and that the operation was heading for failure even before it started. Some have gone so far as to suggest that RAF commanders allowed their enthusiasm, excitement and determination to mount the raids, override their better military judgement about what could realistically be achieved. If, as the sceptics claim, the result achieved by Black Buck were of minimal operational importance, and if, in the final analysis, the raids amounted to nothing more than an over-hyped, long-range, air-power demonstration, then the naysayers may have a point and perhaps the operation should never have been sanctioned.

My take on events is somewhat different to that of the sceptics. The RN and the army were powerless to do anything to assuage the Task Force commander's concerns that Port Stanley airfield could possibly be used by the Argentinians to mount fighter-bomber attacks on his ships. RAF senior officers who were already searching for ways to provide further assistance to Operation Corporate, decided to take up the challenge and set about planning the airfield-denial attack against the airfield. This was the right thing to do. Did those critical of Black Buck really expect the RAF to sit back and adopt a nonchalant attitude? Furthermore, would senior RAF officers have been content to watch their soon-to-be-retired Vulcans gather rust at Waddington if there was the slightest chance that they could be used to disable the runway at Port Stanley? I suggest not. As it was, senior RAF officers got together and devised a plan that, although admittedly tenuous, had the potential to render the airfield unusable, at least for Argentinian fighter-bombers. Having crunched the figures and mulled over the options, they were fully aware that mounting a successful airfield denial operation at Port Stanley would be an extremely difficult undertaking. They were also aware that the AAR effort required from the Victor Tanker Force was going to be massive and not without significant risk. Nevertheless, they concluded that, despite all the negative influences, the task was doable. Although Operation Black Buck would stretch the capability of the UK's Vulcan and Victor aircraft and their crews to their limit, it was decided to proceed. I think this was the correct decision. Furthermore, I am certain that the British public would have expected nothing less.

Regarding the argument that Port Stanley airfield could not possibly have been used to launch fighter-bomber operations against the Task Force, I have yet to see the evidence to support such a claim. It is true that the airfield was not in tip-top condition and its short runway length, poor load-bearing surface and limited manoeuvring area would almost certainly have made its use by fuelled and weaponised Mirage, Dagger and perhaps Dassault Étendard aircraft risky, if not downright impossible. However, we can't be similarly sure when it comes to the A-4 Skyhawk. There is well-documented information that pays tribute to the versatility of this aircraft and its ability to operate from austere runways. However, if an early decision had been made by the Argentinians not to mount Skyhawk operations from Port Stanley, then this only became clear when the Task Force arrived in the area and the Harriers had established air-defence patrols over the islands. As it was, there was no way that the Task Force commander could be absolutely certain that offensive anti-surface warfare operation would not be mounted from the airfield as his ships closed towards the islands. Also, his concerns were aggravated by a lack of up-to-date high-definition reconnaissance photographs of the islands, thus preventing him from seeing what the invading forces were getting up to. A heroic effort to provide this capability by 39 Squadron using their Canberra PR9 aircraft failed for reasons that were political rather than operational. Of course, once within range of the Falkland Islands, Harrier FRS1s from the Task Force would have been able to provide this much-needed reconnaissance service. However, by that time, the Task Force would have already been within range of Skyhawks had they been operating from Port Stanley. Some of the doubters have suggested that the UK must have had access to some high-definition and recent satellite imagery of the

Falklands, but I have not seen anything to verify this. The fundamental point is that the Task Force commander felt he was blind to events taking place at Port Stanley airfield and this was a source of great concern to him and his ship captains.

The claim that those responsible for planning Operation Black Buck failed to adhere to the principles and tenets of warfare is an interesting argument. In my view, the tenets of warfare are not meant to be a mandatory set of conditions that must be met in all circumstances. They are simply a set of ideals that should be considered prior to mounting any military action. So, whilst it could be argued that Black Buck planners should have thought more carefully about these ideals, it does not follow that the operation should not have been mounted. In warfare, as in other walks of life, it sometimes takes monumental effort to achieve minimal results. On other occasions, monumental results can be achieved through minimal effort. It just so happens that Black Buck fell into the first of these two categories.

Moving on, there is the issue of secondary effects. Many say that it has become almost par for the course that when military operations fail to achieve their primary effects, those responsible for planning and mounting them will attempt to justify their decisions by listing a series of advantageous secondary effects. For example, supporters of Black Buck claim that the airfield denial raid on Port Stanley was at least partially successful because it inflicted physical and psychological damage on the enemy. It cannot be denied that the sudden arrival of 21 1,000-lb bombs on and around Post Stanley in the middle of the night was certain to generate some rather acute anxiety amongst those sleeping nearby. Also, the raid must have caused some surprise, if not shock, within the ranks of Argentinian military commanders and politicians on the mainland. I am sure it made them wonder if they had bitten off rather more than they could chew. Nevertheless, while conceding that these secondary effects were beneficial to the UK, they had nothing to do with the primary aim, which was to render the airfield unfit for aircraft operations.

Another secondary effect often claimed is that Black Buck forced the Argentinian air force to move their Mirage III fighters to an airfield further north on the mainland to defend the country from possible Vulcan attacks. This, it is claimed, effectively removed the fighters from the Falklands area of operations, thus relinquishing air superiority to the British. Sceptics argue that this is questionable for two reasons. Firstly, they claim that a UK government official had already informed Argentina that the UK had no intention of bombing the Argentinian mainland and that this effectively removed the stated threat; although, knowing the Royal Air Force, I am sure that some effort was made to prepare a short list of targets just in case political sanction was given. Secondly, according to a very experienced RN Sea Harrier pilot, the Mirage III posed very little serious threat to our forces on and around the Falklands as the fighter was configured for air-to-air combat, not ground-attack operations. Further, it carried barely enough fuel to fly from Argentina to the Falklands and back, let alone indulge in fuel-guzzling dogfights with Harriers. He was also very convincing when he opined that even if the Mirage pilots had chosen to engage the Sea Harriers in low-level subsonic air combat, the British pilots would have run rings around them. The results of actual Harrier-versus-Mirage clashes over the Falklands tend to confirm this argument. While Mirage III fighters were, indeed, moved north, ostensibly to provide some protection against a perceived threat to the Argentinian mainland, one has to seriously doubt whether this had any measurable impact on air operations around the islands. So, once again, this secondary effect bore no relevance to the primary aim which was to render the runway at Port Stanley unusable.

Black Buck will surely be a valid subject for discussion in future military circles, just as it has been since the Falklands conflict took place. 'Evidence' offered up from individuals in the UK, Argentina and other places shows that opinions of the effectiveness of the raids remain divided. In some cases, the evidence has tended to bolster the efficacy of the raids, but on other occasions it has tended to downplay their usefulness. Whatever the truth of the matter, there can be no doubt that once the decision was made to execute the operation it was a case of 'all hands to the pumps' to make it happen. This, in my opinion, is exactly how it should be. When a country becomes engaged in conflict, it is the job of military commanders to decide what they can do to help achieve the outcome desired by their political leaders. This requires careful understanding of what political outcome is being sought and how to translate that into military aims. Furthermore, there has to be a nuanced understanding about what can and cannot be achieved with the military tools at hand, and what the cost of achieving it will be. Cost effectiveness and the adoption of realistic goals is not just jargon for the commercial sector, it applies to the military too, especially when lives are at stake. But if the choice is between winning the war or being cost effective, then winning the war tends to come up trumps every time.

There is still one interesting and overarching question that hangs over the Black Buck operation and it is as follows. If the principal aim of Black Buck was to prevent Argentinian aircraft from using Port Stanley airfield, either permanently or at least for a significant period, then it should have been obvious from the outset that such an outcome was probably not going to be achievable with the forces available, and RAF commanders should have said so. If, on the other hand, the aim was to temporarily disrupt air operations from Port Stanley's runway, even for just a couple of days, then the task was achievable, albeit at a very high cost in terms of assets, effort, and potentially, lives. In fact, it could be argued that this very limited outcome was partially achieved by Black Buck 1. The question that remains, therefore, is why some have claimed that it was sufficient to disrupt the runway at Port Stanley's airfield for just a small number of hours in order to declare Operation Black Buck a success. Was some special event scheduled to happen over that particular period? If not, then why was the attack, that arguably provided no lasting effect and had very limited impact on Argentinian air operations, deemed to be so successful?

I have a strong feeling that there is a lot more to be told about the operational and technological efforts that went on behind the scenes during the lead-up and execution of Black Buck in an effort to bolster the effectiveness of the raids. I am also sure that there is more to know about the political constraints that were placed upon those charged with organising and executing the operation. Perhaps details of this will emerge in book form at some later date. My current feeling is that while Operation Black Buck did not have pivotal relevance to the outcome of the Falklands conflict, it certainly pushed hard in the right direction. For some, the criterion for declaring mission accomplished may not have been met, but there can be no doubt that the efforts made in trying to succeed were wholehearted, magnificent, and in keeping with the proud tradition of the RAF. British people invest a great deal of their taxes to provide the tools needed by our armed forces to defend their country and its overseas interests. So when a call to action comes, our military leaders should not hesitate to answer it by using all of the human and material assets available to them to bring about victory. Failure to do so would rightly cause the British people to question the determination of the military leadership. Some may even be moved to ask why we should bother having armed forces at all.

What is beyond question, is that the ruggedness, adaptability and reliability of the Vulcan B2 proved its worth when the call to action came. Furthermore, the skill, determination and grit of its aircrews, and the dedication, professionalism, and can-do spirit of all the RAF officers, airmen and airwomen, and civilian personnel who helped make the endeavour possible, must be applauded. This, of course, includes the inventiveness and courage of those 'noble-enablers' in the Victor Tanker Force without whom the whole operation could not have taken place. Their wholehearted performance was superb throughout. As a humble ex-Vulcan AEO, I hold all of those who took part in the preparation and execution of the Black Buck raids in the highest possible regard. Indeed, I am envious that I never got the chance to take part myself. Black Buck air and ground crews were given their orders and they carried them out to the very best of their ability. No one can ask for more.

# CHAPTER TEN
# ROUND-UP

My last flight as an AEO in a Vulcan took place on 30 April 1981. During this period the Vulcan B2 was in the process of being withdrawn from service. The Black Buck operation carried out a short while later in 1982 was perhaps a fitting and well-deserved swansong for this iconic and long-serving bomber. A small number of Vulcans were retained in service and converted to single-point AAR tankers in 1982–83, but their service in this role was short-lived and within less than a year, they were withdrawn from use, thus marking the end of the Vulcan's operational service.

As you would expect, individual squadrons held their own disbandment parties and the crews were soon informed of where they would be expected to serve next. Some pilots and navigators moved across to Tornado squadrons, some to VC10s, and some to flying training air and ground roles. Others decided to call it a day and left the RAF. A similar dispersion took place for the AEOs, with some going to the Nimrod MPA, and others adopting air and ground duties appropriate to their specialisation. Also, like some pilots and navigators, some decided to retire from the RAF. Ground personnel, too, were moved to take up new duties at other stations, but again, some just decided to end their service in the RAF. It really was the end of an era.

Most of the Vulcans were broken up for scrap, but some were saved and dispersed to aircraft museums dotted around the UK and overseas in America. One Vulcan B2, XH558, was purchased by David Walton, the owner of Bruntingthorpe airfield. Assisted by a small group of civilian enthusiasts and ex-military volunteers he was able to show the aircraft at Bruntingthorpe's 'Big Thunder' open days. Typically, the Vulcan crew would perform the initial part of the take-off run by accelerating noisily down the runway until it reached the halfway point when the throttles would be closed and the brake parachute streamed. This power and noise demonstration was really appreciated by the crowds. But the true intention of the owner was much more ambitious – he wanted the Vulcan to fly! It soon became clear that this would demand a massive injection of money and voluntary labour. It was at this point that Dr Robert Pleming, technical director of Cisco Systems became involved and, thanks to his wide range of contacts and those of Davis Walton plus a host of – too many to mention – expert and non-expert volunteers, the aircraft was restored to flying condition – with some imitations. As a result, the Vulcan with its team of volunteer air and ground crews were able to perform at many air displays around the UK from 2008 until it was finally retired from flying in 2015. Vulcan B2 XH558 now resides as a static display aircraft in the visitor centre at Doncaster Airport.

# Follow-On Medium and Long-Range Strike Capability

I sometimes wonder if the retirement of the Vulcan was a mistake. Like the similarly aged B-52s of the USAF, the Tu-95 'Bear' of the Russian air force and modified Tu-16 'Badger' aircraft (Xian H-6) flown by the Chinese, two or three squadrons of re-built, updated and cruise missile-armed Vulcans could have provided the UK with a medium to long range, deep strike capability at moderate cost. Like the B-52, updated Vulcans could have been armed with a range of conventional and/or nuclear-armed AGM-86 air-launched cruise missiles (ALCM), and when they became available, other stand-off cruise missiles such as Storm Shadow. Instead of having to penetrate enemy airspace at low level to deliver a single WE.177 bomb, the re-modelled Vulcan armed with the AGM-86 would have been able to remain at high level, well outside an enemy's air-defence envelope, and launch attacks on targets located up to 1,500 miles from the missile launch point, thus in effect, offering a combined Vulcan-plus-AGM-86, unrefuelled radius of action of around to 3,000 miles. I am not sure how many ALCMs the Vulcan could have carried, but I would hazard a guess at four – one on each Skybolt pylon and two carried internally in the bomb bay, thus providing the UK with at least four strike options per Vulcan – a bargain in anyone's eyes! As things turned out, the RAF's medium-range strike capability was relinquished leaving the RN's single on-station SSBN armed with nuclear-tipped SLBMs (a weapon of last resort?) to fulfil the UK's long- and medium-range nuclear strike role on its own. This, in my view, was a mistake.

It is far from clear that the patrol areas currently used by our on-station SSBN to allow it to conduct a rapid nuclear response against Russia are also ideal to allow it to mount a rapid nuclear response against China. With both Russia and China posing, or soon to pose, simultaneous existential threats to the UK and its allies, it is possible that additional SSBNs will have to be procured to cover the simultaneous threats posed by both countries. By scrapping the Vulcans instead of re-building, re-equipping, and re-rolling them, the UK gave up a relatively low-cost, rapidly deployable and flexible capability able to conduct conventional and nuclear strike missions anywhere in the world at very short notice.

When the Vulcan was retired from service, its place was taken by the Tornado GR1, an aircraft that had a much smaller weapon-carrying capability and an un-refuelled, hi-lo-hi radius of action when fully armed of around (I am guessing here)

200 to 300 miles. When it was used to launch Storm Shadow missiles against targets in Libya in 2011, the Tornado required multiple AAR top-ups to reach and return from its weapon launch point. A remodelled Vulcan could possibly have performed the same task – and more – without any AAR whatsoever. This is not meant as a criticism of the Tornado. It was a truly great tactical strike aircraft that served the RAF very well indeed. But when fully loaded, it had a woefully short range; fine for nearby tactical strike missions, but far from ideal for medium- to long-range operations unless supported by a fleet of very costly and increasingly vulnerable AAR tankers.

Today, we find that the final version of the Tornado, the GR4, has been replaced with the Lockheed Martin F-35B Lightning, an aircraft that, assuming it is required to retain its stealth characteristics, will carry an even smaller payload than the Tornado over what I suspect will be an even shorter unrefuelled radius of action. Supporters of the F-35B are keen to remind us that the aircraft will be able to operate from the RN's new Queen Elizabeth class aircraft carriers and this will give it global reach, but this is only partially true. It assumes that future battles will take place no further than 200 or 300 miles from where the carrier is safe to loiter. It also assumes that we can afford to wait for the days or weeks it will take for a task force and its F-35Bs to be made ready for combat and to sail to wherever the conflict is – or was! What our government has done, consciously or unconsciously, is develop a task force mindset that almost perfectly matches that which was required for Operation Corporate. I fear that, once again, the UK has girded its military loins to re-fight our last conflict instead of focusing our defence spending on capabilities that will better reflect the future threats to our country.

Accepting that the UK's aircraft carrier-based attack capability is now a reality, a rather large question mark must be looming over how we intend to use it for maritime-based warfare, bearing in mind that those countries deemed to be an existential risk to the UK also possess very long-range anti-surface warfare capabilities. In particular, we must ask how the new task force will be able to operate and survive close to enemy shores, because that is where it will have to go to allow the F-35B with its limited radius of action to attack its targets? It is obvious to those who study such things that, in time of war, our new aircraft carriers will not be able to survive for more than a day or two if they are deployed into the Baltic, Black, Barents and China Seas, or anywhere else close to Russia and China. Yet by remaining in the relative safety of larger seas and oceans, the F-35B strike aircraft will be rendered almost useless unless a very significant level of land-based, and increasingly vulnerable, AAR support is provided to allow them to fly from the carriers to their targets and back. In fact, the mustering and deployment of such an AAR force could, by itself, provide the enemy with an early warning of impending F-35B action.

Modern long-range SAM systems, such as the Russian S-400, and stealthy fighters armed with long-range air-to-air missiles are already entering service with the air forces of our potential opponents and they will pose a serious threat to tanker, reconnaissance, and other large aircraft types that dare to fly within several hundred miles of the area of conflict. Like our American allies, it is likely that the RN will have to consider acquiring some form of stealthy, carrier-borne AAR capability to give the F-35B the radius of action needed to better perform its mission. Instead of developing a relatively simple, medium-sized, post-Vulcan-era aircraft (Airbus 321LR) armed with modern ALCMs and capable of conducting rapid-reaction stand-off strike/attack missions from medium to high altitude and from well outside the coverage of enemy SAMs and long-range fighters, we have chosen to base our new attack capability on the F-35B, a stealthy pea-shooter that will be tethered by a very short string to its highly vulnerable and expensive aircraft carrier. Also, as the primary threat to NATO countries now comes from both Russia and China – countries with geographical diameters measured in thousands of miles – then it is clear that short-range F-35Bs operations mounted from a task force positioned well outside harm's way will pose no threat whatsoever to them.

As mentioned, the clue was there for all to see many years ago when the USA, Russia and China decided to retain in service their vintage, medium- and long-range bombers. They refurbished them, updated their systems and armed them with modern air-launched anti-ship and land-attack cruise missiles to provide them with the long-range anti-surface warfare capability needed to threaten naval task forces, and to strike targets deep behind enemy shores. None of the above is meant to imply that the UK's naval forces are no longer necessary. The UK will always need a surface force capable of protecting sea lanes and performing international policing, troop deployment, amphibious operations and other tasks. But if government ministers and defence officials think that our new carrier task force represents a valid long-range conventional – and possibly nuclear – counterforce to those countries that pose a threat to our freedom, then someone, somewhere, has misrepresented the case to them.

As we now know, the Vulcan, after being relieved of the nuclear deterrent role in 1969, remained in service for close to 12 years providing the UK with a medium-range, sub-strategic, low-level nuclear-strike capability. To better equip the aircraft for this type of mission, the Vulcan received a number of early system enhancements including the MFS, a fairly modern RWR and an integrated TFR/radio altimeter system and Decca Doppler 72 to replace the obsolete Green Satin Doppler navigation system. However, nothing of any real consequence was done to enhance the aircraft's H2S radar, NBC and ECM capabilities. To compound the matter, the flexibility offered by having a conventional bombing option and the ability to take on extra fuel through its AAR capability were deemed unlikely ever to be required and removed from the Vulcan's repertoire. These decisions effectively reduced the Vulcan to being a one-trick nuclear-armed pony.

Then, out of the blue in 1982, the Falklands conflict erupted and Black Buck was sanctioned. Suddenly, the Vulcan *needed* an INS, as well as modern ECM capability, a conventional bombing option, and the ability to refuel in flight. It was all made to happen almost overnight. Despite the magnificent technical effort that this represented, a number of far-sighted observers were quick to ask why the conventional bombing and AAR capabilities that offered the Vulcan rapid global reach and tactical flexibility had been deleted from the aircraft's profile in the first place. Others forensically asked why the radar, navigation and ECM enhancements deemed to be so vitally important for the Black Buck Vulcans were not seen as being equally important for those Vulcans that had stood ready over many years to provide a sub-strategic strike capability for the UK? Perhaps those in power at the time gambled that the Vulcans would never be launched on their war missions and that authorising additional system upgrades would have simply been a waste of money. But isn't this the classic case for all defence procurements?

As things stood in the mid-to-late seventies, if the Vulcans had been launched on their war mission, the crews, already hampered by the aircraft's lacklustre speed and agility when flying at low level, would also have had to navigate their way to and from the target without the back-up of modern INS systems, without a modern radar that would have provided a sharper view of targets and offsets, without a modern and reliable digital NBC, and without a means to actively counter the plethora of modern AAA, SAM and fighter threats posed by Soviet forces. Not a happy prospect. It is easy, of course, to sit back and pontificate about what should and should not have been done to maintain the credibility of the Vulcan Force over its many years of service. But it must be obvious that when a decision is made to procure and introduce into service an expensive strike/attack asset such as the Vulcan, then those in government responsible for its upkeep should be compelled to make sure that it remains viable throughout its service life by instituting a programme of regular system upgrades. An early attempt at doing this was tried in 1961–62 when the UK joined America in the development of the AGM-87 Skybolt air-launched ballistic missile (ALBM) programme. Unfortunately, this endeavour proved to be a technological step too far, even for the Americans. This left the UK to fall back on Vulcans armed with free-fall nuclear weapons and, later, the relatively short-range Blue Steel stand-off weapon. Subsequent to RN SSBNs armed with Polaris SLBMs entering service, the Blue Steel was removed from service and all the Vulcan B2 squadrons were re-rolled to conduct the low-level laydown nuclear strike mission, a role it continued to fill until its retirement. It was also during this period that the Vulcan's capabilities were left to slowly wither on the vine, or so it seemed to those that were still required to fly and operate the aircraft. By allowing the Vulcan to sink prematurely into obsolescence and by gradually reducing its effectiveness by removing its AAR and conventional weapon options, the UK was left with an aircraft that increasingly lacked the flexibility and capabilities needed to rapidly respond to unexpected operations such as, for example, Argentina's invasion of the Falkland Islands. Surely, as a minimum, two or perhaps three Vulcan squadrons should have been gathered together to form a 'Standby Expeditionary Wing', retaining their AAR and conventional bombing capabilities and being fitted out with modern navigation and other systems necessary to allow worldwide operations. During 'normal' times, these aircraft would have still formed part of the UK's sub-strategic nuclear capability. Alas, it was not to be.

# CHAPTER ELEVEN
# POST-VULCAN DAYS WITH THE NIMROD

In 1981, after ending my tour on 617 Squadron, I was posted to the Vulcan Office at HQ 1 Group which was located at RAF Bawtry, just south of Doncaster. The closing down of Vulcan squadrons was gathering pace and the amount of important administrative work being carried out in the HQ was falling and/or becoming of lesser relevance. Then, in 1982, the Argentinians decided to invade the Falkland Islands and everything within the HQ changed. The minds of senior officers and selected teams of Vulcan B2 and Victor K2 staff officers suddenly became focused on the planning and execution of an operation which, I found out much later, was to be Operation Black Buck. Routine HQ activities seemed to lose importance and I definitely felt surplus to requirements!

So it was with some genuine relief when I was posted away from HQ 1 Group and re-located at the newly formed Electronic Warfare Operational Support Establishment (EWOSE) at RAF Benson near Oxford. Initially, I was told that my work there would be focused on helping to develop the threat radar libraries needed to support new RAF EW systems such as Loral 1017 Yellow Gate ESM for the Nimrod MR2 and the Sky Shadow ECM pod for the Tornado GR1. But no sooner had I started working on this when the plan was suddenly changed and I was told that I was to become one of a small number of Yellow Gate project officers and I would be required to work during weekdays at the Racal factory at Crawley. To help me get started I was sent on a Coral 66, real-time software course at RAF Locking near Weston-super-Mare for which, upon completion, I was awarded an A2 pass. On my return to Benson, I began to organise civilian accommodation close to the Racal factory and I bought a second car to allow me to commute to and from my MQ at Benson. Just as I was about to get started the plan was changed yet again, and I was informed that the project officer position that I had prepared for would, instead, be filled by an RAF engineering officer.

Soon afterwards, EWOSE moved to RAF Wyton[2] where I spent several years as part of a small team tasked to set up an automated worldwide EW scenario generation system. This was considered in some circles to be important to allow the rapid and automatic generation of electronic order of battle (EOB) information and to provide

---

2   EWOSE was eventually subsumed into the Air Warfare Centre at RAF Waddington.

the data needed for the timely re-programming and testing of in-service ESM and ECM systems. However, in 1985, while the system was still under development, I was posted back onto 51 Squadron where I spent the next ten years flying as an airborne supervisor on the Nimrod R1.[3]

# Third Time on 51 Squadron

It was good to be back on 51 Squadron. The squadron was still earning its keep by flying 'milk-run' electronic reconnaissance missions around the eastern periphery of the Soviet Union and many of the crew members that I knew when I was flying on the squadron as a spec op were still there, albeit looking a little bit older. When flying these sorties, it was not uncommon for visiting senior naval, army and RAF officers to fly on the aircraft as guests. On one occasion AVM Peter Harding took a break from his desk duties at HQRAFG to fly on one of the Nimrod R's regular sorties along the IGB. He was wearing a standard olive-green flying suit, just like those worn by other crew members so he melded in perfectly with the rest of the crew. At some point during the sortie, he decided to leave the Nimrod's flight deck area and make his way back into the mission cabin to have a chat with some of the operators.

At the same time, MACR Jim Brown, an experienced COMINT operator who hailed from Scotland, was heating up meat pies in the Nimrod's small oven and dishing them out to the crew. The pies were piping hot which made them rather difficult to handle, so Jim returned to the galley, picked up some paper napkins and a handful of plastic forks, and started passing them to the waiting operators. As Jim made his way forward past the mid-point of the aircraft, he saw a crew member that he immediately recognised as MACR Trevor Siggs – an ELINT operator – bent over and talking to the operator at the aircraft's Aux A workstation. Seizing the opportunity for a perfect 'gotcha' moment, Jim thrust one of the plastic forks into Trevor's backside. Unfortunately, it wasn't Trevor. It is said that AVM Harding jumped vertically upwards with such velocity that he almost created his very own mid-upper gunner position on the Nimrod. Upon descending back to the cabin floor, the air officer spun around, white faced and clearly in shock to confront Jim. "Bloody Hell!" said Jim, when he recognised who the victim of his unprovoked attack actually was. He then went into a form of verbal shock and blurted out a never-ending stream of semi-coherent apologies.

---

3   For some reason after I left, the EW scenario generation task was cancelled as it was deemed not to be a worthwhile effort. Worse still, all the data and software created as part of its development was 'accidently' destroyed during a tidying-up session in preparation for an inspection by a senior officer.

Meanwhile, one of the mission supervisors, oblivious to what had happened, was quietly getting on with the task of processing signals when he noticed that the intercom call-light from an operator sitting close to Aux A had illuminated. He pressed the call-light button and said, "go ahead". "Sir, Jim Brown has just stabbed AVM Harding in the backside with a plastic fork." Long pause. "Err, say that again?" The operator repeated his message. The supervisor, somewhat gobsmacked, but realising the severity of the situation decided it was time to 'pass the buck' and inform the captain. "Captain from supervisor." "Go ahead supervisor." "Captain it would seem that one of our operators has stabbed our VIP passenger in the backside with a plastic fork." "WHAT?!" said the captain. Like the supervisor, he could not believe his ears. The supervisor repeated the message. There was a long pause, followed by a groan, followed by "Oh Christ!" then complete silence. As it happens, OC 51 Squadron, Wg Cdr Michael Feenan, was also on board the Nimrod and he quickly took control of the situation. He interrogated MACR Brown, who was still in shock, to ascertain why he had attacked the AVM with a plastic fork. Jim explained that it was simply a case of mistaken identity and that he really meant to stab MACR Trevor Siggs. Wg Cdr Feenan, now aware of the run of events, explained the situation to the AVM, apologised for the outrageous and unprovoked attack on his person by one of his squadron operators, and generally managed to calm things down. Fortunately, the wound sustained by AVM Harding proved not to be life-threatening, and being aircrew himself, he quickly recovered his posture and saw the funny side of the incident. No disciplinary action was taken against MACR Jim Brown and nothing further was said. However, the incident did lead to some faux-concern amongst the squadron's ELINT operators who were 'worried' about COMINT operators being allowed to handle plastic forks unsupervised. Much later, it was discovered that AVM Peter Harding made frequent and humorous mention of the incident when making speeches at official and unofficial functions.

## Operation Desert Shield/Granby

There existed a long-running and bitter dispute between Iraq and Kuwait about the ownership of tracts of land bordering the two countries. Iraq was also convinced that Kuwait was carrying out excessive commercial exploitation of its oil reserves, some of which it said was coming from wells drilled in the disputed land areas. This, Iraq claimed, was leading to a drop in world oil prices which, in turn, was having a deleterious impact on Iraq's economy. These issues, plus some other festering and seemingly unresolvable arguments came to a head on 2 August 1990, with the Iraqi leader, President Saddam Hussein, ordering his military forces to invade Kuwait.

This shocking and totally unexpected move led to demands from the United Nations (UN) and nearby Arabic countries for Iraq to immediately withdraw its forces. Their demands were ignored and Iraqi forces quickly overran the whole of Kuwait, seizing almost all of its national assets and damaging or destroying some of the country's military and commercial facilities. Increasing the level of defiance against those calling for him to withdraw his forces from Kuwait, President Hussein began to act in a seriously threatening way towards his southernmost neighbour, Saudi Arabia. In response to Iraq's defiance, the UN immediately imposed economic sanctions on the country. Furthermore, having serious concerns that Iraq might also decide to invade northern Saudi Arabia, the USA decided on 7 August 1990 to bolster that country's defences by enacting Operation Desert Shield. Over the next few days, a coalition of other countries including the UK joined in and began to rapidly deploy land, sea and air forces to Saudi Arabia. Other countries from around the world also decided to lend a hand by offering a range of military, logistical and medical support services. The British operation mounted in support of Desert Shield was code-named Operation Granby.

Operation Granby took effect very quickly and within a few days the focus of 51 Squadron's efforts pivoted from monitoring events in and around the Soviet Union to conducting electronic reconnaissance in the Middle East. On 10 August a Nimrod R1 was deployed to RAF Akrotiri in Cyprus from where it immediately started flying reconnaissance missions along the eastern Mediterranean littoral. Meanwhile, the large number of UK forces arriving at Akrotiri plus the high volume of UK and coalition military personnel transiting through the base on their way to Saudi Arabia led to a shortage of accommodation on the station. This problem came to a head in October when it was decided that accommodation was to be allocated on a priority basis. This, for some reason, meant that 51 Squadron aircrew had to vacate their accommodation to make way for Tornado F3 crews that had recently arrived from the UK to provide air-defence cover for Akrotiri. It would seem that, at or around that time, there was some concern that Iraq could mount a disabling attack on the base using Scud missiles and/or attack aircraft. In October 1990, Sqn Ldr Barry Smith – 51 Squadron Flight Commander Plans – took ownership of the problem and fought hard to secure some long-term accommodation for his officers, ELINT operators and a few COMINT operators at the joint RAF/army base at Episkopi, which is located on the coast some four miles to the west of Akrotiri. The number of COMINT operators having 'specific to theatre' language skills were in short supply at that time which resulted in them having to fly on every Nimrod R1 mission. In an effort to minimise their on-duty time, it was decided that they should remain housed at RAF Akrotiri, thus sparing them the pre- and post-flight road transit journey between Akrotiri and Episkopi. Happily, this small and select band of COMINT SNCOs were eventually allowed to remain in a block of rooms called 'The Animal House', a facility famously – or perhaps infamously – known to aircrews from most of the RAF's front-line squadrons.

Whilst the accommodation secured at Episkopi for 51 Squadron officers was excellent, that provided for ELINT operators was poor, cramped and disappointing. Their sleeping accommodation comprised a number of dreary rooms, cellars and tin huts located within and around the Kensington Building – a fairly large brick-built structure located about 100 yards south of the officers' mess. This collection of semi-dilapidated rooms and sheds perched on the edge of the high cliffs overlooking the Mediterranean Sea soon became known as 'Benghazi Towers'. A further disappointment came when, despite our operators holding warrant officer (WO) and SNCO status, they were, for some inexplicable reason, not allowed use of the Episkopi sergeants' mess. This issue was compounded when they were told that they would also have to wait in line with junior NCOs and private soldiers for their meals. As an additional irritant, our WO and SNCO operators had nowhere nearby to relax in the evenings and socialise with their peers. It was all rather unsatisfactory. 'Team 51' was definitely not happy. Taking matters into their own hands, two of 51 Squadron's stalwarts, MAEOp Joe Slade and MAEOp Bill Wade, decided to create their very own recreational/social meeting place. The venue of choice was a long disused and dust-covered hall-cum-lounge bar inside the Kensington Building and, despite some initial opposition from the army, permission for its use was quickly granted. Although this room had been out of use for some time and lacked many much-needed comforts, Joe and Bill, aided by a band of willing squadron SNCOs, soon managed to turn it into a welcoming facility where they could unwind, relax, socialise and even invite army and air force guests. It also served a secondary, but important purpose of drawing those crew members not scheduled to fly the following morning away from the accommodation rooms, thus allowing the next day's flying crew to get some undisturbed sleep.

Determined to get a bar facility up and running on the first night of the move to Episkopi, Joe and Bill approached the manager of the Episkopi sergeants' mess with a view to borrowing some beer pumps, a refrigerator and a few other items needed to get things started. Unfortunately, once again, the sergeants' mess manager was unable or unwilling to help. Disappointed but undeterred, Joe and Bill approached Mr Pat Craft, the Episkopi officers' mess manager, to see if he could help out in some way. In earlier years, Pat Craft had been manager of the officers' mess at RAF Wyton and he was something of a kindred spirit to the squadron. As luck would have it, Pat was a godsend and it wasn't long before Joe and Bill took charge of the basic pieces of equipment needed to set up their bar. Thanks to the sterling efforts made by Joe and Bill, plus the help offered by Pat Craft, the friendly efforts of a 'Mr Fix-It' called

Post-flight refreshments in The Kenny. (Bill Wade)

Michael, and the constant assistance provided by MAEOp Steve Moore, Steve Taft and some of the other 51 Squadron crew members, the Kensington Bar and Social Club – 'The Kenny' – opened for business on the very first night of the squadron's arrival at Episkopi. A brilliant, moral boosting achievement.

Having got The Kenny up and running, some thought was given to how it could be managed in a viable and trustworthy manner. There was no permanent staff available to oversee things so it would have to be run on a self-help and mutual-trust basis. When not flying, Bill Wade looked after the ordering of supplies, delivery notes and invoices. He also established an excellent and friendly relationship with the NAFFI manager and staff at Akrotiri thus ensuring that the bar's regular and varied demands were always met. Being an 'open bar', the number of visitors soon increased and this was enhanced even more by the arrival of crews from No. 42 Nimrod MPA Squadron. As a result, the periodic small deliveries of 'essential supplies' procured from the NAFFI shop at Akrotiri at the start of the detachment soon increased from being a few crates of local beer to being a twice weekly and very sizable set of deliverables including a wider choice of beer, an ever-expanding list of soft drinks, and the all-important nibbles and other consumables needed to support the enhancement of The Kenny's newly established, 24-hour tea and coffee bar service. A television and video recorder were also hired to allow crews to keep up to date with current affairs and to screen films and other types of entertainment.

Cash arrangements for the bar were run by 51 Squadron's very own 'Shylock', MAEOp Tony Pewton, deputised as required by MACR George Lash and a few others. Between them, and with help from other squadron members, they managed to expertly run The Kenny and take good care of its cash arrangements. Such was their success, that at the end of 51 Squadron's involvement in Operation Granby, the proceeds from The Kenny were sufficient to allow a sizable donation to be made to the 51 Squadron fund.

After the initial rush of activity required to establish 51 Squadron flying and technical operations at Akrotiri, and after sorting out the accommodation for both the air and ground crews, life soon settled down to a routine rhythm of flying, socialising and sleeping. After just a few weeks, not only did 51 Squadron aircrews enjoy the luxury of having a well-run officers' mess and the Kenny Bar close by, they were also able to make use of the Episkopi golf course located on the beach immediately below the military base. In the latter stages of Operation Granby, the number of COMINT operators trained in the required languages increased and some of those newly arriving in theatre were able to be accommodated at Episkopi. In a nutshell, despite preparing for war operations, the squadron found itself blessed with reasonably good accommodation and food, excellent bar facilities, a golf course on the doorstep, and easy access to the warm waters of the Mediterranean Sea. While

Bill Wade doing The Kenny's books. (Bill Wade)

most of us who served on Operation Granby felt privileged to be accommodated at Episkopi, we also felt a pang of guilt when we thought about those less fortunate front-line warriors who would have to live in rather austere tented accommodation in the Saudi Arabian desert.

The regular drumbeat of Nimrod R1 operations was maintained throughout the deployment. Early missions flown from Akrotiri in August through November 1990 tended to focus on the eastern Mediterranean littoral. However, as the build-up of allied forces in Saudi Arabia increased and the prospect of war became more likely, the Nimrod R1's tasking was changed and the aircraft started flying reconnaissance patrols along the Saudi/Iraqi border. At some point during the build-up, a second Nimrod R1 joined our detachment thus ensuring that the daily, and sometimes twice daily, patrols could be more reliably sustained. Despite the increasing number of coalition ground forces massing close to the Iraq/Saudi border, and the strenuous diplomatic efforts made by the UN and other political entities to persuade Iraq to withdraw its forces from Kuwait, Saddam Hussein remained stubbornly determined to stay put in the country. As a consequence, the risk of armed conflict drew closer.

On one sortie when I was flying as mission supervisor, a young, enthusiastic COMINT operator suggested that I should allow the metal boxes containing the crew's personal weapons (9-mm pistols and ammunition) to be opened and the weapons issued to the crew. His logic was that if we were shot down but survived the crash, crew members might need to have rapid access to their weapons for self-defence. I could understand his logic, but at that time hostilities had not yet started and, anyway, our patrols were still taking place within Saudi airspace. But more to the point, the idea of over 20 crew members, some of whom were very young, running around the back of the aircraft with pistols and ammunition frightened me more than the thought of being shot down by an Iraqi Foxbat. I therefore decided not to act on his suggestion. Meanwhile, as we flew our daily patrols along the southern border of Iraq, everything and anything that emitted RF energy was intercepted, analysed, located, recorded and reported, and with our American allies conducting similar operations, it wasn't long before the coalition had the electromagnetic environment in southern Iraq pretty well stitched-up.

Back home, the wives and other family members of those serving at Akrotiri did their best to keep the home fires burning. Some of the more experienced wives got together to offer advice and a helping hand to those that were younger and who, for a number of different reasons, were finding it difficult to cope with the sudden departure and extended absence of their husbands. Simple events like coffee mornings all the way through to family welfare meetings were arranged and, in a few cases, domestic help and temporary childcare was organised. Support also came from on-high when HRH Prince Philip visited RAF Wyton. A gathering of families

HRH Prince Phillip chatting with the families of those 51 Squadron members serving on Operation Granby. (George Lash)

from all ranks was held in the sergeants' mess where the prince proved determined to meet as many family members as possible. In his usual relaxed style, Prince Phillip listened, conversed, joked and generally bolstered the morale of all the wives and children that he met. His visit, which had been arranged at fairly short notice, left a lasting impression on everyone.

Tension along the Saudi/Iraq border intensified and Saddam Hussein ratcheted up his bellicosity by threatening to unleash 'the mother of all wars' on the coalition if it dared to intervene in his annexation of Kuwait. On 17 January 1991, with the patience of the coalition finally exhausted, Operation Desert Shield was upgraded to Operation Desert Storm and offensive operations to forcibly remove Iraq forces from Kuwait began. The shock and awe of the initial offensive action against Iraqi military targets and enabling infrastructure was such that by the end of the second or third day, Iraqi military radar and communication emitters in the southern part of Iraq had either been reduced to rubble or had been rapidly withdrawn further north out of harm's way. As coalition ground forces fought their way northwards deep into Iraq, American Rivet Joint, AAR, AWACs, JSTARS, Fighter CAPs and other strategic and tactical air assets had their patrol lines moved further northwards over southern Iraq to maintain close cover over the battlefield and to obtain better access to the signals environment within and around Baghdad. For some reason the UK MoD was reluctant to allow 51 Squadron to follow suit and for many days the squadron's patrol line remained south of the Saudi/Iraq border. It goes without saying that, with all or most of the Iraqi military-associated RF emitters in southern Iraq either destroyed or withdrawn, SIGINT collection activity in the Nimrod reduced markedly. Thankfully, it wasn't too long before the UK MoD caught up with the reality of the tactical situation and the Nimrod was allowed to patrol further north over Iraq to resume its important contribution to the joint intelligence collection effort. One abiding memory I have of Desert Storm is catching sight of the vast, billowing clouds of black smoke rising from the Kuwait oil wells that had been deliberately set alight by retreating Iraqi forces. Seeing this first hand helped to quash my feeling of somehow being detached from the reality of the armed conflict that was taking place on the ground below and to the north of our patrol line.

Another Granby-related event cherished by those squadron members involved, is when the Chief of the Air Staff (CAS) ACM Peter Harding (yes, there was a second Peter Harding!) decided to fly as a guest on one of 51 Squadron's missions. As the aircraft began to taxi out of its dispersal at Akrotiri, a gathering of squadron ground crew lined up facing away from the Nimrod, dropped their trousers and 'mooned' the departing crew. Better still, the airmen had printed on the cheeks of their bottoms letters of the alphabet that, when viewed together, spelt out a birthday greeting for the co-pilot. This display of outrageous, but hilarious, comradery caused some near heart-seizures amongst the senior ranks on the Nimrod's flight deck, but thankfully it went completely unnoticed by the CAS. No. 51 Squadron continued to patrol within Iraq for some time after Desert Storm had achieved most of its aims. But later, and with little left to do, the squadron was withdrawn back to RAF Wyton where it resumed its normal peacetime activity of flying patrols against the Soviet Union.

# Operations Sky Monitor and Deny Flight

In late 1992 the focus of the squadron's effort shifted once more, this time to the area comprising what was the former Yugoslavia. The break-up of Yugoslavia in 1991 resulted in the now-independent nations that made up the federation attempting to re-establish their old borders, their individual political orders and their unique cultures. This gave rise to conflict about where the new borders and political power should lie. It also encouraged elements of Islamophobia. In an effort to limit the fighting, the UN passed Resolution 713 in September 1991 that established an embargo on the delivery of weapons into the region. In May 1992, the UN passed Resolution 757 which bolstered the embargo and authorised Operation Maritime Monitor that called for NATO maritime forces to check that weapons were not entering the conflict zone by sea. This operation started in July 1992. Later that year the UN, having concerns about the use of aircraft by forces in the region, passed Resolution 781 that imposed a total ban on military flights within Bosnian airspace and on 16 October Operation Sky Monitor was officially sanctioned.

The squadron's task was to conduct electronic reconnaissance missions in support of Operation Sky Monitor. Specifically, the objective was to cover principally air, but also ground, operations that were being conducted in the region with emphasis on Bosnia. The squadron was required to detect and report any unauthorised military flights taking place within Bosnian airspace in violation of UN Resolution 781. No. 51 Squadron's share of the tasking required it to mount three or four seven-hour Nimrod R1 flights every week. The Nimrod was based overnight at the Italian airbase at Pratica di Mare, just south of Rome, and the crews were housed in a comfortable hotel in the nearby town of Pomezia. As a result of the continuing violations of UN Resolution 781, in 1993 the rules were bolstered and upgraded in line with UN Resolution 816 which banned all military and civilian unauthorised flights within Bosnian airspace. While this was effective at preventing, or at least reducing, the number of violations by fixed-wing aircraft, the number of helicopter violations remained high, and in some cases increased.

As a result of this, in the spring of 1993, NATO operations were upgraded once more to include actions necessary to enforce the no-fly-zone and Operation Sky Monitor was upgraded to Operation Deny Flight. Whilst ELINT activity in the area under reconnaissance was generally low, our COMINT teams were kept fairly busy. However, as in all wars, attrition tends to thin out the level of radar and communication activity and as the number of SIGINT targets gradually reduced, the sorties tended to become less productive. This led to some changes being made to the size and composition of the crews. Meanwhile, although Operation Deny Flight resulted in a significant reduction in unauthorised flights by fixed-wing aircraft, violation of the rules by helicopter activity continued to be a serious problem.

Furthermore, the war on the ground was spreading and intensifying and by the summer of 1995 things had got so bad that NATO invoked an offensive air campaign called Operation Deliberate Force. This was accompanied by the start of ground operations against the Bosnian-Serb army by the United Nations Protection Force. Both the air and the ground campaign were ended when a peace agreement was brokered – the Dayton Agreement – in late 1995, and soon afterwards, the Nimrod R1 was allowed to settle back into its normal peacetime activities.

# Project Star Window

In 1991–92, whilst the first Gulf War was in progress, I was the appointed project officer for the procurement of a system aimed at replacing both the Nimrod R1's ageing Astral Box Mission Computer, COMINT DF system, and COMINT receivers. Initially, this task comprised two separate activities, one called 'Star Cross' and the other called, if I remember correctly, something like 'Airy Window'. However, it was quickly decided to amalgamate both activities into a single procurement under the new project name of Star Window. This led to my work being shared between flying on Nimrod R1 sorties and working on Star Window procurement.

After a long and thorough selection process, the company chosen to develop and provide the new system was E-Systems, which at a later date would be absorbed into Raytheon Systems. The technical solution provided by E-Systems was largely based upon COMINT systems already in use by the USAF. Work on the project required me and my small team of operators to carry out system acceptance testing in the E-Systems laboratories at University Centre, just west of Dulles Airport in America. To get to and from America, my team and I made good use of the RAF's Brize Norton-to-Washington VC10 service. Excellent as this service was, it resulted in me once again sitting in an aircraft with backward-facing seats. However, this time I completely approved of the arrangement as it was quite obvious that rearward-facing seats enhanced the passenger's chances of surviving a crash.

The author after a Star Window calibration sortie.

Work on Star Window continued apace and it wasn't long before the first aircraft scheduled to receive the upgrade was wheeled into the Electronic Warfare Avionics Unit (EWAU) hangar for routine maintenance work and the installation of the Star Window system. As you will appreciate, in 1992–93, 51 Squadron was heavily involved in operations in the Adriatic, and with the squadron having only three aircraft to work with, the time allowed for installation, testing and calibration of the Star Window system, and for the training of operators and maintenance personnel was very tight indeed. Testing the new receiver systems was straight forward and, to some extent, could be carried out on the ground. However, calibrating and verifying the performance of the DF system was rather more complex and required the aircraft to fly six or more night-time calibration sorties, each lasting around eight hours. These flights involved flying to-and-fro over the south of Wales at around 10,000 feet at night whilst collecting direction of arrival data on signals transmitted from a built-for-purpose transmitter located within the Aberporth Test Range. The results obtained from these flights were subjected to a data smoothing process on the Star Window ground system after which the new data files were installed on the aircraft's Star Window mission disc. A number of DF system verification flights were then flown to confirm the performance of the system and, once deemed satisfactory, the Star Window system was released for operation use.

The pressure of work involved in all of these activities was such that sometimes equipment faults and software problems could not be fully resolved before the aircraft was called forward to fly operational sorties. It is not surprising, therefore, that on early post-Star Window sorties the system's performance failed to meet the operator's expectations in a number of technical areas. However, after some hardware and software changes were made and more experience was gained by operators and the maintenance personnel, the list of faults and niggles raised during post-flight debriefing sessions gradually reduced and the system stabilised.

# Project Extract

Soon after Star Window entered service in 1994, the MoD initiated a technical programme to upgrade the Nimrod R1's ELINT capability. This programme was called Project Extract and, once again, I was ordered to act as project officer. On this occasion, the Defence Evaluation and Research Agency (DERA)[4] at Great Malvern

---

4   In July 2001 DERA at Malvern changed its name to Defence Scientific and Technical Laboratories (DSTL).

was hired to provide technical assistance and scientific oversight of the project. To assist DERA with subject matter support, I was posted to Malvern in January 1995, just before the squadron moved to Waddington. Raytheon Systems, with its recently acquired knowledge about the Nimrod R1 through its involvement in the Star Window project, was selected to carry out development of the Extract system at the company's premises at Falls Church in Washington DC and at the L3 Corporation facility at Greenville in Texas. Once installed, Extract provided operators with an upgraded manual ELINT function (MEF), the development of which was sub-contracted out to Racal Ltd at its Wells facility south of Bristol. Extract also furnished the aircraft with a new automatic tactical ELINT function (TEF). Design of the TEF was based upon the automatic ELINT emitter location systems (AEELS) installed in USAF RC-135 Rivet Joint aircraft. Like Star Window, the Extract programme also included enhancements to the Nimrod R1's on-board computer and display system. It also resulted in upgrades to the rear crew trainer and ground analysis systems. The work associated with Extract involved lots of road travel within the UK and flying to and from America to assist Raytheon and L3 with development and testing of the system. The internal and devolved design and fabrication work programme for Extract (and Star Window and other projects) was shared between British Aerospace (BAe) Systems and EWAU. BAe Systems was design and technical authority for air vehicle aspects of the Nimrod R1, and EWAU was the design and technical authority for the mission cabin element. Both organisations worked in unison to design and implement modifications on to the aircraft and its internal cabin layout in order to accommodate system upgrades. In Extract's case, this required BAe to modify the Nimrod's wing-tip pods in order for them to accept the TEF's array of horns and spiral antennas. Although the Nimrod R1's wing-tip pods looked similar to those that housed the Yellow Gate ESM system on the Nimrod MR2, that is where the similarity ended. At no time was Yellow Gate ever installed on the Nimrod R1. Amongst other things, EWAU carried out design and construction of the equipment racks, revised the distribution of electrical power to the sensor and computer systems, optimised air conditioning within the cabin, and produced the vitally important system interface documents. After the system was installed, a Nimrod R1 was tasked to NAS Patuxent River in Maryland, USA, where it was flown on a number of sorties to calibrate the TEF system. Before this, in 1998, I retired from the RAF having completed 40 years of service. Luckily, I immediately found employment as a civilian contractor working for the MoD/DSTL and I was asked to continue working on the testing and introduction into service of Extract. This included flying on the previously mentioned system calibration flights at NAS Patuxent River.

# Projects Interpret and Helix

At some juncture during my time at DERA/DSTL I was asked to take part in a small study called Project Interpret. The aim of the study was to map out the requirement for a future Nimrod R1 replacement. Despite some 'experts' from the MoD suggesting that the Nimrod R1 could easily be replaced by a roll-on-roll-off system hosted on an RN ship, or even by a satellite-based system, it was always clear to me, and others in the airborne SIGINT community, that the chosen solution would have to be based upon an air vehicle for the following reasons. To be effective, the system had to:

1) Be capable of rapid worldwide strategic and tactical deployment.
2) Be able to intercept radar and communication signals operating at very long range from the host platform.
3) Provide a persistent and adaptable collection capability across a wide part of the RF spectrum.

51 Squadron RC-135 Rivet Joint electronic reconnaissance aircraft arriving at RAF Waddington. This replaced the Nimrod R1 previously flown by the squadron. (Aviation Photo Company)

4) Allow for rapid and simultaneous detection, geolocation, analysis and tactical exploitation of the widest possible range of radar, data and voice systems.

5) Be able to offer direct and immediate SIGINT support to those forces engaged in combat.

Moreover, all of these requirements had to be met whilst the platform remained at a relatively safe distance from the area of conflict. It was clear that sensors on ships and satellites would not be able to satisfy all of these requirements. Some months later, and after some serious analysis, the obvious decision was made to procure a new aircraft-based SIGINT system. This new procurement activity was called Project Helix.

At the start, the Helix project team scoured the market and visited organisations that would potentially be able to conduct the work needed to provide a replacement for the Nimrod R1 and its associated training and ground analysis systems. After studying a number of proposals, the MoD whittled the list down to three companies deemed best suited to be able to fulfil the contract, BAe Systems, Lockheed Martin and Raytheon Systems. All of the proposals were scrutinised in depth, but towards the end of the assessment phase it began to dawn on the MoD that they were in danger of, perhaps unwittingly, re-inventing at great expense a wheel that already existed – the RC-135 Rivet Joint. In what could be called a 'light-bulb moment', the MoD decided that the quickest, possibly the most cost-effective, and certainly the most risk-free solution was for the UK to buy its way into the USAF RC-135 Rivet Joint community. It would accomplish this by purchasing three suitable, but no longer required, Boeing KC-135 airframes and having them rebuilt and then modified by L3 Corporation at Greenville in Texas to RC-135W Rivet Joint standard. With Rivet Joint being a well-established programme of long standing, I felt that I no longer had a role to fill and I retired for good in 2008. Subsequent to my retirement, three Boeing airframes were eventually purchased, overhauled and modified and the first aircraft entered service in 2014. Thus, the RC-135W Rivet Joint became the UK's new airborne SIGINT asset, re-vitalising the role that the Nimrod R1 had performed from 1975 through to its retirement in 2011. Better still, the RAF's three Rivet Joint aircraft were integrated into the USAF's Rivet Joint maintenance and modification schedule, thus ensuring the aircraft's future capability and mission effectiveness.

Although my flying career had effectively ended when I was posted to DERA/DSTL in January 1995, I did manage to get some flying hours added to my logbook. As previously mentioned, I flew on a number of Nimrod R1 TEF calibration sorties at Patuxent River. I also flew on board a Cobham Ltd Falcon 20 twin-jet from Bournemouth Airport to assist in a research project being carried out by DSTL. But better still, in 2001 I decided to renew my private pilot's licence. This allowed me to fly regular pleasure and touring flights around the UK in rented light aircraft such as the SOCATA Rallye 180, Cessna 152, Piper Arrow and Cherokee, and SOCATA TB9 Tampico. I also became a tug pilot for the Cambridgeshire Gliding Centre and over a period of four years flew over 1,300 glider-tows flying Piper Pawnee, Rallye and Robin DR400 aircraft that had been modified for glider towing. What a pleasure it was to end up flying forward *and* facing forward.

# APPENDIX
# RADAR BAND NAMES
# MILITARY vs INTERNATIONAL
# TELECOMMUNICATIONS UNION (ITU)

| NEW AND OLD RADAR BAND NAMES | | | |
|---|---|---|---|
| MILITARY BAND NAMES | BAND FREQUENCY | ITU BAND NAMES | BAND FREQUENCY |
| A-BAND | 0 — 250 MHz | HF | 3 — 30 MHz |
| B-BAND | 250 — 500 MHz | VHF | 30 — 300 MHz |
| C-BAND | 500 — 1,000 MHz | UHF | 300 — 1,000 MHz |
| D-BAND | 1,000 — 2,000 MHz | L-BAND | 1,000 — 2,000 MHz |
| E-BAND | 2,000 — 3,000 MHz | S-BAND | 2,000 — 4,000 MHz |
| F-BAND | 3,000 — 4,000 MHz | C-BAND | 4,000 — 8,000 MHz |
| G-BAND | 4,000 — 6,000 MHz | X-BAND | 8,000 — 12,000 MHz |
| H-BAND | 6,000 — 8,000 MHz | Ku-BAND | 12,000 — 18,000 MHz |
| I-BAND | 8,000 — 10,000 MHz | K-BAND | 18,000 — 27,000 MHz |
| J-BAND | 10,000 — 20,000 MHz | Ka-BAND | 27,000 — 40,000 MHz |
| K-BAND | 20,000 — 40,000 MHz | mm WAVE | 40 MHz — 300,000 MHz |
| L-BAND | 40,000 — 60,000 MHz | | |
| M-BAND | 60,000 — 100,000 MHz | | |

# ACRONYMS AND DEFINITION OF TERMS

| | |
|---|---|
| **AAA** | Anti-Aircraft Artillery |
| **AAPP** | Auxiliary Airborne Power Plant |
| **AAR** | Air-to-Air Refuelling |
| **AD** | Air Defence |
| **AEELS** | Automatic Electronic Emitter Location System |
| **AEO** | Air Electronics Officer |
| **AEOp** | Air Electronics Operator |
| **AGI** | Auxiliary Gatherer of Intelligence |
| **AGM** | Air-to-Ground Missile |
| **AI** | Airborne Intercept |
| **AIRPASS** | Airborne Interception Radar and Pilot's Attack Sight System |
| **ALBM** | Air-Launched Ballistic Missile |
| **ALCM** | Air-Launched Cruise Missile |
| **AM** | Amplitude Modulation |
| **AMTC** | Aviation Medicine Training Centre |
| **ANZAC** | Australian and New Zealand Army Corps |
| **ARAR/ARAX** | French-made Electronic Support Measures System |
| **ARI** | Air Radio Installation |
| **ARM** | Anti-Radiation Missile |
| **ASV** | Air-to-Surface Vessel |
| **ASW** | Anti-Submarine Warfare |
| **ATC** | Air Traffic Control |
| **ATCC** | Air Traffic Control Centre |
| **AVM** | Air Vice-Marshal |
| **AVS** | Air Ventilated Suit |
| **AWAC** | Airborne Warning and Control |
| **BAe** | British Aerospace |
| **BTR** | Basic Training Requirement |
| **CAP** | Combat Air Patrol |

| | |
|---|---|
| CAS | Chief of the Air Staff |
| CASEX | Combined Anti-Submarine Exercise |
| CENTO | Central Treaty Organisation |
| CFB | Canadian Airforce Base |
| CO | Commanding Officer |
| CW | Continuous Wave |
| COMINT | Communications Intelligence |
| DERA | Defence Evaluation & Research Agency |
| DF | Direction Finding |
| DME | Distance Measuring Equipment |
| DSTL | Defence Scientific & Technology Laboratories |
| ECM | Electronic Countermeasures |
| ELINT | Electronic Intelligence |
| EOB | Electronic Order of Battle |
| ESM | Electronic Support Measures |
| EW | Electronic Warfare |
| EWAU | Electronic Warfare Avionics Unit |
| EWOSE | Electronic Warfare Operational Support Establishment |
| FAW | Fighter All Weather |
| FIS | Fighter Identification System |
| FMS | Full Mission Simulator |
| FOB | Forward Operating Base |
| FRC | Flight Reference Cards |
| GCI | Ground-Controlled Intercept |
| GDR | German Democratic Republic |
| GPI | Ground Position Indicator |
| HF | High Frequency |
| HMS | Her Majesty's Ship |
| HRS | Heading Reference System |
| HTP | High Test Peroxide |
| ICBM | Inter-Continental Ballistic Missile |
| IDL | International Date Line |
| IGB | Inner German Border |
| IFF | Identification Friend or Foe |
| INS | Inertial Navigation System |

| | |
|---|---|
| **IP** | Initial Point |
| **IR** | Infrared |
| **IRIS** | Inspector of Radio Installations and Services |
| **ITC** | Initial Training Course |
| **JSTARS** | Joint Surveillance Target Attack Radar System |
| **LOA** | Local Overseas Allowance |
| **LROFE** | Long-Range Operational Flying Exercise |
| **LRU** | Line Replacement Unit |
| **MACR** | Master Aircrew |
| **MAD** | Magnetic Anomaly Detection |
| **MAEOp** | Master Air Electronics Operator |
| **MAWS** | Missile Approach Warning System |
| **MEF** | Manual ELINT Function carried on board the Nimrod R1 |
| **MFS** | Military Flight System |
| **MHQ** | Maritime Head Quarters |
| **MoD** | Ministry of Defence |
| **MPA** | Maritime Patrol Aircraft |
| **MQ** | Married Quarter |
| **MRR** | Maritime Radar Reconnaissance |
| **MU** | Maintenance Unit |
| **NAS** | Naval Air Station |
| **NATO** | North Atlantic Treaty Organisation |
| **NBS** | Navigation Bombing System |
| **NCO** | Non-Commissioned Officer |
| **NOTAM** | Notices to Airmen |
| **OC** | Officer Commanding |
| **OCU** | Operational Conversion Unit |
| **PAN** | International Urgency Call |
| **PEC** | Personal Equipment Connector |
| **PD** | Pulse Doppler |
| **PFCU** | Powered-Flying Control Unit |
| **PPI** | Plan Position Indicator |
| **PSI** | Pounds per Square Inch |
| **QRA** | Quick Reaction Alert |
| **RADAR** | Radio Detection and Ranging |

| | |
|---|---|
| RAF | Royal Air Force |
| RAAF | Royal Australian Air Force |
| RAFLO | Royal Air Force Liaison Officer |
| RAT | Ram Air Turbine with 22kVa alternator |
| RATT | Radio Tele-Typewriter |
| RBSU | Radar Bomb Score Unit |
| RF | Radio Frequency |
| RN | Royal Navy |
| RSF | Radio Servicing Flight |
| RSS | Radar Signal Simulator |
| RWR | Radar Warning Receiver |
| SAC | Strategic Air Command |
| SACEUR | Supreme Allied Commander Europe |
| SAM | Surface-to-Air Missile |
| SAR | Search and Rescue |
| SEATO | South East Asian Treaty Organisation |
| SIGINT | Signals Intelligence |
| SIF | Selective Identification Feature |
| SIMDEFATO | Simulated Double Engine Failure on Take-Off |
| SIOP | Single Integrated Operational Plan |
| SLBM | Submarine-Launched Ballistic Missile |
| SLR | Self-Loading Rifle |
| SNCO | Senior Non-Commissioned Officer |
| SONAR | Sound Navigation and Ranging |
| SOP | Standard Operating Procedure |
| SRAM | Short-Range Attack Missile |
| SRD | System Requirements Document |
| SSB | Single Sideband |
| SSBN | Ship Submersible Ballistic Nuclear |
| SSR | Secondary Surveillance Radar |
| TACAN | Tactical Air Navigation |
| TACEVAL | Tactical Evaluation |
| TEF | Tactical ELINT Function fitted on the Nimrod R1 |
| TFR | Terrain Following Radar |
| TNT | Trinitrotoluene (A high explosive chemical compound) |

| | |
|---|---|
| TRU | Transformer Rectifier Unit |
| TWS | Track While Scan |
| UHF | Ultra-High Frequency |
| UK | United Kingdom |
| UN | United Nations |
| USA | United States of America |
| USAF | United States Air Force |
| USAFE | United States Air Force Europe |
| USN | United States Navy |
| USSR | Union of Soviet Socialist Republics |
| VECTAC | Vectored Attack |
| VCCP | Vapour Cycling Cooling Pack |
| VHF | Very High Frequency |
| WO | Warrant Officer |
| WP | Warsaw Pact |
| WRAF | Woman's Royal Air Force |

| | |
|---|---|
| Astral Box | A late 1970s programme to provide the Nimrod R1 with a COMINT DF system and a computer-based data management capability. |
| Blue Danube | The UK's first national, aircraft delivered, atomic bomb that offered a yield of around 10 to 15 kilotons of TNT. |
| Blue Steel | A rocket-propelled medium-range nuclear-armed stand-off missile fitted to a number of Vulcan and Victor bombers of the 1960s era. |
| Black Buck | Code name for Vulcan B2 raids on Port Stanley airfield in support of Operation Corporate. |
| Corporate | Code name for the UK's operation to retake the Falkland Islands. |
| Deny Flight | A NATO operation initiated in April 1993 to enforce the No-Fly Zone over Bosnia and Herzegovina, and later to provide close-air support for UN troops in Bosnia. |
| Deliberate Force | A NATO air campaign initiated in August 1995 that, in unison with the United Nations Protection Force, aimed to reduce the military capability of the Bosnian Serb army. |
| Desert Shield | Code name for coalition action to prevent Iraqi forces taking aggressive action against Saudi Arabia. |

**Desert Storm**   Offensive operation by coalition forces to remove Iraqi forces from Kuwait.

**E-boat**   A torpedo-armed fast patrol boat.

**Firestreak**   A British infrared air-to-air missile that was carried by UK Gloster Javelin and English Electric Lightning fighters.

**Gepard**   German-built radar-controlled AAA system used by Germany and the Netherlands. German version had a S-band radar for search and a Ku-band radar for tracking. The Dutch system used an X-band radar for search and an X/Ka-band radar for tracking.

**Giant Voice**   A strategic bombing competition hosted by the USAF in which RAF Vulcans were invited to participate.

**Granby**   Code name for UK forces taking part in Gulf War One.

**Green Satin**   An early Doppler navigation radar employed for many years on the Vulcan. It provided the navigator with an accurate measurement of ground speed and drift. It was eventually replaced with the Decca Doppler 72.

**Gun Dish**   The NATO code name given to the Soviet radar that controls the ZSU-23/4 mobile AAA system.

**HAWK**   Raytheon-built medium-range, semi-active radar homing SAM system used by many nations. System has undergone many electronic, mechanical and radar upgrades over the years.

**Head Net**   Soviet Era E/F-Band air and surface surveillance radar.

**Helix**   A project to replace the Nimrod R1.

**Interpret**   A UK MoD/DSTL programme initiated early in 1999 to capture the key requirements for a system to replace the Nimrod R1 electronic reconnaissance aircraft. Superseded by Project Helix.

**Maritime Monitor**   NATO operation to observe and deter the supply of arms to countries within the former Yugoslavia.

**Polaris**   American submarine-launched ballistic missile used in early American and British SSBNs.

**Red Shrimp**   A D/E-Band barrage noise-jamming ECM system fitted on Vulcan B2 and Victor B2 bombers.

**Red Snow**   A British thermonuclear warhead based upon the design of the American W-28 warhead. It was used as the warhead in both the Yellow Sun Mk. 2 free-fall nuclear weapon and the Blue Steel supersonic stand-off missile.

**Red Steer**   A sector-scanning I-Band search radar used on Vulcan B2 and Victor B2 bombers to warn of aircraft approaching behind the host aircraft.

**Red Top**          A UK-designed and built infrared air-to-air homing missile used on later marks of the English Electric Lightning.

**Rivet Joint**      American-built RC-135 electronic reconnaissance aircraft used by the USAF and the RAF.

**Sky Monitor**      A NATO operation authorised by United Nations Security Council Resolution 781 to monitor the No-Fly Zone established over Bosnian airspace.

**Sky Shadow**       Marconi-built ECM pod carried by the Tornado IDS aircraft.

**Spec Op**          ELINT operators on the Nimrod R1 electronic reconnaissance aircraft.

**Star Window**      A project to update the COMINT DF and mission computer systems on the Nimrod R1.

**Storm Shadow**     Anglo-French low-observable, subsonic, air-launched cruise missile that can operate over ranges in excess of 250nm.

**Tall Boy**         A WWII 12,000-lb high-explosive bomb designed by Sir Barnes Wallis and used on special missions by the RAF Nos. 617 and 9 Squadrons.

**V1**               Early sub-sonic flying bomb (cruise missile) used by Germany during WWII. Typical range was around 150 nautical miles.

**V2**               The world's first long-range, rocket-powered ballistic missile built and used by Germany against the UK during WWII.

**V3**               Large-calibre gun built by Germany for attacks on the UK. Initial emplacements were built at Pas-de-Calais in France, but they were rendered unusable by RAF and allied bombing raids.

**WE.177**           A UK-designed and constructed nuclear bomb based upon the American W59 warhead.

**Yellow Gate**      Loral-built ESM system carried on the Nimrod MR2.

**Yellow Sun**       Casing for UK, air-delivered nuclear bombs. Yellow Sun Mk. 1 used the Green Grass physics package giving the bomb yield of around 4/500 kt. Yellow Sun Mk. 2 used the Red Snow physics package that offered a yield in the order of 1 Mt.

# INDEX